TABLE OF CONTENTS

this is the alaskan malamute

joan
mcdonald
brearley

Cover:
Ch. Inuit's Sweet Lucifer, owned by Sheila Balch, Best of Breed at the 1974 Alaskan Malamute Club of America Specialty. Photo by Alton Anderson.

Back Cover:
Inuit's Wild Thing and Inuit's Our Man Flint pictured at ten weeks of age. Owned by Sheila Balch. Photo by Alton Anderson.

Frontispiece:
American and Canadian Ch. Zardal Baranof, bred and owned by Audrey I. Thomas of Zardal Kennels, Penfield, N.Y. Photo by Streeter.

ISBN 0-87666-650-0

© 1975 by T.F.H. Publications, Inc. Ltd.

Distributed in the U.S.A. by T.F.H. Publications, Inc., 211 West Sylvania Avenue, P.O. Box 27, Neptune City, N.J. 07753; in England by T.F.H. (Gt. Britain) Ltd., 13 Nutley Lane, Reigate, Surrey; in Canada to the book store and library trade by Clarke, Irwin & Company, Clarwin House, 791 St. Clair Avenue West, Toronto 10, Ontario; in Canada to the pet trade by Rolf C. Hagen Ltd., 3225 Sartelon Street, Montreal 382, Quebec; in Southeast Asia by Y.W. Ong, 9 Lorong 36 Geylang, Singapore 14; in Australia and the south Pacific by Pet Imports Pty. Ltd., P.O. Box 149, Brookvale 2100, N.S.W., Australia. Published by T.F.H. Publications, Inc. Ltd., The British Crown Colony of Hong Kong.

4

DEDICATION

to

SUSAN LYNN BLAUVELT

my godchild

and the other great lover
of animals in our family.

ACKNOWLEDGMENTS

The author wishes to acknowledge her sincere appreciation to those who contributed so greatly to this book. First and foremost, thanks are due to Sheila Balch for the huge amount of research material offered and for her efforts in securing important photographs and statistics; to Janet Edmonds of England for the research and photographs essential to presenting the breed in her country; to Alice Jean Lucus for material and photographs on chondrodysplasia and her courage in revealing its presence and cause; to the staffs of the Museum of Natural History, the American Kennel Club, and New York Public Library; to Robert R. Shomer, D.V.M. for expert counsel, to Stephen McDonald for special material, and to the owners of the Malamutes proud enough to want photographs of their dogs presented in this book dedicated to their intelligence, beauty, and their important role in the world of dogs.

The author and noted columnist/critic/animal welfarist Cleveland Amory and his Alaskan Malamutes at the Amory apartment in New York City.

ABOUT THE AUTHOR. . .

JOAN McDONALD BREARLEY

Joan Brearley has loved animals ever since she was old enough to know what they were. Over the years there has been a constant succession of dogs, cats, birds, fish, rabbits, snakes, turtles, alligators, squirrels, lizards, etc., for her own personal menagerie. Through these same years she has owned over thirty different breeds of purebred dogs, as well as countless mixtures, since the door was never closed to a needy or homeless animal.

A graduate of the American Academy of Dramatic Arts, Joan started her career as a writer for movie magazines, actress and dancer. She also studied journalism at Columbia University and has been a radio, television and magazine writer, writing for some of the major New York City agencies. She was also a television producer-director for a major network on such shows as *Nick Carter, Master Detective*, and has written, cast, directed, produced and, on occasion, starred in television film commercials. She has written material for such personalities as Dick Van Dyke, Bill Stern, Herman Hickman, Dione Lucas, Amy Vanderbilt and many others prominent in the entertainment world.

Her accomplishments in the dog fancy include being an American Kennel Club approved judge, breeder-exhibitor of top show dogs, writer for various dog magazines, author or co-author of many breed books including *This is the Afghan Hound, This is the Shih Tzu, This is the St. Bernard, This is the Bichon Frise, This is the Old English Sheepdog, This is the Siberian Husky, This is the Skye Terrier*, and many others. For five years she was Executive Vice-President of the Popular Dogs Publishing Company and editor of *Popular Dogs* magazine, the national prestige publication for the dog fancy at that time.

Joan Brearley is just as active in the cat fancy, and in almost all the same capacities. She is editor of the Cat Fanciers Association Annual Yearbook and writes for the various cat magazines as well. Joan Brearley speaks at kennel clubs and humane organizations on animal legislation and has received many awards and citations for her work in this field, including an award from the Morris Animal Foundation.

At present Joan lives in a penthouse apartment overlooking all Manhattan in New York City with three dogs and a dozen or more cats, all of which are Best in Show winners and have been professional models for television and magazines. Joan is proud of the fact that in her first litter of Afghan Hounds she bred a Westminster Kennel Club Group winner, Champion Sahadi (her kennel prefix) Shikari, the top-winning Afghan Hound in the history of the breed for many years.

In addition to her activities in the world of animals, Joan Brearley is a movie buff and spends time at the art and auction galleries, the theatre, creating needlepoint (for which she has also won awards), dancing, the typewriter—and the zoo!

1. ANCIENT HISTORY

Alaska and Siberia, separated only by 55 miles of Bering Sea—with some of the smaller islands in the straits as close to each other as only 2 miles—have all through the ages shared their ancestry, a way of living and their life-preserving dogs.

Some 35,000 years ago the people of Central Asia migrated farther and farther north to the extreme-most regions of Siberia and the Arctic, and brought with them their jackal-type dogs (*Canis aureus*). Cross-bred with the Arctic wolves (*Canis lupus*), these animals developed over the centuries into what later came to be referred to as the Northern breeds, including the Malamute, Samoyeds, the Spitz, Keeshonds, Elkhounds, the Nootka dogs of Iceland and the Russian Laikas.

By the Neolithic age, 3500 to 2000 B.C., the Northern dogs had become established with their own type and characteristics which, with periodic breedings to the wolf, managed to endure down through the ages. All of these dogs were referred to as "huskies." The term husky is a corruption of "esky," a slang word for Eskimo; it covered all the sled-pulling breeds that had rough, shaggy coats, pointed faces and plumey tails. Their coats were thick and woolly to protect them from the elements, and they came in almost every color; solids, brindles, white with spots, black with white, white with black patches, reds, yellow, yellow spotted, red spotted, etc. Today the term husky applies only to the Siberian Husky breed.

From the first days of the Eskimos' existence on earth the dogs had been there at their sides, living with them and hunting with them, thousands of years before sleds were thought of or necessary to their existence. As far back as Mesolithic times men traveled on skis, and there are also evidences that they used the travois for ages before they got around to building sleds.

As the wilderness opened up before them, and as their numbers grew, they began to develop a dog bred to meet the requirements of their specific needs, a dog with the necessary conformation to provide endurance over great distances with the least expenditure of energy.

And so the Mahlemut Indians in the vast Alaskan territory, with their settlements along the Kotzebue Sound in upper Western Alaska,

Arctic Dog and Fox is the title of this 1819 rare print from the collection of the author.

took the husky dog and began by process of elimination to develop what we have come to know as the Alaskan Malamute breed. It was almost a case of the survival of the fittest, since only the strongest of the litters came to survive the elements and the work schedule given to them by their owners. Through this continuous culling program we now have the distinctive, strong, powerful working dog that is hailed as the king of the working dogs.

We must remember that this native Innuit tribe called Mahlemuts lived in what was then called Alashak, or Alyeska. It was owned by the Russians, and was sold to the United States for $7,200,000 in 1867. At first it was called Russian America; some time had to pass before the more "native" name of Alaska was made the official name, just as the name Mahlemut has become Malamute.

Most of the tribes consisted of three "divisions": the marine or maritime people, who were largely fishermen and lived along the river where the dogs were used to pull the umiaks, or large skin boats, along the shore; the sedentary people, who remained in one place and traded to make a living; and the nomadic tribes, which wandered far and wide following the huge herds of reindeer. Travelling by reindeer became less and less satisfactory to the nomads, who became more and more dependent on their dogs not only to help them hunt and herd but also to get them from village to village to trade.

The Mahlemuts were said to treat their dogs with great care and kindness, much as the Samoyed tribes, not like the rest of the inhabitants of the Arctic region. The dogs were described as being affectionate and seemingly tireless in their desire to work. The Mahlemuts were highly respected among other Innuits, and so were their dogs. It was only at the beginning of the 20th century and the Alaskan Sweepstakes races that the breed once again became partially involved with breedings with the other Northern breeds.

While many of the tribes were hostile toward one another, there were times when the tribes depended upon one another and their dog teams for their very survival. When food was scarce, they would join their dogs to one sled when it became necessary to move entire villages and all their belongings from one location to another. At times the women and children would get into harness and pull right along with the dogs to facilitate the move. Their dogs were held in such high esteem that only the babies, the sick or the elderly were allowed to ride.

Northern dogs in an Arctic setting constructed for the 1904 World's Fair in St. Louis. Photo courtesy American Museum of Natural History.

Drivers led or walked behind the teams guiding their worldly goods to a new less hostile location. In heavy snow or bad weather the drivers would often blaze the trail with their snow shoes ahead of the lead dog, and the teams would follow in his footsteps along the man-made trail. These Northern dogs were seldom fast runners, as it was more important that they maintain the long pull from one village or camp to the next by moderate speed to assure their getting there with their cargo intact. Today as well the Alaskan Malamute is at his best when he can cover great distances with a heavy load at a moderate speed. Under these conditions he has no peer. Pound for pound, the Alaskan Malamute is the strongest draft dog of them all!

TYPES OF HARNESSING

There were basically three kinds of harnessing in ancient times, as there are today. One type of harnessing was attaching the dogs in pairs on both sides of a main line that was attached to the middle of the front of the sled. This was, of course, the ideal method of hauling large, heavy loads.

The second method of harnessing the dogs was with them attached singly, alternately placed on a single tow line to the sled. They used about six or seven dogs on this single team haul. The logic behind the single line was to avoid excessive loss in crevasse accidents and to prevent dogs from going over the precipices during snowstorms.

The third harnessing method was the fan attachment, where several dogs ran side by side, being attached at a single point and with a single tow line to the sled. This method was satisfactory only on clear wide open terrain.

EARLY SLEDS

The first sleds, or komiatics, were made from whale bone or driftwood gathered from ice floes or from the tundra during the thaws. The runners were usually wooden, preferably hickory, and extended as far as 5 to 30 feet in length with 12 feet being the average. Reindeer antlers tied to the sled with strips of walrus hide were sometimes used as handle bars. The baskets were made of seal or walrus hide; on some sleds, when wood was not available, runners were made from parts of the jawbones of whales. In an emergency sleds could be made from cutting of ice, frozen together and carved to their individual needs.

HARNESSING THE PUPPIES

Harnessing began when the puppies were a few months old, sometimes as early as two months. It was not uncommon to see entire litters of puppies tied up behind their mother learning to pull in unison even at this early age. These teams often made the best and most

Sheila Balch's American, Canadian and Bermudian Ch. Inuit's Wooly Bully with a friend. This typical photograph appeared in an advertisement in *Time* magazine in 1968.

efficient workers. Geldings frequently suffered the additional indignity of having their tails cropped, since the Kamchadal and Koryak tribes believed it added to their speed. The Koryaks also put their new-born puppies in underground dugouts and kept them there in total darkness until they were old enough to be harnessed, the result being that the moment the puppies saw daylight for the first time they were so exuberant there was no holding them.

SLED DOG'S CAREER A SHORT ONE

Seven years was about the limit of service for a sled dog, though some of the stronger dogs were used for a dozen or more years. But it was strictly downhill from about seven years on. Others were lost to frostbite, hunger, accidents on the trail, dog fights, ending up second best in a bout with a bear or other animal, or disease. More still fell victim to their owners' cruelties and neglect.

HARDSHIPS OF EARLY TEAM DOG LIFE

In the wilds of the North the Alaskan Malamute team dogs were completely different from those we see in more modern times. They were scrappy and vicious, and brutal fights among the dogs were commonplace. All life was a challenge: a defense against the elements or a cruel master, the winning of a female, a fight for its food, its own territory or its status among the rest of the dogs.

If there was a fight for pack leadership between two dogs, it would be a fight to the death. The entire pack would swarm around waiting eagerly to demolish and devour whichever dog turned out to be the loser. No amount of beating on the part of the owner can hold off the pack when the loser in a dog fight goes down. The same applies when for some reason the pack ostracizes a dog in its midst. It may lag behind the rest at first, but sooner or later the pack will gang up on it, close in and finish it off. And what's more—the dog will know it is a goner and will do little to defend itself.

The lead dog realizes this as well. The moment it shows the first sign of weakness or illness or oncoming age it must immediately be replaced or it will meet the same fate as the outcast dog. Life for a working sled dog was a demonstration of the survival of the fittest in its most extreme context.

GELDINGS

The above represent a few reasons why more and more frequently geldings were used on the teams. They ate much less food, did not fight as much among themselves and could be quartered together in small places. The dogs were gelded with an iron knife, and at times only the lead dog on a team was a whole male, making his job of maintaining law and order much easier.

EARLY TEAM TRAINING

On occasion there were dogs which never could "make the team." These dogs were killed, and probably eaten. Quarrelsome dogs had their teeth pulled out or the points broken off. By the time they reached 18 months of age the new young dogs were ready to join the teams in prominent positions, and the older dogs were weeded out.

With this eventual and complete turnover every so often you can readily understand the importance of the lead dog. He leads; the rest follow *him*, not the driver. The team is only as good as the lead dog. And it was perfectly possible for a lead dog to bring that team home when the driver was lost on trail, and against the most unbelievable odds. They may turn up snowblind during a blizzard, but they've kept to the trail and have gotten the team home safely.

Well treated, well fed dogs take great pleasure in their work, and

This early Eskimo dog, rendered around 1920, is reproduced from a lithograph in the collection of the author.

the closer the relationship between the driver and the lead dog the better the team will function. The winning drivers in the racing events never forget this!

TREATMENT OF THE DOGS

In ancient times, just as today, treatment of dogs varied from person to person, family to family, tribe to tribe. While all tribes were aware of the importance of the dogs to their very existence, many treated their dogs horribly. Dogs which became ill or wouldn't run up to standard were abandoned on the trail and left to die. The rare exception was the extraordinarily good runner, who might be forgiven and put on the sled for the ride home.

Some disobedient dogs had their tails cut off on the spot, leaving a trail of blood all along the way. Obedience was taught with a stick, and many severe beatings had to be endured before the dogs came to realize what was expected of them.

Some drivers preferred whips, vicious instruments with lashes reaching anywhere from 18 to 24 feet, with a one-foot handle. With such a whip the driver, by cracking it on either side of the lead dog while shouting and repeating certain guide words, could pretty well hold the team in complete control. The whip handles were frequently used to hit the dogs over the head if they didn't shape up. In place of the whip handle, the driver often used the sled's brake to beat the dog; the brake was usually four feet long and very sturdy, so one can imagine the savagery of the beatings.

Other disobedient dogs would have a rope with a knot in it tied around their throats; the rope was pulled tight until they fell senseless. Dogs that chewed their harnesses were hung up until they lost consciousness, and then the tips of their rear molars were knocked off so they could no longer chew. While this method was terribly brutal we must recall that in olden times the teeth of the dogs and the wolves were a great deal larger and sharper. Domestication has reduced the size and sharpness of dogs' teeth, largely due to difference in diet.

The Northern tribes which treated their dogs kindly went to other extremes. The children were allowed to play with them, and the women were instrumental in the upbringing of the puppy; some tribes would even build shelters for their dogs for protection against the elements. The Samoyeds were known to bring their dogs into their huts to live with the family, each member taking a dog to sleep with him for warmth.

While these Eskimo (also called Esquimaux) dogs were virtually slaves to their owners rather than allies and help-mates, their hard work did at times make them balky and refuse to move. If there was, perhaps, an especially heavy load women were frequently called upon to entice the dogs to move. The women, having very likely played with them more as puppies and cared for them when they were sick, could often get them to "give their all."

At times a woman would walk ahead of the sled throwing bits of animal skin which she had first placed in her mouth and chewed on. The dogs would think it was food and pull toward it. Certain tribes have been known to harness the women and young girls to the sleds, and they helped pull right along with the dogs.

Later, when the explorers began to arrive in the North and demonstrated to the Eskimos that better results could be achieved through training and special care, the man-dog relationship reached its full potential and ceased to be just a case of man's will and dominance over a wild animal.

While some of the tribesmen built shelters for their dogs, others merely staked them out somewhere near their housing. In the face of violent storms or raging blizzards the dogs were set free to avoid being buried in the snowdrifts or freezing to death for want of exercise. In summer the dogs were set free to fend for themselves. They would dig holes in the ground to keep cool or lie in water to avoid the mosquitoes. Some did well for themselves, especially if the seal hunts were successful and they had scraps thrown to them, while others were good at fishing and managed to survive on their own skills. Others had to scrounge for their food, and still others succumbed.

FEEDING IN ANCIENT TIMES

The diets of the Northern tribes consisted largely of seal, whale or walrus meat, and whatever scraps of meat or blubber were left over would get tossed to the dogs. If they were putrid so much the better. When food was scarce the dogs would devour whatever came in front of them in the way of solid food. Hunger during hard times often led to their chewing up and eating bits of their harness or the thongs that tied the sleds together.

The farther south the dogs were the better they fared, naturally. If fishing was good they survived quite nicely on whole dry fish. The dogs got along on very little food; this was fortunate, because if they got too heavy they could not pull as well or as much. As winter approached the drivers watched to see that the dogs lived off their own

This engraving by Lizars was made from a drawing by H. Smith, circa 1840, and features a Northern dog quite different from our Northern breeds as we know them today. From the collection of the author.

fat if they had eaten well over the summer months. During the winter, when the dogs were cared for, they might be fed a sort of soup made from dried salmon bones, with a piece of blubber thrown in, and slopped in a trough. It is a wonder the dogs survived at all, much less that they were capable of pulling the great burdens they were expected to haul!

NATURAL INSTINCT

Food was always ravaged by these half-starved dogs, and, of course, more food was required by a dog living and working in a cold climate than by those in a more temperate zone. The Eskimo knew his dogs would be in trouble working on a full stomach or after drink-

An old drawing by R.H. Moore of Perla, a Lapland sledge dog owned by the Prince of Wales. From the collection of the author.

ing large quantities of water, so they were fed after the day's work was done. Instinctively, the dogs knew that licking snow was a substitute for water. Licking snow caused less contraction of the stomach and lessened cramping and distress while relieving the hunger pains caused by these contractions. Many of the dogs came back from the long hauls not having been fed for days; they were weak and hungry and would die of exposure or starvation.

WHELPING IN THE WILDS

Unless the women took pity on them, bitches often were pulling sleds up to the moment of delivery. If their puppies were born while they were out on the trail they were usually destined to die. If born at home, the wives would frequently care for them as well as take pity on the dam. The women have been known to take it upon themselves to nurse the puppies along with their own children if the dam were to die or be unable to perform this vital function herself.

BITCHES IN SEASON

Since the bitches were smaller and could not pull the weight the dogs could, they were usually not put in a lead position. However, if a male team was reluctant to pull, a bitch in season would be put in the lead to give the males an incentive to pull. Bitches in season were sometimes tethered out where male wolves would have access to them when the tribesmen thought it necessary to reintroduce wolf blood to the pack to strengthen it. With the foregoing exception, the lead dogs were given first opportunity to cover the females.

THE SACRIFICIAL DOG

There is little doubt that vast numbers of the dogs were sacrificed to the gods. There seems to be a question only as to what was done with the remains once the sacrifice had been offered. We are well aware that the skins of dogs were used for clothing and that in times of famine the flesh was eaten by man and dog alike. And we also know that while the dogs were bred in great numbers, each family seemed to have fewer dogs than they bred. Over the years, had this not been the case, the dogs could have well outnumbered and devoured the tribes.

The Museum of Natural History in New York City has on file a series of photographs of what was referred to by the villagers as the most perfect example and specimen of a husky dog ever seen up to that time. It was to have been sacrificed to the gods on the very day it was photographed, but it was literally snatched from the arms of death by an explorer who purchased him for a bottle of whiskey! This dog, whelped at the turn of the century, is noticeably more like a brindle Chow Chow than any Samoyed or Siberian Husky, Spitz, Alaskan Malamute or Eskimo dog that we have seen in our time!

MYTHS AND LEGENDS

We have heard various fantastic stories about the part animals play in religious rites and ceremonies in various cultures all over the world. We have just mentioned the husky as a sacrificial dog. Beyond this there are other legends which the people of the Far North put great stock in, and these legends have been passed down from generation to generation.

Many northern tribes believe that there are dogs guarding the gates to paradise. These dog-loving people tell tales of the Eskimo women who had unknown lovers which are dogs by day, men by night. Many Eskimos also believe that Indians and Europeans are descended from a dog. The story is that at the beginning of the world a woman had ten children by a dog, five of which became inlanders, and the other five she set afloat on a raft—and they became Europeans!

Lapp women would offer dog sacrifices to the goddesses of childbirth just before they delivered to insure a healthy baby.

Sled dog huts made from barrels that have the open end framed and attached to lateral rails for stability can be considered to be adequate quarters for a Malamute, but in many cases the dogs stay outside in the snow anyway.

STONEHENGE ON THE ESQUIMAUX DOG

One of the most famous writers on the dog in ancient England was a man who used the pen name of Stonehenge. Actually he was the editor of *The Field*, a major dog publication in England in the nineteenth century. He wrote books about individual breeds and enormous editions covering all breeds as they were known up to that time.

In the preface to *The Dog In Health and Disease*, dated July 1, 1859, he expounds at great length about his extensive and reliable sources; with this in mind it is fascinating to read the account of The Esquimaux Dog, which states as follows:

"This dog is the only beast of burden in the northern parts of the continent of America and adjacent islands, being sometimes employed to carry materials for hunting or the produce of the chase on his back, and at others he is harnessed to sledges in teams varying from seven to eleven, each being capable of drawing a hundred weight for his share. The team are harnessed to a single yoke-line by a breast-strap, and being without any guide-reins, they are entirely at liberty to do what they like, being only restrained by the voice of their master and urged forward by his whip. A single dog of tried intelligence and fidelity is placed as leader, and upon him the driver depends for his orders being obeyed. In the summer they are most of them turned off to get their own subsistence by hunting, some few being retained to carry weights on their backs; sledges are then rendered useless by

Sergeant Preston of the Yukon was one of the most popular series on television during the 1950's. Sergeant Preston's lead dog, Yukon King, was a popular favorite with children of all ages.

the absence of snow; and as there is a good subsistence for them from the offal of the seal and walrus which are taken by the men, the dogs become fat at this season of the year. The Siberian and Greenland dogs are nearly similar to those of Kamtschatka, but somewhat larger, and also more manageable, all being used in the same way. The Esquimaux dog is about 22 or 23 inches high, with a pointed, fox-like muzzle, wide head, pricked ears, and wolf-like aspect; the body is low and strong, and clothed with long hair, having an under-coat of thick wool; tail long, gently curved, and hairy; feet and legs strong and well formed; the color is almost always a dark dun, with slight disposition to brindle, and black muzzle."

Stonehenge went on to include brief mention of other Northern dogs in a one-sentence paragraph entitled *"Iceland and Lapland Dogs"*:

"There are nearly similar to the Esquimaux, but rather larger, more wolf-like, and far less manageable."

THE SOCIAL HIERARCHY

All descendants of either the wolf or the jackal are dogs which belong to a group which adheres to communal family living; in other words, they lived in packs. And each pack had its leader.

It was the function of the leader not only to protect his position but also to guide, keep order, discipline, and excel in every way over all the rest of the pack. The leader, therefore, was always the strongest, most intelligent and certainly the bravest and most aggressive of the lot and had to take on all comers at all times, since other males were constantly challenging his position. Since the leaders were first with the females as well, it assured the breeding of the best and strongest specimens within the pack. This "law of the jungle" is as old as time.

While there seems to be little doubt that the ancestors of domestic dogs were the wolves, there is good reason to believe that there was also jackal blood introduced through the centuries. This supposition is based on research in observance of the Asian wolves. The Northern wolf, for instance, blends into the Tibetan wolf, the Tibetan wolf shades into the Mesopotamian desert wolf and so on . . . and all of them are similar to the jackal.

There is also a supposition among a number of historians that jackals and wolves were actually the same, that jackals were merely wolves which went off in an opposite geographical direction and to a different way of life, developing qualities and characteristics necessary to survive in a particular region. Those which migrated toward the North developed into shaggy, wolf-like creatures that could withstand the colder climates and made conformation adjustments accordingly. When they became domesticated by the Eskimos they were regarded as the Northern breeds of dogs. The wolf-jackal-dog species all can interbreed and produce fertile get, so it was not an impossibility.

Hutchinson's Encyclopedia offers the theory that while the wolf coloration of the Husky may bear out the general impression that Huskies at least were frequently wolf-crossed, if that were the case most Huskies would be all white, because the Arctic wolf is white. Also, the Arctic wolf is a much larger animal than the Husky, often weighing 150 pounds. They also carry their tails down while the Husky dogs carry them up and over their backs. And strangely enough, the Arctic wolf is the only animal a Husky is afraid to attack.

Additionally, pure-bred wolves have been trained and used to a limited extent as sled animals. They proved most unsatisfactory, since they did not have the endurance so necessary for a good sled dog! The only conclusion can be that while the Husky may have originally descended from wolves, there has since been only what could be considered as occasional cross-breedings.

According to Dr. Edward Moffat Weyer, Jr., one of the foremost students of the Eskimo, "It seems altogether likely that the dogs have crossed to some extent with wolves. The skeletal similarity points to a relationship."

Perhaps the most obvious difference seems to be in behavioral pattern of the wolf and of the jackal. While both the wolf and the jackal packs recognize a leader, the wolf packs support a graduated order of superiority from the leader down, in a one, two, three "pecking order." The jackals, on the other hand, are said to recognize a leader, but the rest of the pack share equally in rank, with no dog taking second place to any other dog in importance.

With this comparison in mind, and going beyond the wolf-like physical appearance of today's Malamutes and knowing that they have been interbred with wolves over the centuries, we must also note that their social behavior resembles that of the jackal. In spite of the virtually complete domestication of today's Malamutes, they observe the "leader of the pack" social pattern, which is one of the reasons they fit in so nicely with our family living. The dog joins the family "pack" and recognizes the dominant member of the family as his "leader." This is the person to whom obedience is paid and to whom his allegiance belongs. But it also upholds the jackal social behavior pattern in that he gets along equally well with all other members of the family "pack," a trait attributed to animals descending morphologically from the jackal.

EARLY EXPLORERS AND EXPEDITIONS

It was the Northern type dog which the Russians used during the 17th century when they succeeded in charting the Siberian coastline. All the dogs were described to be merely domesticated wolves and had the same instincts and characteristics as the sled dogs used and described by the members of the Western Union Telegraph Expedition of 1865, 1866 and 1867.

Apparently they did not differ from any of the dogs found along the entire route of the expedition, which extended from its starting point at the lower Kamchatka Peninsula to the top northeastern tip of Siberia. We can be sure that the colonization of the northeastern part of Siberia by Czarist Russia during the last few centuries played a part in improving the lot and expanding the uses of these native dogs.

In actuality there is no different description of the Northern sled dogs in the diaries of Marco Polo written in the thirteenth century while describing their use in relay teams as a means of rapid transportation in the Arctic.

As late as 1900 only slight, very superficial differences could be discerned among the Northern breeds. They were all described by the early explorers as having long, shaggy coats and very definite wolf or fox-like appearance. The very earliest photographs and drawings of these dogs and writings by explorers such as Olaf Swenson, Vilhjalmur Stefanson, Waldemar Jochelson, Valdemar Borgoras (writing on the Jessup North Pacific Expedition in 1904), George Kenner, Washington B. Vanderlip, Irving Reed and the rest of them seemed to have a single picture in mind of the breed.

Opposite:
A five-dog team during a sled dog training session at a War Corps training center during World War II.

Sledge dogs staked out at their training quarters photographed in March, 1943. These dogs were assigned to the Quartermaster Corps War Dog Reception and Training Center at Camp Rimini, Montana during World War II.

A lovely family scene from several years ago. . . Mrs. Lorna Jackson's month old puppies and some full grown Alaskan Malamutes at her kennel in Toronto, Ontario, Canada. Photograph by Evelyn Shafer.

2. THE ALASKAN MALAMUTE IN THE TWENTIETH CENTURY

The turn of the century marked the era of the great Alaskan Gold Rush. By 1906 a little village named Nome had burst into a boom town! It was the leading gold mining town in the world but once winter set in and froze the Bering Sea, it had little more than the telegraph and native dog teams with which to keep in contact with the rest of the world.

The dog teams suddenly became an essential means of transportation for the natives as well as the members of the mining companies. In order to assure the stamina and performance of the vitally necessary dogs, the Nome Kennel Club was organized in 1907. The man responsible was a lawyer named Albert Fink, who was to serve as the first president of the club. The All-Alaska Sweepstakes races were the means devised to create interest in the dogs, and the Club set the first running for 1908.

THE ALL-ALASKA SWEEPSTAKES

A race course between Nome and Candle on the Seward Peninsula was drawn, which would represent a 408-mile trail round trip with a $10,000 first prize! It was to be run each April, the exact date depending on the weather conditions. The course was to follow as closely as possible the Nome to Candle telephone line, and presented every possible kind of terrain.

In 1908 a man named Goosak, a Russian fur trader, imported a team of small dogs from Siberia; driven by a man named Louis Thustrup, this team won third place in this running of the Sweeps, in spite of 100 to 1 odds against them! There was great speculation that Thustrup might have done better if he had not become snowblind before reaching the finish line.

At this time a young Scotsman named Fox Maule Ramsey, in Alaska to supervise, with his two uncles, Colonel Charles Ramsey and Colonel Weatherly Stuart, his family's investments in the gold

31

fields, showed up on the scene. The second son to the Earl of Dalhousie, he was fascinated by the excitement of the races and chartered a schooner for $2500 to cross the Bering Sea. He brought back 70 dogs of mixed breeding (several of which he claimed swam out to the ship to meet him) in the Siberian settlement named Markova, 300 miles up the Anadyr River.

He had driven his own team of dogs in the 1909 event and had not placed, so on the advice of his friend Ivor Olsen he trained his new mixed breeds and entered three teams in the 1910 event. He drove one team himself and placed second. One of the two other teams, entered in the names of his uncles, placed first. He hired John "Iron Man" Johnson to drive one of the teams, and Johnson won in the record time of 74 hours, 14 minutes, and 37 seconds. Third place went to the mixed breed Malamute team entered by Allen and Darling.

After the race he turned the dogs over to the drivers, never to compete again; he eventually returned to Scotland, where he succeeded to the Earldom of Dalhousie upon the death of his older brother.

1911 saw the entry of two Siberian dog teams, one by Johnson and Madsen and driven by Charles Johnson. Scotty Allen won the race with his mixed-Malamute team entered by Allen and Darling; second position went to another mixed-Malamute team driven by Coke Hill, who later became U.S. District judge for the 4th Judicial Division. Charles Johnson and his team of Siberian Huskies were third. Iron Man Johnson with his team of Huskies did not place in the top three this year, and there was much talk and rumors that he had thrown the race, since there was so much money bet on the outcome of this one, based on his remarkable record the year before.

The enthusiasm waned the next year. . . only four teams entered the 1912 All-Alaska Sweepstake Race. Scotty Allen won with the Allen Darling mixed-Malamute team, and Alec Holmsen, also with a mixed-breed team, placed second. Charles Johnson and his Siberians placed third.

The sixth running of the Sweepstakes in 1913 was won by the mixed-breed entry of Bowen and Delzene, driven by Fay Delzene. Iron Man Johnson and his Siberians took 2nd place and Scotty Allen was third with the Allen-Darling team. 1914 was Iron Man Johnson's year once again; the Allen-Darling team was second, and third spot went to Fred Ayer with an entry of half-Malamute and half-Foxhound team. This was also the year a stalwart young man named Leonhard Seppala arrived on the scene with his mixed-breed team, although after several misfortunes he was obliged to drop out of the competition.

The 1915 All-Alaska Sweepstakes was a different story, however. Leonhard Seppala entered and won with his Siberians. Second to Seppala was a mixed-breed entry of Bowen and Delzene, driven by Fay

Delzene, and third was the Fred Ayer Malamute-Foxhound team.

This triumphant and satisfying win by Seppala in 1915 was one which he repeated in 1916 and 1917. Probably he would have repeated in 1918 but the World War had hit Nome hard, and the greatest dog team races ever run at this annual Alaskan event came to an end.

RACING WITH DEATH IN ALASKA: THE GREAT SERUM RUN IN 1925

One of the greatest tales of heroism ever to come out of the frozen North is the story of the great Serum Run of 1925, when a group of drivers and their stalwart dogs fought their way through fifty below zero weather and an 80 mile an hour blizzard to get serum to the inhabitants of Nome to halt the march of diphtheria.

In spite of the waist-high drifts and the mountainous crags of the pack ice, they covered the distance of 655 miles in five and a half days under the most excrutiating circumstances, safely delivering the 20-pound package containing the precious three hundred thousand units of antitoxin serum. At 5:30 A.M., on the morning of February 2, 1925, Gunnar Kasson and his half-frozen team of dogs with bloody, torn feet pulled into Nome and handed over the serum to Curtis Welch of the United States Public Health Service. Welch was Nome's only doctor, and together with a handful of nurses in an area containing 11,000 inhabitants, stretching one thousand miles to the east and as far north as the Arctic Ocean, they got busy putting the serum to work. The epidemic *had* to be halted, since diphtheria is certain death to Eskimos. . .

Prayers of thanks were echoed throughout the area and all over the world, for this crisis was big news everywhere. Newspapers had carried the progress reports of the relay teams of Eskimo Pete Olsen, Leonhard Seppala, Gunnar Kasson and the rest of those involved in the run, and everyone seemed to realize instinctively the icy terror in the black Alaskan night these brave men were facing. The names of Titus Nicolai, John Folger, Jim Kalland, Tom Green and Bill Shannon became household words as the journey proceeded to Nome by the Bering Sea.

Not only did the names of the drivers remain foremost in the minds of the people, but so did the names of the dogs which led and pulled on the teams. There were the names of Togo and Scotty, Seppala's two lead dogs, and the most famous of all, Balto, the dog which pulled into Nome with Kasson. The moment the team halted at the end of their 60-mile run, Kasson fell into the snow beside his dog and began pulling the ice splinters from Balto's torn and bloody paws. Exhausted, Kasson still paid tribute to his lead dog. Newspapers all over the world carried his words of praise for Balto: "Damn fine dog! I've been mushing in Alaska since 1903. This was the toughest

The commemorative state of the canine hero Balto, famous for helping to deliver the serum during the 1925 Alaskan diphtheria epidemic, was photographed by Edmond Vianney on February 5, 1926, in New York City's Central Park.

I've ever had on the trails. But Balto, he brought us through."

Kasson was referring to Balto's scenting the trail when Kasson got lost on the bare ice and had run into an overflow while crossing the Topkok River. Balto had proved his worth before on more than one occasion. He had led Kasson's team in 1915 when they won the Moose race, and two years before had led the team which carried explorer Roald Amundsen north from Nome when he planned an airplane flight over the North Pole. He well earned and deserved his title of the best lead dog in Alaska.

Seppala's dogs had come through for him on many occasions also. Togo and Scotty were the leads on his teams and were known throughout Alaska as the very fastest dogs. At the start of the run Seppala had been warned by officials not to cut across Norton Sound, since weather officials had reported the ice was breaking up and drifting out to sea. There was a storm raging over the area at the time as well. He was urged to take the longer distance around which circled Norton Bay, but Seppala preferred to throw caution to the winds to gain speed. He felt his dogs were in good condition to make it although they had already mushed 80 miles.

The crossing of Norton Bay was hazardous and stormy, but once they reached the other side they headed for Isaac's Point. Seppala pulled the sled into a cabin and by a roaring fire, undid the wrappings around the package containing the serum and warmed it as best he could. His instructions were that the serum had to be warmed up at intervals and the wrapping could be removed down to a certain seal which could not be broken. Once the heat had penetrated the last wrapping which he was authorized to remove, Seppala once again rewrapped the package in its canvas coverings, several thicknesses of reindeer skin, and a final wrapping of a full fur sleeping bag. Then, once again, he started on his way.

Seppala delivered the precious cargo into the hands of Charlie Olson at Golofnin. Olson then with his team of seven Huskies ran the twenty-five miles from Golofnin to Bluff, where he turned over the package to Kasson. Every one of Olson's dogs pulled into Bluff frozen in the groin. They could not have gone on much farther, but true grit made them run on until their mission was completed, even though they all pulled up stiff and sore.

Olson lived in Bluff. He owned a quartz mine and stamp mill there and when he and Kasson met they took the package into a cabin and warmed it before Kasson struck out in the 28 degree below zero temperature and a raging wind. They had waited two hours for the storm to abate, but Kasson finally decided to buck the snow rather than lose the trail or have it become impassable. He was advised not to attempt it, but he was adamant. The ice was in constant motion from the ground-swell, and it was at this point that he soon ran into trouble crossing the Topkok River. They hit an overflow, and the winds and snow had become so severe that he could not see even as far as the wheel dogs. His right cheek became frozen and he lost the trail completely. But Balto came to the rescue. He kept to the trail and ploughed on through snow and over ice, allowing nothing to alter his direction. Kasson recalls that he himself did not even know when they passed right by Solomon, where they were to have picked up a message from Nome which would advise him not to go on until the weather improved.

When Kasson finally pulled into Port Safety, Ed Rohn was waiting to take off as relay, but Kasson felt his dogs were doing so well that he decided not to awaken Rohn and drive right on the final 21 miles from Port Safety to Nome. The trail ran along the beach of the Bering Sea, and it was at this point that two of the dogs which had been frozen on another trip began to stiffen up. Kasson had rabbit-skin coverings for them, but the cold was so severe it still penetrated.

Three volunteer flyers were standing by with their airplanes at Fairbanks for the shipment of serum when the dog-teams went through. They knew, however, that weather conditions being what they were, the planes could never get through. Governor Scott C.

Bone of Alaska, in a special dispatch to the *New York Times*, stated that any attempt to fly would have been a hazardous undertaking because their flying equipment was inadequate and only unskilled flyers were available.

Once again, the mushers and their legendary sled dogs came through. Man and animal had fought a bitter battle against the elements—and had won! Another epic tale had become part of the history of the vast Yukon country in the Far North.

THE TRIBUTE TO BALTO

In New York City's Central Park there is a magnificent bronze statue of Balto with a trace hanging over his back; it bears the following inscription:

"Dedicated to the indomitable spirit of the sled dogs that relayed anti-toxin six hundred miles over rough ice, across treacherous waters, through arctic blizzards from Nenana to the relief of a stricken Nome in the winter of 1925. Endurance—fidelity—intelligence."

WHO GOT TO THE NORTH POLE FIRST?: THE PEARY-COOK CONTROVERSY

Hutchinson's Encyclopedia pays tribute to the Northern breeds as helping to make the remarkable strides in exploration at both the North and South Pole regions, declaring that it was indispensable to its owner as no other breed. The same holds true with the explorer. Every expedition had to depend largely on the use of the sled dogs, and therefore it is very probable that no other breed has had such a wide natural distribution.

The year was 1909 when two creditable, adventurous men claimed to have reached the North Pole. . . Navy Commander Robert E. Peary and Dr. Frederick A. Cook each put in his claim to fame. Comm. Peary was steadfastly backed by the Peary Arctic Club, composed of 21 millionaire sportsmen who all secretly yearned to have accomplished the feat themselves. Dr. Cook, backed by a notorious gambler, John R. Bradley, lost the honor in a raging controversy which ensued.

Dr. Cook was discredited, ridiculed and on the verge of a breakdown as all his previous accomplishments were placed in doubt and he was dubbed the "prince of losers." The campaign waged against him by Peary's wealthy backers led him to desperation and despair to the end of his days.

Cook returned to civilization first to announce his achievement. Cook was a "loner" and made the journey with two Greenlanders, doing all the charting and navigating himself. Peary had 25 men go along to support his claim. It worked. Years of trying to clear his name of the Peary accusations, and a prison sentence for stock fraud, all took their toll on Dr. Cook. The sentence was commuted by President Franklin D. Roosevelt on Cook's deathbed. He rallied upon hearing this news, but it was mild consolation to this dedicated explorer.

The paths of Peary and Cook had crossed before. In 1892 Cook had been signed on as medic on one of Peary's expeditions to Greenland. During the journey Peary sent Cook and another man back, while Peary and a few of the others went on with three sledges and 14 dogs until 34 days later they reached 82 degrees north latitude. Peary believed he had proved that Greenland is an island, and when he and his party reached a great body of water he proclaimed it Peary Channel. In 97 days Peary had traveled 1130 miles. In 1915, however, Peary Channel was removed from the maps, as Danish explorers proved that Greenland went a great deal beyond Peary's calculations. His first expedition thus discredited, his second was also a failure. In 1893-1895 they tried again, but were forced to return, having to eat some of the dogs on the return journey. In 1898 he made another unsuccessful attempt to reach the Pole and met the famous Norwegian explorer Otto Sverdrup when their ships both became frozen in the ice about 700 miles south of the Pole.

Before sailing, on July 6, 1908, Peary said goodbye to President Theodore Roosevelt, who said to him, "I believe in you , Peary, and believe in your success—if it is within the possibility of man." At this time news of Dr. Cook's departure reached him. Dr. Cook had come up with a new way to reach the Pole and had written, "There will be game to the 82 degree point and there are natives and dogs for the task, so here is for the Pole." On March 18, 1908, he reduced his party to two 20-year-old Eskimos, two sleds and 26 dogs and started for the North Pole. This was 3½ months before Peary sailed from New York.

When Peary arrived at Etah, the starting-off point in the North, he claimed it was difficult to get Eskimos and dogs because Cook had gotten there first. This simply was not true, since Peary left Etah with 49 Eskimos and 246 dogs. A pair of dogs could be had in a trade for a tin cup and saucer.

The cold was excrutiating for Cook and his group. The dogs' tails, ears and noses drooped and perspiration froze and coated their bodies with ice. A hundred miles from the pole, Etukishook and Ahwelah, the Eskimos, decided they did not want to go on. The knife and gun each was to receive as payment no longer seemed enough. But they trusted Cook, who convinced them to go on.

On April 21, 1908 Cook and his two Eskimos reached the Pole. Cook later said, "I strode forward with undaunted glory in my soul. . . The desolation was such that it was almost palpable. . . What a cheerless spot this was, to have aroused the ambition of man for so many years."

He buried a short note, mentioning the good health of the men and dogs, and part of a flag in a metal tube. He later admitted that he felt a "sense of the utter uselessness of this thing, of the empty reward of my endurance," which had followed his exhilaration at his accomplishment.

Peary on his last assault had with him four Eskimos and his Negro servant Matthew Henson, along with 5 sledges and 40 dogs. Peary also expressed almost the same disappointment in the face of his success. He recorded in his diary: "The Pole at last. The prize of three centuries. Mine at last! I cannot bring myself to realize it. It all seems so simple and commonplace."

Peary also buried a jar with a piece of the flag in it and took possession of the territory in the name of the President of the United States. Their route back was aided somewhat by following the urine stains left by the forty dogs which accompanied him to the North Pole.

MACMILLAN ON THE HUSKIES

Lieutenant-Commander Donald B. MacMillan, an Arctic explorer whom Peary referred to as an excellent dog man, made several trips to the North Pole. In 1908-1909 he went with 250 dogs, during 1913-1917 with 400 dogs, 1923-1924 with 60 dogs. His 1927-1928 journey to Northern Labrador gives us considerably more information regarding the part the dogs played in these expeditions. He definitely claimed the dogs from Labrador were better looking and the best of all the Northern dogs he had seen. MacMillan, who is accredited with running an authentic trip of 100 miles in less than 18 hours, had nothing but good to say about the ability and endurance of the dogs.

He noted that for fast travelling they limited the load to approximately the combined weight of all dogs in the team. For ordinary hauls they limited to 1½ times the team's total weight, and for heavy hauling the limit was double the weight. When the going was good, and with a light load, the team made six to eight miles an hour.

He further stated: "The usual gait is a fast steady trot, which they keep up hour after hour. Some dogs will frequently shift from this trot to a pace, evidently as a measure of rest. Occasionally too, they will gallop, probably for the same reason." He also made the same observation that most of us have; that once a lead dog is trained, he never forgets. Photographs of all expeditions show piebalds, solid blacks and all variations of color and color combinations. Their value is further evidenced by a paragraph contained in *Hutchinson's Encyclopedia* which reads: "As poor Captain Scott and his brave companions were struggling to their death after reaching the South Pole (in 1911) Amundsen was riding back in comparative comfort with his team of 11 Greenland Eskimo dogs."

ADMIRAL BYRD AND THE HUSKIES

Rear Admiral Richard E. Byrd, USN, was the first man to fly over the North Pole and the South Pole and the only man to fly over both. He gazed upon more square miles of unknown, uncharted territory than any other human being in all history. During his wartime duties he was decorated four times, receiving the Congressional Medal of Honor, the Congressional Lifesaving Medal, three specially voted Congressional medals, and many others.

In an article in *National Geographic* magazine in October, 1947, Rear Admiral Byrd wrote extensively about his 1946-1947 return to the Antarctic. Entitled "Our Navy Explores Antarctica," the article refers only briefly, but no less significantly, to the role of the dog in that exploration.

Over 4,000 men and 13 ships played a part in this particular expedition, Operation Highjump, which was the largest polar expedition

Admiral Richard E. Byrd, center, accepts two puppies as mascots for his ship *East Wind* (pictured in the background) as the expedition departs for the Antarctic from Boston on Operation Deepfreeze. Mrs. Seeley provided thirty sled dogs for the expedition from her Chinook Kennels in Wonalancet, New Hampshire, where many of the dogs for the Byrd expeditions were trained and conditioned.

Rear Admiral Richard E. Byrd, the explorer who headed a number of the polar expeditions that used the Northern breeds.

Admiral Byrd had undertaken up to that time; it even was accompanied by an aircraft carrier, the *Philippine Sea*. The objective was to sail as far as possible around the 16,000-mile coast of the continent, since most of the coastline up until that time was mostly conjectural. Expedition leaders proposed to send seaplanes from sea plane tenders to explore the coast and make flights inland and to have their ships establish a base for ski-equipped land planes which would make photo-reconnaissance flights across the unmapped interior of the continent.

On this trip all the aircraft were equipped with the latest inventions which World War II had provided: new weapons and photo-reconnaissance tools and aerial cameras which could photograph about 100,000 square miles of territory in one shot. All this equipment, plus the wide use of snow tractors, produced remarkable information. But there was still a "dog town" in Little America! The marvelous husky dogs were still useful and very necessary on the rough,

The plaque on the Admiral Byrd Memorial for the sled dogs he used on his various expeditions to the Poles over the years! It reads:

Admiral Byrd Memorial
to
All Noble Dogs
whose lives were given on dog treks
during the two expeditions to
Little America, Antarctica
to further Science and Discovery
1928-1930   1933-1935
Dedicated October 8, 1938.

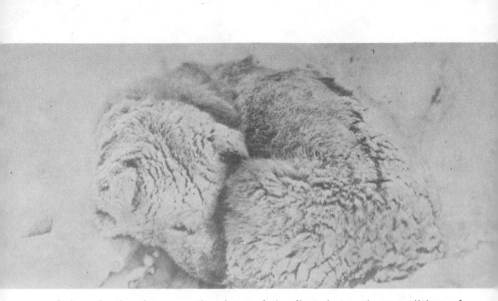

Asleep in the deep. . . the deep of the first Antarctic expedition of Admiral Richard E. Byrd to Little America in 1928-1930. This typical sleeping pose shows how the Northern breeds curl up to sleep with their plumey tails covering their noses. It is said that the tail hair helps to warm the air so it does not chill the dogs' lungs.

crevassed terrain, where no mechanical equipment could function to full advantage.

Large dogs were usually chosen, because it was thought they could better withstand the ardors of the Antarctic climate.

ED MOODY AND ADMIRAL BYRD

Ed Moody, prominent racer and sled-maker, had accompanied Admiral Byrd on his earlier 1933 expedition during which the sled dogs played an important part. They took along nine dog sled teams, as well as fifty tons of Purina Dog Chow to feed them. Admiral Byrd later referred to the dog teams as the backbone of the expedition. At that time they could not have done without the dogs. Here again, mechanical equipment broke down while the dogs did not.

Weather, claimed Moody, was even for the dogs the biggest problem they had to overcome on the trip. Blizzards, crevasses, ice breaks. . . all played havoc with their progress, but the crucial point in the journey came in the Bay of Whales. The dog teams were hauling 1,000 pounds a load and finally even they could not work when the temperature dropped to sixty degrees below zero. Below that their lips and foot pads froze. But there is, there was and there always will be a place for dog teams among the inhabitants of the extreme frozen lands of the Arctic and Antarctic.

3. MILTON AND EVA B. SEELEY — THE PINNACLES IN THE BREED

Arthur Treadwell Walden left his home in New Hampshire and headed for the Alaskan gold fields in 1896. He was not as caught up in the idea of striking it rich as he was with the idea of what could be accomplished by using the native dogs and sleds for freighting purposes. His endeavors along these lines won him renown as one of Alaska's best-known dog-punchers.

In later years he was to gain additional fame with a book he wrote titled *A Dog Puncher on the Yukon*, the story of the freight dogs and their uses in Alaska. Later still he handled the training and the conditioning of the dogs for Admiral Byrd's expeditions; the training was carried out at his Chinook Kennels in Wonalancet, New Hampshire. It was at his Chinook Kennels that Milton and Short Seeley got to know the breed, and they eventually purchased and took over Walden's kennels, still being operated by Short Seeley in the mid-1970's. The Seeleys also became involved here in the training and conditioning of the Byrd expedition dogs. Walden firmly believed that a dog team could go farther "on its own food" than any other team in the world and did much to prove his belief.

Walden's most famous dog was Chinook, after whom he named his famous kennel; it still carries that name today. Walden said of his dog, the great-grandson of a wolf: "One of the best dogs I ever owned was Chinook, a large half-bred MacKenzie River Husky. I got him in Dawson in 1898. The man who owned him had used him as a one-man dog. He wouldn't sell him for money, but I traded him for three sacks of flour, worth sixty dollars a sack, and two sacks of rolled oats, making two hundred dollars in all. He claimed that Chinook could start a heavier load than any other dog in the Yukon. He cried when he left, carrying his food." Walden rejoiced at his good fortune!

Chinook later became Walden's lead sled dog on the team that won the dog sled race of the first international competition between

Canada and the United States in Berlin, New Hampshire, in 1922.

Eva Brunell Seeley, known today as Short Seeley, was born and brought up in Worcester, Massachusetts, and prepared herself for a teaching career. In 1922 she was Director of Sports at the Bancroft School in Worcester. At Bancroft she met Milton Seeley, also on the school staff and a brilliant chemist, and they were married in May, 1924. It was while they were on their honeymoon mountain climbing in New England that they first met Arthur Walden and his dog team. They ordered a son of Chinook before their visit had ended, and they knew they were "hooked" on sled dogs!

For reasons relating to Mr. Seeley's health, in 1928 they moved to Wonalancet, where there was a great activity going on at the Chinook Kennels. Intensive training was underway for dogs which were to accompany an Admiral Byrd expedition.

Milton Seeley instantly saw the need for a substantial diet for dogs which would be expected to endure the hardships of the frozen North, and he brought all his knowledge of chemistry to bear in order to perfect just such a diet for them. While his formula was never patented, it was undeniably the basis for some of our best commercial dog foods today.

Arthur Walden went along with Byrd on one of the expeditions and took Chinook with him. Unfortunately, Chinook did not return. Short and Milton went into partnership with Walden before he left and kept the inn and the kennel running while he was in Antarctica. It was during their first winter at the Chinook Kennels that Short learned to drive a team, and her interest in racing and sled dogs became firmly established in her heart.

The Seeleys also made a few trips to Alaska in an effort to record the early pedigrees of the Alaskan Malamutes, and Short also wrote a book with Martha A.L. Lane, published in 1930 by Ginn and Company, titled *Chinook and His Family—True Dog Stories*.

When Arthur Walden returned from the Byrd expedition, he sold his share of the kennel to the Seeleys. They built new kennels on the site and, when their house burned down in 1932, moved into what was intended to be the museum and trophy building.

At least three more expeditions were made by Admiral Byrd, with the dogs all being trained at Chinook Kennels, and it was during this time that the friendship between Admiral Byrd and the Seeleys developed. The Seeleys' interest in the Alaskan Malamute broadened, and it was largely through their efforts that this breed became recognized and registered by the American Kennel Club in 1935. It was in 1932 that Short drew national attention to the breed when she drove a team of Malamutes in the Olympics at Lake Placid, New York. A second Chinook team was also entered at this event.

With World War II raging in 1942, Army dogs were being assembled at the kennel. Dogs for search and rescue units used in the war were trained at Chinook. Many dogs were offered by members of the

Mrs. Milton "Short" Seeley, right, and WAC Lt. Virginia Rees hold sled dog puppies which she presented to Admiral Byrd for the icebreaker *East Wind* expedition to the Antarctic. These puppies, two of thirty that Mrs. Seeley presented to the expedition, became the ship's official mascots.

New England Sled Dog Club drivers, and several went off to Camp Rimini in Montana for training.

Milton and Short were very active with the New England Sled Dog Club; Short served the club as secretary for many years, while Milton served as president and as a member of the executive committee. Eventually both were made life-long honorary members. All during their time as active officers and racing participants with the group, their interest extended to include the children of the members of the club. They were successful in establishing a Junior Sled Dog Club. This juvenile extension of the parent Club is still most active today, with as many as 60 teams competing at their events.

In the early 1930's Short organized a breed club for the Alaskan Malamute in New England which eventually became the Alaskan Malamute Club of America, parent club for the breed.

Milton Seeley died in 1944, but Short never had any doubt in her mind about maintaining the kennel herself; she continues to do so with help from the young people in the area who have enabled Short to make the Chinook Kennels a popular tourist attraction for dog lovers from all over the world.

Short Seeley's interests extend beyond the dog world. For many years she was an active worker for the Republican Party on all levels, and she included representatives, senators, governors and presidents among her personal friends. Short Seeley deserves her title of Matriarch of the Breed. In 1971 she celebrated her 80th birthday and almost a half century of devotion to the Malamutes and Siberian Huskies. Her efforts in behalf of Northern dogs in general and Siberian Huskies and Malamutes in particular were celebrated to the degree that they provided an occasion for acknowledgment of them by President Nixon; the letter is reproduced here.

THE WHITE HOUSE
WASHINGTON

October 5, 1971

Dear Mrs. Seeley:

On your eightieth birthday I am delighted for the opportunity to join your many friends in wishing you every happiness and all the satisfaction that a full, active life such as yours has earned.

As you look back on a half a century of dedication to showing and raising sleddogs you have much to be proud of. Your special work in helping to perpetuate the Alaskan Malamute and Siberian Chukchi Sleddog is to be applauded as an important contribution to the preservation of the heritage of the native peoples in the American and Asian Arctic.

I know that I am joined by countless fellow citizens who value and appreciate your efforts in wishing you all the best on this milestone and in the years ahead.

Sincerely,
Richard Nixon

Matriarch of the breed. . . Eva "Short" Seeley and an armful of puppies at her Chinook Kennels in Wonalancet, New Hampshire, photographed by Bob Duncan several years ago.

SHORT SEELEY TESTIMONIAL

In October, 1971, in Philadelphia, a testimonial dinner was given in Short Seeley's honor to commemorate her 80th birthday and to pay tribute to her many accomplishments in the fancy. Some of the milestones mentioned in a "This Is Your Life, Short Seeley" pageant were her initiating of the Siberian Husky and Alaskan Malamute Clubs, her formation of the New England Sled Dog Club, being a breeder-owner of the first Siberian Husky bitch to become a champion, being owner of the first registered Alaskan Malamute and the first Malamute champion, being the only woman to be given a military award by President Eisenhower and receiving the award from Admiral Richard Byrd as Chief Consultant for the Sledge Dog Divison of Operation Deep Freeze.

An acknowledgment of this testimonial dinner and a list of these accomplishments was read into the Congressional Record on October 29, 1971, by the Hon. Norris Cotton of New Hampshire.

Eva B. Seeley's team of all AKC-registered dogs including five champions and the foundation stock of many of our present-day kennels. This rare old photograph was taken at the Chinook Kennels training trail at Wonalancet, New Hampshire. All the dogs pictured were house pets, brood bitches and studs as well as top show and racing dogs, with many bearing the Alyeska name, the oldest established foundation stock in the breed.

Receiving the awards presented to her for her outstanding contributions to dogs—Alaskan Malamutes and Siberian Huskies in particular —Short Seeley reflects on her years of activities in the dog fancy. Judy Rosemarin and Sy Goldberg deliver two more plaques to commemorate her achievements.

The members of the committee for the testimonial dinner for Short
Seeley's 80th birthday banquet were, left to right: Joseph Ensminger,
Bob Shirone, Phyllis Buoneillo, Violet Schirone, Debby Ensminger, Sy
Goldberg, Judy Rosemarin, Martin Rosemarin, Jean Fournier, Peggy
Grant, Beryl Allen, Vincent Buoneillo. Photo by F. Dysart.

Perhaps as fate decreed it, on the very night of Mrs. Seeley's Tes-
timonial Dinner an Alaskan Malamute (American, Canadian and
Bermudian Ch. Inuit's Woolly Bully) placed First in the Working
Group at the Vacationland Dog Club in Maine under judge Melbourne
Downing, and at another dog show in the United States a Siberian
Husky also triumphed in the Working Group—a fitting tribute to the
lady who did so much for so many years to establish these two breeds
in the American dog fancy.

It is especially significant when we remember that Woolly Bully,
owned and bred by Sheila Balch—who spoke and paid her own personal tribute to Mrs. Seeley at the dinner—traces her stock back to Mrs.
Seeley's original foundation stock in the breed.

The matriarch of the breed. . . Mrs. Eva B. "Short" Seeley, photographed on the occasion of her 80th birthday by Judy Rosemarin.

One of the lighter moments at the Short Seeley testimonial dinner came during Mrs. Sheila Balch's tribute to her. Mr. and Mrs. Martin Rosemarin, Mrs. Peggy Grant, Mrs. Seeley and handler Robert Cullinane look on.

American and Canadian Champion Bearpaw Elk of Tote Um, the first red and white male champion in the United States.

4. FAMOUS FIRSTS IN ALASKAN MALAMUTE HISTORY

Over the years as various breeds of dogs have developed and caught on in popularity there have always been a number of fine dogs that lead the way. They stand out above the rest and establish certain records that set the pace for the rest to follow. So it was in the Alaskan Malamute breed as it came into its own identity from its background in what had previously been referred to as the Northern breeds.

A gray and white dog named Gripp of Yukon led the way for the Alaskan Malamute. Bred and owned by Mrs. Milton Seeley, Gripp brought great recognition to the breed as a member of a team of Malamutes she ran in the 1932 Olympics at Lake Placid, New York. Mrs. Seeley campaigned Gripp along with several other Malamutes from her Chinook Kennels to bring the breed to public attention and to help gain recognition from the American Kennel Club.

Gripp was also used to set the Standard for the breed, and in 1936, at the age of 7 years, he was recorded as the first Alaskan Malamute champion in the breed as well as the first registered Alaskan Malamute.

A bitch named Ooloo M'Loot was the first female champion in the breed. Whelped on February 27, 1946, she was 25 inches at the withers and weighed 85 pounds. Bred by P.G. Voelker, she was co-owned by him and Ralph and Marchetta Schmitt.

The first champion of record on the West Coast was Ch. Sierra Blizzard. From the M'Loot breeding this 95-pound, 25-inch male was bred by D.R. Gordon and campaigned by Betty Lou Scalet. He was later owned by Mr. and Mrs. W. Sherrif. He was whelped in December, 1947.

The first red and white Alaskan Malamute to make his championship in the United States and Canada was Bearpaw Elk of Tote-Um. Whelped September 21, 1963, he was bred by Minnie Graham in Canada and was owned by Mrs. Alice Jean Lucus of Seattle, Washington. This powerful 105-pound, 26½-inch dog was a lead dog on a team and a weight-puller as well. His pedigree carried many champions from the top bloodlines of the day, and his sire was also a champion in both Canada and the United States. His sire was Ch. Kodara El Toro and his dam was Siska of Erowah.

The first red bitch champion was Ch. Kodara's Scarlet Panda.

The first Alaskan Malamute champion in Canada, any color, was Lorna Jackson's Ch. Lorn-Hall's Oogerook M'Loot.

The first Malamute to earn championships in three countries was Beth Harris' American, Canadian and Mexican Champion Beowulf Thosca of Snow Foot.

MOVING UP IN THE SHOW WORLD

While progress was being made in the 1930's, no Malamute managed to capture a place for the breed in the Working Group until the 1940's. The dog to do it was Ch. Mulpus Brooks Master Otter, owned by Jean Lane. Sired by a dog named Mikiuk *ex* Noma M'Loot, he was bred by Paul Voelker (M'Loot Kennels) and Ralph Schmitt (Silver Sled Kennels). Otter was 25 inches at the withers and weighed 80 pounds. He was whelped on February 27, 1946.

While Master Otter was the first to place in a Working Group at an A.K.C. point show, it was another Mulpus Brooks dog which managed to win First Place in a Working Group. Whelped in January, 1952, Ch. Mulpus Brooks the Bear, a son of Master Otter, won the Working Group in December, 1954 under judge William Kendrick. Bear was owned by Mrs. James W. Dawson. His dam was Mulpus Brooks Dusty Lane.

The second Malamute male to win a Working Group was Ch. Aabare of Redhorse, whelped in 1953 and bred and owned by H.B. Pearson, Jr.

The first bitch to place in a Working Group was Ch. Barb-Far Marclar's Machook. She was owned by the W.R. Gormleys and was sired by Ch. Apache Chief of Husky Pak *ex* Ch. Cheyenne of Husky Pak.

The first bitch to win First Place in a Working Group was John Vanyo's Ch. Eldor's Pretty Miss Penny.

The first bitch to place in a Working Group in Canada was American and Canadian Champion Tote-Um's Shawna Tu. Shawna was owned and bred by Dianne Ross of the Tote-Um Kennels in Cle Elum, Washington. This win was made in October, 1967.

There was also a Malamute which placed in the Group from the Puppy Class. This was Brenda Malesa's Ch. Malesa's Silver Chalice. Chalice's sire was Ch. King Nikki of Northwind, C.D.X.; the dam was Ch. Glacier's Tisha Lyng, C.D.

Ch. Malesa's Silver Chalice also was the youngest (6½ months) Alaskan Malamute to place in a Working Group. Chalice eventually went on to be the sire of 9 champions from his first three litters; he

One of the earlier important Alaskan Malamutes, Ch. Mulpus Brooks Master Otter, pictured winning under judge William Kendrick, handled for owner by Jane Kamp Forsyth for this early 1950 show win.

was also #2 Alaskan Malamute in the 1969 Phillips System ratings. He finished for his championship in just 63 days, which made him one of the youngest Alaskan Malamutes to achieve championship; he was 8 months old on attainment of his title. He had 11 Bests of Breed and 5 Group Placements before he was a year old. He was bred by Lois and Hames Olmen and owned by Brenda Malesa and Marchetta Schmitt.

The youngest Malamute to achieve championship was a bitch, Ch. Alcan Applause; she finished in five shows at 7 months and 7 days old from the Puppy Classes. She was bred by Frederic Seyfarth and owned by the Michael Scotts and Carol, Dian and Nally McComb.

The first Alaskan Malamute placed in the Group at the world-famous Westminster Kennel Club Show in 1969, when Joseph and

Janice Whitacre's Ch. Alyeska Su Son placed fourth. Su Son was a Best in Show-winning dog and a sire of champions. In 1974 and 1975 Ch. Talak of Kotzebue, handled by Myrna Pearson and co-owned by the William Millers and the Charles Sullivans, placed Third in the Working Group at that show both years. Talak was also #10 Working Dog in the Nation for 1973, having amassed over 15,000 points in *Popular Dogs* magazine's famous Phillips System ratings for top United States show dogs.

The first Alaskan Malamute to place in a Group in Cuba was also Cuba's first Malamute champion, Ch. Kobuk's Erkluk, owned by Lois

Best of Breed at an Alaskan Malamute Club of America Specialty Show a few years back was Ch. Aabara of Redhorse, owned by H.B. Pearson, Jr. Mr. Pearson handled Aabara to this important win under the late judge Charles A. Swartz.

Ch. Barb-Far Marclar's Machook pictured winning Best of Opposite Sex at the May, 1958 National Specialty Show. Owned by Mr. and Mrs. W. Robert Gormley of Barberton, Ohio. Norton of Kent photograph.

Ch. Kelerak of Kobuk, bred by Earl and Natalie Norris and owned by the Robert Zollers. The sire was Ch. Toro of Bras Coupe *ex* Helen of Bras Coupe. Mrs. Zoller handling.

The 1953 Specialty Show of the Alaskan Malamute Club, held in conjunction with the Westchester Kennel Club, saw judge Mrs. Rudolph Engle award Best of Breed to the bitch Ch. Arctic Storm of Husky-Pak and Best of Opposite Sex to the dog Ch. Apache Chief of Husky-Pak. Both Malamutes, owned by Mr. and Mrs. Robert J. Zoller, were from the same litter. William Brown photograph.

and Bill Dawson. He was sired by Ch. Mulpus Brooks the Bear *ex* Ayi-yak of Roy-El. It must be remembered that before Castro, Cuba was exceptionally active in the sport of showing dogs. Close to the U.S. border, the dog shows in Cuba and Mexico were just like another circuit in those early days, with fanciers and their dogs from other countries showing as readily in one place as another. The moneyed people of both countries were proud of their breeding, and their shows were the ultimate in hospitality and efficiency.

One of the most prominent fanciers in Cuba was Mario Fernandez, breeder and exhibitor of Cocker Spaniels, who after fleeing the Castro regime came to live in Philadelphia and became head superintendent for the Foley Dog Show Organization, staging the majority of the dog shows on the eastern seaboard.

FIRST ALASKAN MALAMUTE BEST IN SHOW WINNERS

The first Alaskan Malamute to win the first Alaskan Malamute Club of America National Specialty Show was Ch. Toro of Bras Coupe in 1952. Bred by Mrs. Milton Seeley, he was owned by Earl and Natalie Norris of Anchorage, Alaska. Toro's breeding was mainly pure Kotzebue, his sire being Ch. Kim of Kotzebue and his dam Kotzebue Cleopatra. He was whelped in 1945 and is known also for his other accomplishments in the breed.

The first bitch to win the parent club's National Specialty was the following year, 1953, and the winner was Ch. Arctic Storm of Husky Pak. Storm was sired by Ch. Spawn's Hot Shot of Roy-El. Bred by Elsie A. Truchon, he was owned by Alice M. Spawn of Newark Valley, New York. The Hot Shot was only 10 months old when he attained his championship.

In 1963 the breed celebrated its first all-breed Best in Show winner. Ch. Sno-Crest's Mukluk was the dog, and Martha Guiffre was his proud owner; he was sired by Ch. Cochise of Husky Pak *ex* Kobuk's Dark Beauty. (Beauty was top Brood Bitch in 1962 and in the history of the breed.) Mukluk won his first all-breed Best in Show on August 25, 1963. He won a total of 3 Bests in Show. Whelped in 1958, he was during his time the top show dog in the breed history and was always owner-handled. He was also lead dog on a 4-dog team.

The first Best in Show-winning Alaskan Malamute in Canada was Dr. and Mrs. Kenneth Bourn's Ch. Boru's Erkloonook.

The first Alaskan Malamute to win a Best in Show in Alaska was owned by Kay Moustakis from Anchorage, and the dog's name was Ch. Kougarok. He was top-winning dog in Alaska for 1971 and the first Malamute ever to win a Best in Show in Alaska. The judge was Dr. Frank Booth and the show was October 10, 1971. Kougarok was sired by Ch. Kee-too *ex* Kee-nah. Kougarok was also a sled dog; he weighed 96 pounds and stood 25 inches.

BRACE AND TEAM WINNERS

The first Best in Show Brace win was made in September, 1969 by Nancy Russell and her Ch. Glacier's Storm Kloud, C.D. and his grandson, Ch. Timberlane's Storm Kloud. This beautiful brace also won the Best Brace in Show award at the 1972 Westminster Kennel Club show at Madison Square Garden in New York City.

It was Nancy Russell who also won the first Best Team in Show award for the breed in 1972. She won with the two dogs mentioned above and with Ch. Timberlane's Pamiiyok and Russell's Yveti Rose, C.D. added.

Yveti Rose was top-producing dam in the breed for 1968 with five champions to her credit and many more pointed. Timberlane's Storm

First Alaskan Malamute Brace to win a Best in Show at a Westminster Kennel Club Show was Nancy C. and Robert G. Russell's Ch. Timberlane Storm Kloud and Ch. Glaciers Storm Kloud, C.D.

Kloud was also a weight-puller and won second place in the 1970 International Kennel Club of Chicago contest.

FAMOUS FIRSTS IN OBEDIENCE

It was inevitable that the Alaskan Malamute would become involved with obedience work as time went by. While they are naturally better at pulling and racing, their temperament also lends itself to obeying commands, and for those who didn't work their dogs in harness, obedience was another excellent way to "work" them.

The first Alaskan Malamute to win a "Best in Obedience Trial" was Coldfoot Ponoka, C.D. Ponoka later became a leader dog for the blind.

The first Alaskan Malamute to earn a Companion Dog, or C.D. title, was Ch. Husky-Pak Blackhawk, whelped in 1950 and owned by Mr. and Mrs. Roy Truchon of New Jersey and bred by the Robert Zollers. Sired by Kayak of Brookside *ex* Ch. Arctic Storm of Husky Pak, Blackhawk was the sire of 3 champions. His dam, Arctic Storm, was the first bitch to win the AMCA National Specialty in 1953.

The first Alaskan Malamute to win the Companion Dog Excellent, or C.D.X. title, was Ch. Cliquot of Husky Pak, bred by the Robert

Ch. Arctic Storm of Husky-Pak with owner Robert J. Zoller of Blue Ridge Summit, Pennsylvania.

Zollers and owned by Alizabeth Aninger of Somers, Connecticut. Bred in 1952, he is also the dog represented in the Alaskan Malamute Club of America emblem, drawn by Drew Drasher.

American and Mexican Ch. Beowulf Thaera, C.D., was the first Alaskan Malamute to win a "Highest Scoring Dog in Trial" award. Bred by Vera Goldsmith and owned by Beth Harris, Thaera was also a sled dog.

The first Utility Dog, or U.D. winner, was Ch. Coldfoot Minto, U.D.T. As you can note from the complete title just given, he went on to earn his Tracking Dog title as well, though the first Tracking Dog titleholder in the United States and Canada was another Coldfoot Kennel dog, Ch. Coldfoot Oonanik, owned by Wilfred and Desneiges Anctil. Oonanik won his T.D. title in the United States in October, 1968 and in Canada the same year. Minto was owned by the Coldfoot Kennels and was sired by Stikeen of Tyree *ex* Ch. Coldfoot Chevak and won the title in December, 1966.

The first Utility Dog bitch title-holder appeared in 1967. She was Ch. Tigara's Nucah of Arctica, U.D. She was owned and handled to this advanced title by Joan Byrne. Nucha's sire was Ch. Tigara's Sadko the Tartar *ex* Tigara's Tsena of Arctica.

The first Triple Obedience title-holder was Ch. Beowulf Thytaen of Sno Hawk, owned by Beth Harris. Thytaen held obedience titles in America, Canada and Mexico.

THE MOST TITLED DOG IN THE WORLD

The most titled dog in the world—of any breed—was owned by Wilfred and Desneiges Anctil, and mentioned earlier. The dog was International Ch. Coldfoot Oonanik , cited as the first dog in the United States and Canada to earn a T.D. title. In addition to the International Championship, he had his C.D. title in Bermuda and his U.D.T. and the C.A.C.I.B. (*Certificat d'Aptitude au Championat Internationale de Beaute*) championship in Mexico. Oonanik was wolf gray and white and is the only dog ever to earn both a C.A.C.I.B. championship and also a U.D.T. title. Nikki was 27½ inches at the withers and weighed 150 pounds. He held 19 titles and 102 "Breed First" achievement awards and—perhaps the most significant of all—he was always owner-handled! His sire was also a famous dog in his own right, Ch. Coldfoot's Lucky Strike Mine, C.D.

THE MOST TITLED BITCH IN THE BREED

American, Bermudian, Canadian, Mexican, C.A.C.I.B., F.C.I., International Champion Beowulf Thosca of Snow Foot, American, Canadian, Bermudian and Mexican C.D., American C.D.X. is her name. Bred by Vera Goldsmith and owned by Beth Harris of Fair Oaks, California, Thosca has 10 titles in 42 countries and was #1 Bitch in the United States for 1970. Thosca was whelped in 1965.

THE STORY OF STORM KLOUD: A SUCCESS STORY TO BE PROUD OF

During the second half of the 20th century it became the vogue for more and more Americans to attend and exhibit at the famous Monte Carlo dog show each year. The members of the royal family of Monaco—which for some time now has also included our own Grace Kelly—have always been known dog fanciers, so it was only a question of time before the Monaco dog show event would become one of the prestige shows to attend when one traveled.

During my years as editor of *Popular Dogs* magazine, I had a correspondent covering the various dog show events in Europe, and I naturally instructed him to cover the Monte Carlo show on a regular basis. He would always send me a post card with the news that Princess Grace had asked for me, and the post card bore a dog stamp which heralded this event each year. The cards and the stamps became some of my most treasured dog fancy possessions. Princess Antoinette, sister of Prince Rainier, is the show chairman, and either Grace or Prince Rainier or Princess Antoinette herself presents the trophy for Best in Show each year.

In 1973 Mrs. Nancy Russell of Sussex, Wisconsin was one of the Americans who attended the Monte Carlo show and took in the entire

Ch. Glacier's Storm Kloud, C.D., one of the all-time top Alaskan Malamutes. Owned by Nancy Russell.

European circuit including Sam Remo, Italy and Nice, France. With her was her magnificent Alaskan Malamute, American, Mexican and Canadian Champion Glacier's Storm Kloud, C.D. To make a lovely long story short—he cleaned up at the shows. He won the top awards at Italy and Monaco and was Best of Breed in France, making him an International Champion. There were 773 dogs from 14 countries at Monte Carlo, and Mrs. Judy de Casembroot of England, who judged the Malamute Best in Show said:

"The Malamute absolutely dominated. He had character and quality." The award was presented at the Garden's Hall, built in 1966 to celebrate Monte Carlo's centennial. Over 1500 people stayed to observe the final judging.

The eight-year-old "Bear," as he is called, was the first Malamute ever shown in Italy and the big seal-gray dog brought down the house with applause whenever he moved out across the ring.

Bear now holds the record for top prizes in the history of the breed. His first victory was in 1970; he then went on to win 11 Groups in the U.S., 6 in Canada, 2 in Mexico and now one each in Italy and Monaco. Bear was Best of Breed at Chicago's International show four years in a row and with his son, Ch. Timberlane's Storm Kloud, has been Best Brace in Show at Westminster; 10 out of 17 times shown as a brace they were Best in Show and won 15 Groups.

Bear is truly a dog with a record to be proud of!

THE STORY OF "PRETTY BOY FLOYD"

No recording of the Alaskan Malamute breed would be complete without the telling of the story of "Floyd," a winner that has had a tremendous influence on the breed in the dog show world as we acknowledge the breed's fiftieth year in the United States during the 1970's.

American, Canadian and Bermudian Ch. Inuit's Woolly Bully, during his decade in the show ring, has won 11 Specialties—more than any other Malamute—and under respected judges in the breed such as Eva Seeley, Lorna Demidoff and Lawson Williams. His later wins were made from the Veteran's Class and at 9 and 10 years of age. Floyd was 10 when he completed his Canadian championship and was still placing in the Group at the shows.

Floyd was bred, owned and shown most of the time by Sheila Balch, owner of the Inuit Kennels in Valley Cottage, New York, a kennel which has won more Specialty Shows than any other kennel. The kennel's foundation bitch was Ch. Balch's Ingrid of Brenmar, dam of Floyd and granddam of Floyd's most famous son, Ch. Inuit's Sweet Lucifer. Lucifer is following in his father's footsteps by winning handsomely and was #3 Malamute in the Phillips System at the beginning of 1975. Lucifer has won the National Specialty and is the current star at the Inuit Kennels.

FIRST COVER DOG

The first Alaskan Malamute to appear on the cover of a modern book devoted exclusively to the breed was Ch. Kimbra's King Notak. The book was a soft-cover volume entitled *How to Raise and Train an Alaskan Malamute*; it was written by Charles J. Berger and published in 1963 by T.F.H. Publications, Inc., publishers of this book. The dog was bred by Dorothy Dillingham and owned by Mary Wiebe of Anaheim, California. Whelped in 1958, he weighed 90 pounds and was 25 inches at the withers. Dark wolf gray and white in color, his pedigree is almost entirely Tigara bloodlines.

Ch. Balch's Ingrid of Brenmar pictured winning Best of Breed at the New York-New Jersey Area Specialty Show in 1967 under esteemed judge Lorna Demidoff. This lovely bitch is the dam of champions and is 100% Kotzebue breeding. Owned and shown by Sheila Balch, Inuit Kennels, Valley Cottage, New York, who also bred her.

American, Canadian and Bermudian Ch. Inuit's Woolly Bully pictured taking the Breed at the 1970 Bucks County Kennel Club show under the esteemed judge Mrs. Eva "Short" Seeley. Owner-handler Sheila Balch, Inuit Kennels, Valley Cottage, New York. Shafer photo.

We can all be very proud of these dogs. They have brought to the breed its royal heritage. We can also be very proud of their sires and dams and breeders and trainers. But we must also look to the future. Records are made to be broken, but famous firsts carry on in the history of the breed. We can hope there will be more famous dogs who will carry the breed forward in the future and join the ranks of these worthy ancestors who did so much to distinguish the Alaskan Malamute in the hearts of all dog lovers.

5. THE ALASKAN MALAMUTE AS A FREIGHT DOG

In the early days in the Arctic the explorers were the first to know—after the Eskimos, that is—that no animal of any size could do the job the huskies could. . . working to help their owners live, protecting them and providing the only practical means of transportation.

The explorers learned the hard way that even horses could not endure the weather conditions in the Arctic regions, and when they did learn their lesson they began to concentrate on the best possible dog to do the arduous labor required to penetrate the miles of ice and show that covered the desolate lands near the Pole. They chose the Alaskan Malamute.

While it was generally agreed that the Siberian Husky was tops at pulling faster, his forte was a fast steady pace for the long haul. The Alaskan Malamute came to be the unsurpassed choice for the heavier load over the farthest distances because of his strength and seemingly endless endurance.

The average freight Malamute could be counted on to pull two hundred pounds. . . perhaps as much as eighteen hundred pounds when part of a six-dog team. None of the animals available in the past centuries could do this job. Today, of course, airplanes, snowmobiles, and the like are being used more and more and can do the job. Even the natives are using the dogs almost exclusively for local travel or racing and weight-pulling contests for recreational purposes rather than as necessities of survival.

It is gratifying to note that the dogs which have not been allowed to become just pets or show dogs still possess the desire to run and pull, whether it is just for fun or to deliver medical supplies to an endangered village in the far reaches of the North country! We hope they never lose this exceptional spirit and instinct, which stems from their earliest days on earth. It is a noble heritage.

THE WEIGHT-PULLING MALAMUTE

It is known that the Siberian Husky makes a faster racing team, so there is not quite the incentive for Malamute drivers to compete. When racing clubs today give races for all-Malamute teams the races are slightly better attended and draw a few more entries than before. But in the freighting races, which feature Malamutes required to carry a specific amount of weight, the interest is keen. There is less opportunity for the dogs to scrap among themselves, or to take on another team in a battle, and their interest seems piqued when there is excessive weight to pull. It is almost like a challenge to them, and they respond to it.

Perhaps the attraction of owning a freighting Malamute is that you don't need to maintan an entire team of Malamutes to have a good time! Weight-pulling can be done by small teams or with a single dog, as with a pack dog. It is just as competitive and certainly a lot less expensive, and the results can be equally impressive.

Training for the weight-pulling dog can be done in the back yard with a proper harness, and the physical conditioning which results certainly enhances the dog's good health. Conditioning for the show ring is a must, and there is nothing like a good sturdy dog doing what he was bred to do to give it the muscle-tone the judges look for in the show ring.

Just as the winning racing dog has to have the desire to run above all else, the successful Malamute must have "heart" to win at weight-pulling. They can't have an ounce of give-up in their bodies! The desire to pull must be innate, and the desire to succeed must be more important to them than anything else at the time.

THE PHYSICAL STRUCTURE OF THE WEIGHT-PULLING DOG

Since not only Malamutes but also St. Bernards, Newfoundlands, etc., succeed at pulling, there is a lot to be said for "size" in pulling. Harnessing and traction, or footing, are important, and heavy bones and cobby bodies denote power in the most successful dogs. The rest is up to the trainer, and early training can be almost as important as training in the older dog.

TRAINING METHODS

There are almost as many methods of training a dog to pull weight as there are trainers. Several can be effective, and a lot depends on matching the best method with each individual dog. But the best start is to have the dog pull logs of increasing size and, of course, the neighborhood children in carts.

While they are learning this basic training they are also learning the various commands necessary for the later performance in com-

Conditioning for weight-pulling. Beach-running is important to the muscle development necessary for pulling and general all-around physical fitness for the show ring. Weight-pulling Canadian Ch. Bearpaw Lobo, son of Elk, poses on a beach to which his owners, Phil and Alice Jean Lucus of Seattle, Washington, take him for training.

petition. Sled dogs will usually know the commands and excel in weight-pulling, since they are used to pulling, but actually many trainers claim that dogs which have never worked with a team are easiest to train to freighting, because they have no previous work pattern to deviate from. At any rate, the gee, haw, whoa and hold commands will be necessary for weight-pullers.

THE ALL IMPORTANT HARNESS

Ideally the harness should be made to fit each specific dog, being fitted as the work on the harness progresses. The harness should feature a spreader in the back to prevent the lines from touching the dog's hindquarters or pulling over the back. The harness is usually padded, fashioned after the old-fashioned horse collars, weight evenly distributed all around and fitting low on the neck so as not to interfere with the breathing. There is also a harness called a Siwash which can be used.

SPECIAL COMPETITION RULES

If you are planning to enter your dog in a competition or contest event, it would be wise the first time to ask for printed rules applying to the particular club. Some clubs do not allow leashes, others do not permit encouragement from the owners, etc. It is wise to know these things before entering as well as while training so that nothing comes as a surprise the day of the show! You might have the best weight-puller in the history of the breed, but no one is going to know it if the dog won't move unless he sees your youngest child with a soggy pretzel in his hand at the end of the course!

CONTEST SLED WEIGHTS

While logs, carts, and carriages are used in training, in personal work at home, along with car tires and sleds, depending on locale and weather conditions, sleds are packed with other weights in an actual contest. Sometimes cinder blocks, people or sandbags are loaded onto the sleds.

Some clubs stipulate either live or dead weight, while other clubs allow a combination of both. Again we point out the importance of finding out the rules of each contest before the day of the race.

THE REWARD SYSTEM

While praise and encouragement are essential in early training, and many trainers offer a pat on the head as well as a bit of something to eat as a reward, it is also important that the dog will pull without any added incentive from a member of the family or his trainer. Needless to say, punishing or hitting the dog is not permitted or to be tolerated.

OVER-DOING IT

We hope it is also needless to say that making the dog pull too much weight too soon will not only discourage but also can injure your dog, even kill him. Undue stress and strain can damage the heart and spoil his chances permanently, if not kill him. Patience as well as training is required from the owner for future success.

A WORLD CHAMPIONSHIP???

While concentrated efforts are being made by interested parties all over the nation, there has never been an "end of the year" competition which could in any way determine a World Champion Weight-Puller. Winners from various competitions all over the country would have to be present, competing under exactly the same rules and regulation in order to determine a top winner. So far this has not been possible, and we have only our area winners to acclaim. Perhaps in the future a national group can organize to present just such a competition. Meantime, we can only record winning pulls and hope for such a contest in the future.

SOME WEIGHT-PULLING WINNERS

In December, 1959, Dr. and Mrs. Leo Rifkind whelped Kodara El Toro and later sold the dog to Richard and Dianne Ross of the Tote-Um Kennels in Cle Elum, Washington. Toro became an American and Canadian champion as well as a famous weight-pulling dog. At ten years of age Toro served as lead dog on a 7-dog team for the Walt Disney movie *Lefty the Ding-A-Ling Lynx*. At 11 years of age, to further prove his all-around personality and potential, he entered the show ring and won Best of Breed and Group Second from the Veterans Class at a trophy show. His fame was the pulling of 1,375 pounds in contests during his heyday.

Ch. Arctic Frost of Erowah, whelped in January, 1960, was another early dog which achieved fame for pulling weight. Bred by Jean Clark and owned by Dick and Marilyn Wooten of Oregon,Frost was also the sire of champions, a sled dog and undefeated in competition. He was trained by pulling a telephone pole around the property!

Ch. Kink of Ro-Ala-Ken was bred by Beulah Robel of El Monte, California in 1961. He was also an all-around dog that starred in television commercials, was a lead dog on a sled and played a part as a wolf in a motion picture. He was also owned by Beulah Robel and pulled 1500 pounds.

The Rosses of Tote-Um Kennels also owned Ch. Pak N Pulls Kaltag. Bred by Martha Guiffre, he pulled 1200 pounds in competition and was a sled dog and sire of 5 champions during the 1960's.

Ch. Vallee's Snow Bandit, bred and owned in the mid-1960's by Leon Navarro, made his mark in fields other than weight-pulling. In 1968 he was the sixth ranking Alaskan Malamute in the Phillips System ratings and in 1969 he was #5. This was after winning a 1966 weight-pulling contest at 14 months of age by pulling 1,460 pounds.

In 1965 Ch. Traleika of Tundra was bred by Katherine and Edward Rodewald of the Sky Fyre Kennels in Arvada, Colorado. Traleika finished for her championship with 4 majors and Group Placements and was an area Specialty Show winner in 1970. In 1970 and 1971 Traleika was all-breed weight-pulling record holder in the Rocky Mountain Sled Dog Club. Holder of the Golden Bone award, Traleika broke the club record for weight-pulling in 1971.

The Rodewalds also owned Ch. Snow Plumes Nayani of Sky Fyre, bred by A. and E. Kirsch. Owner-handled to her championship at 13 months of age, Nayani was Top Puppy Award winner in 1970 from the Alaskan Malamute Club of America and went on to win the Weight-Pulling Award from the Rocky Mountain Sled Dog Club for 1970-1971.

Tundra Boy of Sugar River, a black and white 110-pound dog bred and owned by Jerry and Judy Winder of Durang, Illinois, was never defeated in weight-pulling competition. He was mid-west sled dog champion for 1971 and 1972, pulling over 1,000 pounds.

In 1966 Ch. Squankan's Moose was whelped and destined to be-

American and Canadian Ch. Bearpaw Elk of Tote Um and his litter sister Bearpaw Eechouka. Elk is owned by Alice Jean and Philip Lucus of the Elk's Pinetop Kennels, Seattle, Washington.

come renowned as both wheel dog on a race team and as a weight-puller of 1,450 pounds. Bred by Fran Epley and Jean Sandwell, he was owned by Richard and Dawn Woods.

Through the years Roger and Malle Burggaf have been active in weight-pulling competition. Perhaps their most famous competitor was a bitch they bred named Taaralaste Naki Neiu. Whelped in 1966, Naki broke records by herself and as a lead dog on a 3-dog team. At the 1970 North American Championship Race in Fairbanks, Alaska, she pulled 2,200 pounds. At this event in 1971 she pulled 1,400 pounds uphill! At the 1971 Anchorage (Alaska) Fur Rendezvous she pulled 1,525 pounds, defeating 37 other dogs including St. Bernards and New-

Canadian Champion Bearpaw Lobo, winning on the way to his championship, which was completed in January, 1973. Owned by Alice Jean and Philip Lucus, Elk's Pinetop Kennels, Seattle, Washington.

foundlands which were twice her weight. She outpulled them by 300 pounds!

The Burggafs of College, Alaska, also owned Ch. Tote-Um's Littlest Hobo. Bred by the Rosses of Tote-Um Kennel fame, Hobo finished his championship in 1970 with four Group Placements. This 27-inch, 102-pound sable and white was whelped in February, 1965 and was used extensively for freight trips throughout his lifetime. Hobo also participated in North American Sled Dog Championship weight-pulling contests. This 2-day event, in which each dog pulls 100 pounds of dead weight over an 18-mile course, is a major event in the North and among those in the breed interested in weight-pulling competition.

Other names such as Bearpaw Elk and Ch. Pak N Pull's Hyak of Tote-Um also should be mentioned in a chapter devoted to weight-pulling dogs. Hyak was also a sled dog, sire of champions and a top weight-puller. He was owned by Dr. and Mrs. L. Bosshardt of Yakima, Washington, where weight-pulling contests are a very popular sport.

There have been many other weight-pulling winners over the years, including, last but not least, Ch. Shuyak Caro of Gold Foot, C.D. Obedience dog, sled dog and show dog with Group Placings, Caro also held the weight-pulling record for 5 consecutive years with the G.L.S.D.A. club.

POPULARITY GROWS

Weight-pulling contests have become so popular in the sports world that by 1970 over one hundred competitions were being scheduled almost every year. In these contests the dogs pit their strength and endurance by pulling increasingly heavy loads over measured distances within a specified time limit to become winners. This is done either singly or in teams, and the winner is declared when the sled, not the dog, crosses the finish line. Incredible accounts of strength are recorded during these events.

THE FAMOUS "BUCK"

Perhaps the most famous and best loved story of weight-pulling in the early days was the story of writer Jack London's dog Buck. Members of the Anchorage Mushers Club in Alaska claim he pulled one thousand pounds in Nome, Alaska, during the Gold Rush days. It was this dog on which Jack London based one of his most famous books, *The Call of the Wild*, which was made into a movie of the same name. While 1,000 pounds is nowhere near the weight out top dogs today can pull, *The Call of the Wild* has always been a popular story.

Canadian Ch. Bearpaw Lobo, son of Elk, shown with Philip Lucus after winning another weight-pulling contest. Lobo is co-owned by Alice Jean Lucus and Philip Lucus, owners of the Elk's Pinetop Kennels in Seattle.

Photographer Bob Duncan captures on film a team of Malamutes training for the races. In the absence of snow, owners use rigs or motor vehicles as pictured above to keep the dogs in top condition.

6. THE ALASKAN MALAMUTE AS A RACING DOG

Relatively few Alaskan Malamutes become outstanding racing dogs. If they are good, it is usually because top quality racing dogs are in their background and show in their pedigree. Just as a good "nose" is almost always hereditary with a Beagle, so is the desire to run inherent in the Alaskan Malamute.

If they are good racers they are usually well angulated, with longer legs and lighter bones, with large and strong feet, a long and deep chest and an independence that sets them apart from others in the kennel.

If these qualifications are wrapped up in your dog, you are still only half way there! You must remember that the dog still has to be properly trained and be able to run with all the other dogs on the team, and *then*, if you don't have a top notch lead dog you probably won't win anyway, especially if the dog doesn't have the most essential ingredient of all—the innate desire to run! The most worrisome thing about the breed today is that so many of the Malamutes being bred just do not have that desire to run above all else. Without it, you can never have better than a good team; you will never have a top-winning team!

STARTING THE PUPPY

There are probably few better breeds for pulling than the Alaskan Malamute, because of his stamina and sustained power. Whether your dog will race or pull weight, training should start around two or three months of age. Start with a soft harness and let him drag a small log or board around. Judge the weight of the log by the weight of the dog. Don't let it be so heavy that the puppy could not possibly move it without a struggle; if you do that, he'll lose interest or get discouraged. By the same token, don't let it be so light that it will catch up with him on the down grade, or he'll never learn the meaning of what it is to "pull." Try what you think is just right, and then observe the puppy's behavior with it for a while; make any necessary adjustments at this time and, of course, as the puppy continues to grow.

Kotzebue of Chinook and (sitting down) Ch. Kotzebue Kuyan of Chinook with their owner , Irene Delamater.

Nikkai's Kahn, a normal puppy resulting from a test breeding from a dwarf female and a high probability champion male. Kahn was later neutered to prevent the spread of this terrible hereditary disease. Kahn is photographed in a model sled built by Phil Lucus, Elk's Pinetop Kennels, Seattle, Washington. The Lucuses have crusaded against this disease since 1964.

Alice and Phil Lucus of Seattle, Washington, take their dogs down to the ocean for sled racing practice. From left to right is Tote-Um's Muktuk, Sitka and Chouka. Muktuk, clear of hip dysplasia but a carrier of dwarfism, was important in the establishment of the dwarfism project at Washington State University in 1969.

At this time, while the puppy is learning to pull, he should be encouraged to pull along a given path, so that the idea of a trail can be established in his mind should you wish to enter competition in the future.

EARLY TRAINING FOR THE RACING DOG

I have just stressed how important it is that each dog destined to race have the innate desire to run and win. This eagerness to compete will enable the trainer to start his harness training at an earlier age and thereby give a head start to the dog on the training as well as conditioning him to his purpose of running and pulling.

If you are fortunate enough to live in snow country, your sled, harness and towline will be your initial equipment for training. If you live in a comparatively snowless area you will need a three-wheeled balanced substitute for training. Training should be a serious matter and in no way the same as or comparable to playtime. Start with each dog individually pulling some weight. This individual training will help you determine which of the puppies has the strongest desire to pull ahead in spite of the weight. You will find that invariably the dog with the strongest desire to pull will make the best lead dog by the time your training nears completion.

THE TRAINING GROUND

One of the most difficult aspects of training will be finding the proper place to train the puppies. If you do not live in the country it will be necessary to locate a park or wooded area, or better still, a local race track where the dogs can run a distance with minimum danger of interruption by uncertain terrain. Too many distractions in populated areas will throw puppies or young dogs off until they are used to what is expected of them. With too many spectators around there is always the danger of having the team bowl them over if they get in the way. Therefore, until the puppies get used to running and keeping on the trail, bridle paths, fields and or farm lands are best places to work out. Remember the safety of others when tearing down a path with a team of sled dogs! Under no circumstances train

Sheila Balch and her two sons pose with the then two-year-old Wooly Bully and his racing sled.

your dogs on the street or a concrete surface. The irritation to the pads of the feet somehow prevents the dogs from reaching out to their full stride, so they never become good distance runners in a race. Ideal conditions are snow or sand, but if such surfaces are not available, train on dirt surfaces to prevent the hackneyed gait of the dogs which are trying to preserve their own feet, or which will pull up with bloody pads if forced to run on pavement.

As the puppies grow and begin their working together, you will undoubtedly have joined a club in your area where members are equally interested in racing. You will learn a great deal from your association with other members, and it is advisable to take full advantage of their advice, knowledge and experience. But there still are going to be many hours of training on your own where a few essential rules will apply.

Important to remember in your training is this: do not teach too many commands. Young puppies can not retain too many words, and expecting too much of them too soon will only confuse them and perhaps make them lose interest entirely. Remember to praise them lavishly for their good work and efforts. Remember to keep your puppies and dogs in top racing condition so that they will be able to give what is expected of them without draining every last bit of energy. Remember common sense rules which apply to racing as well as obedience or show training; namely, do not feed or water immediately before training, and exercise the puppies before starting the training so there will be no interruption. And perhaps most important of all, do not go on to another command or lesson until the dog has already learned the last one!

You will find that your puppy can cover a mile comfortably by the time he is eight months old, which should increase to 15 or 16 miles at the peak of his training and performance at two years of age.

DISPOSITION AND ATTITUDE

One of the determining factors in selecting your team will be each dog's disposition. The training may have gone along very well, but if the dog is a "scrapper" and will be undependable when harnessed with other dogs in a team, you will eventually run into trouble. While it is allowable to remove a dog from a team during a race, it would make more sense to have all members of your team able to finish if you really want to win and need that full team to do it!

When we talk about Malamutes being smart in their own special way, we must explain that at times there is an almost obvious "holding back" or lack of complete communication between you and the dog, which manifests itself noticeably in their training for racing competition. When a Malamute is being trained to race he will usually pace himself to fit the distance he must cover on his own. Therefore, it is wise when training the dog for the race to steadily increase the distance each day, rather than varying the ground mileage to be covered from one day to the next. Increasing distance each day will increase his desire to always "go further," and to the end of the race.

FORMING YOUR TEAMS

A tenet in animal behavior studies acknowledges that there is a leader in every pack. So it is with a racing team. Your lead dog must be the most respected member of your kennel or the other dogs simply will not give their all and "follow the leader." Whatever the sex of the lead dog, put your next two fastest dogs behind the lead dog and your biggest, or strongest, two at the wheel positions.

While your lead dog will assert himself to keep order in the pack, to maintain a good team you must have harmony among all members of the team. Drivers will find that on occasion if they buy dogs from other teams to add to their own, the new dog is apt not to pull and will be dragged by the rest unless he feels he has been accepted by the other dogs as a member of the pack. Puppies from the same litter, trained together, often make the best teams for this reason. They "grow into the saddle."

Practice makes perfect, as the saying goes, and hours of practice and training are necessary to get all your dogs working together as a team. There is no easy way to accomplish this other than hard work. It is a magnificent challenge.

SECURING RACING INFORMATION

If you have decided that you wish to enter a team in a race, you must write to the race-giving club well in advance asking for all pertinent information along with an entry blank. Ask the race marshall for specific information regarding not only the race, but information on joining the club, which you will want to do eventually, if you haven't already. State the size of your team, and ascertain at this time whether it is necessary to be a member of the club in order to enter the race. With some clubs this is a requirement.

While waiting for this information to reach you, consider once again whether or not you are *really ready* to enter your first race. Ask yourself whether your dogs are sufficiently trained, run well together, fight in harness, stick to the trail, tangle with other teams, can be distracted by people or other animals on the sidelines? And perhaps most important of all, are all the dogs equal in strength and endurance, and do they all really want to run more than anything else?!?

THE DAY OF THE RACE

You've entered your first race and have received your notification and rules regarding the race, time, place and requirements. Needless to say, the beginner should arrive early to observe the pro-

First in both Stud Dog and Veteran Dog classes at the 1974 A.M.C.A. National Specialty Show under judge Roy Kibler was American, Canadian and Bermudian Ch. Inuit's Wooly Bully. He is the sire of the Best of Breed winner at this show and also sire of the Best of Winners dog as well as the grandsire of the Winners Bitch and Reserve Winners Bitch. Bred and owned by Sheila Balch of Inuit Kennels, Valley Cottage, New York.

cedures others follow and have plenty of time to ask questions. Be sure you park in the correct area, stake your dogs out in the proper area, exercise them, and determine within plenty of time when the drivers' meeting will be held so that you can attend it.

While you are waiting for the meeting to begin, take the time to reread the rules of the race. As a beginner you may forget. . . and knowing what to do when and where can make a difference! Also check out your equipment.

Always include a complete substitute for your harness and tow lines, collars, leashes, etc., in your tack box. Accidents do happen, and it would be a shame to miss your first experience because a break left you without complete equipment. Don't be afraid to ask questions or to ask for help. Remember that everyone else was a beginner once also, and most of them remember how much it meant to them to have a helping hand or a genuine good word of advice.

Remember good manners during the race. Don't spoil someone else's chances because of your mistake or mistakes. They will be watching out for you if they know you are new at the game, but it is your responsibility not to spoil the race for others. You are expected to know the passing rules, re-passing rules, etc., and you will gain more respect for your sportsmanship and knowledge than you will for trying to stick it out when you should get out of the race. No one expects you to win your first race anyway! But whether you win or lose, once you've gotten into the competition you will become addicted to the sport and sooner or later you will win if your dogs are good and properly trained.

RACING MANNERS

Need we say that bad language, complaining and excuses, rough handling of your dogs (for any reason whatsoever!) drinking or pushing your dogs beyond their endurance are strictly taboo? How you conduct yourself under any and all conditions will determine how much help and respect you win from your fellow drivers, and if you want to continue in the racing field you had better stick to the rules or you will find yourself strictly an outsider. And that isn't the name of the game!

VARIATIONS ON THE RULES

Racing rules can sometimes vary according to local conditions, and geographical conditions also enter into it. Some races feature three classes: Class A, teams having a minimum limit of five dogs, with the trail usually 15 to 20 miles, and run in two or three heats on successive days. Total elapsed time determines the winner; Class B, runs from four to seven dogs over an approximate 7- to 10-mile run. This class is also run in heats, with the fastest total elapsed time determining the winner; Class C, or what is referred to as the Novice

Class, has a two or three dog limit on a 2- to 3-mile course. This class usually awards trophies rather than money prizes. One of the most important things for the beginner to remember is to enter his team in the proper class.

PROFESSIONAL RACING TEAMS

You must realize that racing for fun and pleasure or in local club meets or contests is entirely different from the professional racing meets where the stakes and purses are high and the owners and drivers are out to win. Professional racing teams are serious business, and it is a completely different world for the professional racing dog!

The trainers and drivers of the professional teams are usually those dedicated to doing nothing else but training and racing the dogs. It is their profession; the lives of the dogs are dedicated to racing and winning.

Two-dog racing team of Eileen and Chris Gabriel of Golden Bridge, New York. Littermates Wicked Witch and Ironhorse are working and show dogs.

This intent and purpose begins with the picking of the dogs which show—above all else—the natural desire to run and to win. The training is more rigorous, the culling more ruthless, and the proper rearing and selection of the dogs even more essential. Professional team owners will spare no expense and will travel the globe to acquire just the right dog to enhance their team. The studying of pedigrees becomes almost a science, and the health, care and feeding of their teams is of major concern.

While the purses for the winners of the big races are large, so are the costs of maintaining a professional team. The costs far exceed the winnings, and before one considers getting into the professional aspect of this sport, financial considerations must be taken into account.

With the professional racing teams there is also a more strict, concentrated training schedule. The dogs must be kept in top racing condition all the time, not just before racing seasons, which means they must not become overweight. Bad dispositions are weeded out at the first moment of discovery, grooming and training are on a regular schedule and more frequent, and the serious racing training begins in earnest at six or seven months of age.

Most racing dogs are staked out at about three to four months old, and the confined conditions seem to heighten their desire to run.

PROFESSIONAL RACING DOGS

While there is more interest in professional racing teams now than ever before, there are not as many as one would expect. There are reasons for this... the owners of the professional teams are interested to a great extent in the money prizes and will use any dog—purebred or otherwise—if the dog will run to win. Expenses are high to maintain and breed racing teams exclusively while waiting for the top ones to come along. Mixed breeds offer more opportunities to buy up the fastest dogs in spite of their ancestry, giving the owners a "faster team faster!" So unless money is no object, more of the pros will not stick to one breed, but will shop around. Though price may be no object, there is a time limit involved. It is only the dedicated racing enthusiast who can afford to support a team of purebreds who brings out a matched team that has a good chance of winning!

Two-dog team with Ch. Sena-Lak's Miss Tardy on the right. The team is owned by Eleanore DuBuis, Valois, New York.

SLED DOG RACING EVENTS
Sled Dog Racing in Idaho

1917 was the first year of the American Dog Derby in Ashtown, Idaho. This event is still held for racing enthusiasts. Today, however, the club holds several racing events in several different towns each year. They feature ten mile courses each day for two days. This is quite a different schedule from the 1917 event, when a half dozen teams of mixed breeds raced from West Yellowstone, Montana to Ashtown, Idaho—a distance of 75 miles!

Frostfield Kotzebue Kayo, Best of Breed from the puppy class at the North Eastern New York Alaskan Malamute Trophy Show in 1973 under judge M. Cresap. Handled by owner Jerry Wisefield, Frostfield Kennels, Avon, Massachusetts.

Sled Dog Racing in Minnesota

The St. Paul, Minnesota, Winter Carnival in 1962 was the site of the first sled dog racing in the state, in conjunction with the special events at the State Fair.

In 1965 the North Star Sled Dog Club, Inc. was started as a racing club, and by 1969 the club decided to sponsor a major national racing event at the Winter Carnival; they called it "East Meets West." A total of 55 teams competed that year in St. Paul, representing 11 states and Canada. The event was a major breakthrough for racing enthusiasts and has been growing in popularity and competition ever since. The purses get larger each year and the spectators increase notably as well.

While a reasonably new group, the club membership keeps increasing and participating in other racing events, and plans for the future are bright.

Mutt Races

Each year the All American Championship Sled Dog Races are held in Ely, Minnesota, and feature mutt races as part of the special events program. These mutt races are usually held following a torchlight parade, and are run for boys and girls from six to eight years of age, eight to ten years of age, and children from ten to twelve years of age. Each child runs a single hitch, and the one dog may be of any type or breed. The only differential is that they separate the experienced and trained sled dogs from the amateur dogs and run them in separate categories.

There is no entry fee and, of course, trophies are provided for the winners. This is always a popular event with racing enthusiasts of all ages.

Beauty Queens

The Ely event also has been known to feature a beauty queen to appear in the torchlight parade. In 1971, and a repeat performance in 1972, it was Brit-Inger Johannsen, a former Miss Scandinavia and former Miss Sweden, invited by the Sled Dog Committee to head up the parade and to judge such events as a "beard contest" where she rubbed cheeks with those racing participants who sported "beavers."

Special Events

The sled dog gathering usually opens with a community center show which features the latest in sleds, equipment, accessories and demonstrations of anything and everything pertaining to racing, including items which can be purchased.

This is followed on Friday night by a torchlight parade, with the aforementioned beauty queen, sleds, snowmobiles, floats, and the like. The parade is followed by the special events program, which features weight pulling contests, celebrity races, ski-jorring, a scramble race, a beard contest and the kids' mutt races. Entertainment of the indoor variety follows the activities in these categories.

Saturday sees the first heats of the All American Championship Sled Dog Race. Usually over 100 teams compete. Saturday night there is a banquet and entertainment, and on Sunday the second heats are run; prizes are awarded at the completion of the day's events.

There is over $5000 in prize money awarded to the racers as well as hundreds of dollars worth of trophies to the winners who manage to triumph on one of the finest racing trails in the world. The best known racers from all over the United States (including Alaska, of course) and Canada manage to show up to compete.

Because of the great beauty of the dogs, and the excitement of the chase, there is always a great deal of spectator enthusiasm as well as newspaper, radio and television coverage and stories in major magazines all over the world. Over 20,000 fans show up to cheer on their favorite dog teams. The Chamber of Commerce of Ely, Minnesota, can be proud of their Expo-Mini Sports Show and Sled Dog races which are the biggest winter sports events in northern Minnesota.

Two-month-old puppy bitch owned by Georgia Brand. Sire was Ch. Tigara's Black Baron of Tumleh *ex* Ch. Inuit's Mehitabel.

WORLD CHAMPIONSHIP SLED DOG DERBY

On the eastern seaboard the sledding event takes over the main street of Laconia, New Hampshire when the racing enthusiasts participate in this major event. Snow making machines cover the main street with snow if none has fallen from the sky. Laconia also presents a Musher's Ball and crowns a Musher's Queen amid much fanfare.

RACING IN ALASKA

The first All-Alaska Sweepstakes race was run in 1908, with the Nome Kennel Club providing pennants and each team choosing its racing colors to gain instant recognition to win glory. Training began in the late fall for the spring races, and many hours were spent over the long winter months training the dogs for this big event.

The only communication with the outside world was by radio and with the dog teams which brought the mail. In those days the teams left at two-hour intervals, but this wide difference was later reduced to the point where the teams left within minutes—or even seconds— of each other.

In extremely cold weather the dogs were rubbed down with alcohol; they sometimes even wore blankets and flannel moccasins for their feet or eye covers for their eyes. So important was the winning of the races that the drivers fed and bedded down their dogs before they considered their own comforts, so that the dogs would be in good condition to run again the next day.

Even today Alaska considers sled dog racing as its very own sport and features two of the world's most famous races, the North American Championship Race, held in Fairbanks, and the Fur Rendezvous, or the Rondy, in Anchorage. The Fur Rendezvous began in 1936, and by the following year fur trappers in the area were selling their furs *and* racing their dogs. The rendezvous became a virtual festival for everyone, with a fur auction, parties, dances, and exhibitions all being held at the one gathering place. But even from the beginning the dog racing was the main event, and today the 75-mile race still is!

There was a brief halt in the festivities from 1924 to 1936 when only the races were held with the carnival atmosphere, and again during World War II (1942 through 1945) but the annual event was eagerly resumed in 1946 and is gaining in popularity with each year! The schools close on the Friday of the Rendezvous, and the city turns out *en masse* to watch the four-dog team demonstrations which became the regular feature in 1946.

The North American race is 70 miles in length and both events are run in three heats which divide the distance in three parts, over three days. After the third day the winner is announced and the celebrating begins anew!

There are also state championship races held in Kenai and Soldotna, and also one in Tok. In 1967 the Iditarod Trail Race was also held; it was referred to as an "endurance" event and used part of the trail used years ago to bring gold from Iditorod to Knik at the turn of the century. There are attempts being made to open up this rugged trail once again as an 800-mile endurance race. Plans are to restore the shelter cabins to house food for the dogs every fifty miles. Participants will use sleeping bags and carry survival equipment and the committee looks toward $2000 in gold as the reward for the winner!

Racing in Alaska, which had diminished during World War II, picked up again with new enthusiasm in the late 1940's, when the Alaska Dog Musher's Association was formed in Fairbanks. In 1949, in Anchorage, the Alaska Sled Dog and Racing Association was organized.

CHILDREN AND RACING IN ALASKA

At the end of December each year in Anchorage, Alaska, the Junior Alaskan Sled Dog and Racing Association opens its season. The club holds a meeting each Friday night to discuss weather and trail conditions and to draw for starting positions for the race at the Anchorage Tudor Track. Races are held each week throughout the month of January.

Ch. Inuit's Wooly Bully after a swim; this photo was taken when Floyd was one year old.

These juniors must adhere to all the rules and regulations followed by the adults, which are held on the same trails as the adults run and are often eight to twelve miles long. To be a junior musher, the child must be from six to eighteen years of age. There are five classes of junior races consisting of one-, two-, three-, five- and seven-dog teams. The one-doggers race for a quarter of a mile on a straight track, while the two-dog class and most of the three-dog classes run three miles. The five- and seven-dog classes increase the mileage still farther, running a six-mile trail for the opening race with a vote determining the length of future races.

Christmas at the home of Alice Jean Lucus, where her Ch. Bearpaw Lobo of Elk poses by the Christmas tree.

RACING IN CANADA

In Canada the major race is the PAS held in Manitoba. This race is not widely known but is acknowledged to be the longest and the toughest in the world. The dogs travel a distance of anywhere from 100 to 150 miles during the three-day race.

The Quebec race, while not as long, covers a 100-mile distance. The purses for these races are large and the drivers take the winning of these two events very seriously.

THE HUSLIA HERITAGE AND THE HUSLIA HUSTLERS

The Athabascan Indian village named Huslia, which has given to the racing world in Alaska so many of its top dogs and top drivers, is situated 260 miles northwest of Fairbanks on a river about one mile from the Koyukuk. The village remains very remote, still steeped in its Indian culture, but with modern ways and communications now gradually creeping up on it.

Jimmy Hunington was a trapper originally but gained fame for Huslia when in 1939 he entered the dog derbies in Nome. Jimmy borrowed dogs, got a team together and by mushing and getting a ride on a mail plane (along with his 14 dogs!) arrived in Fairbanks to race in the North American Race intent on winning enough money to open his own trading post in Huslia. He placed fourth but went home broke because he was unable to collect his prize money.

The desire to race stayed with him, and in 1956 the villagers urged him to try again and loaned him their best dogs; he emerged the winner of the North American Race in Fairbanks and the Fur Rendezvous in Anchorage. He thereby became known as The Huslia Hustler, until 1958, when George Attla, Jr., also from Huslia, appeared on the scene; George now carries the title as well! Looking at the line-up of any big Alaskan race today, you'll probably find either a winning team of dogs and/or drivers from Huslia!

In 1958 George Attla, Jr. appeared in his first Rondy Race and won handily with a 12-dog team. He owned only one of them, his lead dog named Tennessee. The rest of the dogs belonged to members of his family. Today, after having won the Rondy again in 1962, 1968 and 1972, George is the Huslia Hustler—the greatest hustler of them all!

George Attla was born in 1933, one of eight children born to George and Eliza Attla. A form of tuberculosis caused the fusing of the bones in George's knee, but the defect in no way stopped him from sled racing; in addition to the four Rondy wins, he has captured the number one spot in just about every other major race in Alaska.

George is also known as a great dog trainer. In addition to training his own dogs, he sometimes trains dogs for his competition! He excels in training lead dogs which have made winning teams for many of his competitors in the major races. . . some of which have beaten his team!

George has recently authored a book titled *Everything I Know About Training and Racing Sled Dogs*, in collaboration with Bella Levorsen, a racing enthusiast in her own right, which reveals George's secrets of success as a World Champion Racer four times to date! His 1972 racing records at Bemidji, Minnesota, Ely, Minnesota, Kalkaska, Michigan, Anchorage, Nenana, Fairbanks, Tok and Tanana, Alaska, earned George Attla the Gold Medal from the International Sled Dog Racing Association's first annual competition for a Point Champion.

WOMEN MUSHERS

It seems women have always shared their husbands' interest in driving dog teams and racing. Dog racers are all familiar with the successes of Short Seeley, Lorna Demidoff and Louise Lombard, who in 1949 was the only woman entered in the 90-mile Ottawa, Canada, Dog Sled Derby, competing right along with her husband.

Mrs. E.P. Ricker, now Mrs. Nansen, was driving dog teams in 1928 and placed second at the Lake Placid fourth annual Sled Dog Derby in 1931. Bunty Dunlap, Mrs. Ricker's daughter, went on to follow in her mother's footsteps and became a top sled dog driver. And don't let us forget Jean Bryar, a winner of the North American Women's Championship in Alaska, the first woman from the States to do it. She also gave a good account of herself in many of the gruelling Canadian races, not to mention New Hampshire events. Millie Turner was active at the New England events in the 1930's and 1940's, and Natalie Norris and Joyce Wells have been active at the Rondy races.

Today's representatives are Kit Macinnes, Rosie Losonsky, Vera Wright, Barbara Parker, Shari Wright, Shirley Gavin, Anne Wing, Carol Lundgren and Carol Sheppard. In addition, let's stand by to see what Darlene Huckins will do!

No doubt about it, the women are active in the sport and play by the men's rules. A strong case for sled dog racing as a family sport!

THE WOMEN'S WORLD CHAMPIONSHIP

1953 was the first year of the Women's World Championship Sled Dog Races in Alaska, an event that has been run every year since except for 1956. The same rules apply to the women's races as apply to the regular races, and the women train their own dogs.

In the beginning the purses were small, but by 1972 the winner walked away with a $1000 prize. But then again, the race was not

American and Canadian Ch. Nikik Du Nordkyn, show dog, pack dog, wheel dog and noted sire, owned by Dianne Ross and Len Miller in Washington. Nikik's sire was Skol du Nordky *ex* Koller's Sisak du Nordkyn.

Frostfield Kotzebue Kayo pictured winning Reserve Winners at the 1975 Westminster Kennel Club Show under judge Virginia Hampton. Kayo is handled by M. Ambrose for owners Jerry and Wendy Wisefield.

always as long. The early days featured a two-day race of 20 miles, but by 1972 the winner is determined after three days of racing twelve miles each day for a total run of 36 miles. The total time is tallied to determine the winner.

The teams usually average 9 or 11 dogs, and there are on an average of ten to fifteen teams competing for the purse and the title of top female musher in Alaska—and the world!

THE RONDY RACES

As racing became more and more popular in the late 1940's, the Rondy Races came into being officially in 1946. It is still popular today, and the winning of the Rondy Race is considered of major importance. We list here the annual winners since the event's inception:

1946 — Jake Butler
1947 — Earl Norris
1948 — Earl Norris
1949 — Jake Butler
1950 — Gareth Wright
1951 — Raymond Paul
1952 — Gareth Wright
1953 — Clem Tellman
1954 — Raymond Paul
1955 — Raymond Paul
1956 — Jim Hunington
1957 — Gareth Wright
1958 — George Attla
1959 — Jimmy Malemute
1960 — Cue Bifelt

1961 — Leo Kriska
1962 — George Attla
1963 — Dr. Roland Lombard
1964 — Dr. Roland Lombard
1965 — Dr. Roland Lombard
1966 — Joe Redington
1967 — Dr. Roland Lombard
1968 — George Attla
1969 — Dr. Roland Lombard
1970 — Dr. Roland Lombard
1971 — Dr. Roland Lombard
1972 — George Attla
1973 — Carl Huntington
1974 — Dr. Roland Lombard

The Women's World Championship Race Winners

1953 - Joyce Wells
1954 - Natalie Norris
1955 - Kit Macinnes
1957 - Rosie Losonsky
1958 - Vera Wright
1959 - Kit Macinnes
1960 - Kit Macinnes
1961 - Kit Macinnes
1962 - Barbara Parker
1963 - Barbara Parker
1964 - Barbara Parker
1965 - Sheri Wright
1966 - Shirley Gavin
1967 - Shari Wright

1968 - Anne Wing
1969 - Shirley Gavin
1970 - Shirley Gavin
1971 - Carol Lundgren
1972 - Carol Sheppard

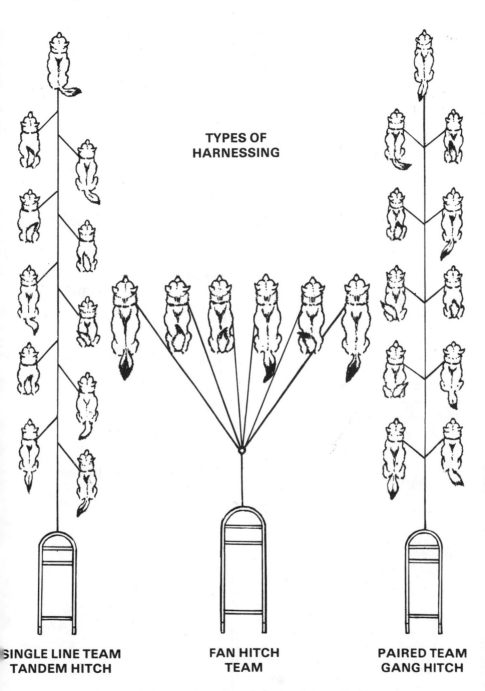

**TYPES OF
HARNESSING**

**SINGLE LINE TEAM
TANDEM HITCH**

**FAN HITCH
TEAM**

**PAIRED TEAM
GANG HITCH**

Types of harnessing. Drawings by Ernest H. Hart.

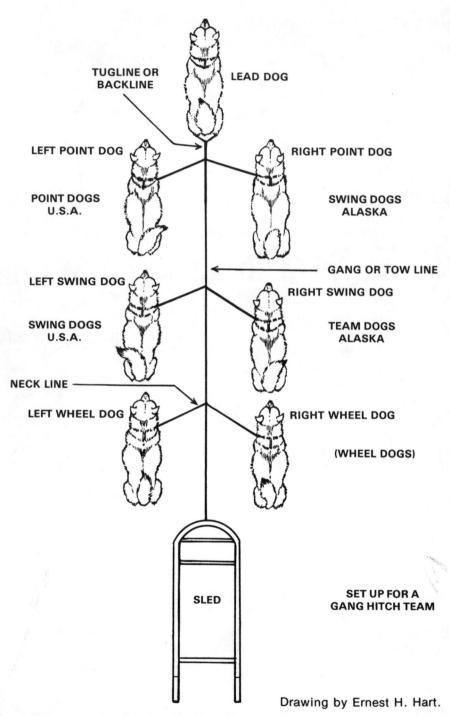

TUGLINE OR
BACKLINE

LEAD DOG

LEFT POINT DOG

RIGHT POINT DOG

POINT DOGS
U.S.A.

SWING DOGS
ALASKA

GANG OR TOW LINE

LEFT SWING DOG

RIGHT SWING DOG

SWING DOGS
U.S.A.

TEAM DOGS
ALASKA

NECK LINE

LEFT WHEEL DOG

RIGHT WHEEL DOG

(WHEEL DOGS)

SLED

SET UP FOR A
GANG HITCH TEAM

Drawing by Ernest H. Hart.

A GLOSSARY OF RACING TERMS

ALASKAN HUSKY: A name appled to any Arctic-type cross-bred dog, usually a Husky, Malamute, Samoyed or Eskimo cross.

ALASKAN MALAMUTE: Used more for hauling than racing because of its great size and endurance.

ATTITUDE RUN: A short "fun" race.

BABICHE: Strips of rawhide used to join the parts of a sled.

BACKLINE: A line from the harness to the towline. Sometimes referred to as a tugline.

BASKET: The section of the sled which carries either passenger or cargo.

BRAKE: The metal fork stepped on by the driver to bring the sled to a halt. A fork on the underside of the sled which hits the ground and stops the sled.

BRIDLE: The collection of ropes gathered with a ring to which the towline is attached.

CART TRAINING: When there is no snow, training dogs with a three- or four-wheel cart is undertaken. Also carts are used in racing in warm climates.

CHAIN: Lengths of chain are used to stake a dog outdoors; usually about six feet in length and attached with snaps at the dog's collar and to the stake.

CHIEF STEWARD: Chief steward takes the other stewards out to their posts. He remains at start and finish lines.

CHUTE: The first several feet beyond the starting line is referred to as the chute.

DNF: Letters standing for Did Not Finish, which means a racer did not finish the race.

DOG BOX: The compartment mounted on a truck in which the dogs are transported to and from the racing site.

DRAGGING: When a dog is dragged along by his neckline, either after he falters, or if he is merely lagging behind.

GANGLINE: Center line fastened to the sled and to which the dogs are hitched. Also known as towline.

GEE: A term used with the dog to indicate a right turn.

GO: Same as start, begin, etc. Response to this word can mean the difference between getting off to a head start or merely starting along with the others.

HANDLE BAR: Topmost portion at the rear of the sled to which the driver holds on.

HARNESS: The webbing which covers the dog and is attached to the lines.

HAW: Term used to indicate a left turn.

HEAT: A heat is one race.

HOLDING AREA: A section near the racing site where dogs are staked until race time.

Eight-week-old Inuit's Rocky Raccoon takes Best of Breed puppy win at the 1969 Rockland County Match Show.

HOOK, SNOW HOOK: A metal hook attached to the bridle of the sled by a line to hold the team in place. It can be driven into the ground or attached to a stationary object.

HOOK-UP AREA: Same as holding area—a place where the dogs are held until race time.

INDIAN DOG: A dog bred and owned by an Indian in an Indian village.

JINGLER: A collection of bells or noisy trinkets used to get the attention of the dogs and spur them on.

LEAD DOG: The dog at the head of the team, usually the fastest, most experienced and best trained.

LEADER: Same as a lead dog.

LOWER 48 or LOWER 49: Term used when referring to racing in any of the United States other than Alaska.

MARSHALL: A term used when referring to the racing official in charge at the race.

MUSH: Originally a French term meaning to walk or to march. While mush can be a term used for starting a team, more often "Let's Go!" or "Take Off!" work just as well. Usually only in the movies do the drivers yell Mush!

MUSHER: The term applied to the driver of a team.

NECKLINE: A light line that hooks the dog's collar to the towline.

NO: Word used to keep the dogs on the trail should they start to veer off, or to stop them from chewing on the line, to ward off a scrap, etc.

PEDALING: When the driver keeps one foot on the runner of the sled and pedals or pushes with the other.

PUMPING: A term used meaning the same as pedaling.

PUNCHING THROUGH: When the dog's feet break through the crust of ice on top of the snow they are said to punch through. The term punchy is the word used for the snow.

RACE MARSHALL: Man in charge of the races.

RIGGING: All the lines collectively to which dogs are hooked.

RUNNERS: Two bottom strips of wood on which the sled runs and are covered with steel or plastic strips called runner shoes.

SIBERIAN HUSKY: Purebred dog used extensively in sled racing.

SKI-JORRING: A short race with the driver on skis rather than with a sled. Line is attached around his waist with a slip knot.

SLED BAG: The canvas bag which holds items necessary to the race and usually carried in the basket.

SNOW BERM: The ridges of snow made along the side of the roads by the snow plows.

SNOW FENCE: Fencing made of wooden upright slats fastened together with wire used to mark off areas or to prevent heavy drifting of snow.

SNOW HOOK: A hook used to stake a team temporarily.

STANCHIONS: Vertical parts of a sled.

STARTER: The man who starts the race.

STAY: Same as Whoa, or stop or halt. Used to stop the dogs at end of race or any other reason. Choose one and stick with it.

STEWARD: One of the officials placed along the trail to avoid trouble at traffic spots, sharp curves, etc. They must stay on the trail until the last team has passed.

STOVE UP: When a dog pulls up lame, or stiff.

SWING DOGS: Dog that runs directly behind the leader either on the right side of the tow line (right swing dog) or on the left side (left swing dog).

Ch. Rogue of Tigara, owned by Dorothy Dillingham of California. A Joan Ludwig photograph.

TEAM DOGS: Dogs hitched into the team between the swing dogs and the wheel dogs.

TO MUSH DOGS: To drive a team.

TOWLINE, OR GANGLINE: The center line fastened to the sled and to which the dogs are hitched.

TRAIL!: Term shouted by mushers to ask another driver for the right of way.

TUGLINE OR TUG: Line from harness to the towline, same as backline.

VET CHECK: Before each race a veterinarian checks over each dog to see that it has not been drugged, if it is in good health and running condition, etc.

WHEEL DOGS: The two dogs directly in front of the sled which determine the direction of the sled.

WHIP: Usually whips are not permitted, but if they are, they must be under three feet in length so that they cannot touch the dogs.

WHOA!: With dogs, as this horses, this means one thing—STOP!

RACING CLUBS IN THE UNITED STATES
International Sled Dog Racing Association
P.O. Box 55
Watertown, New York 13601

New England Sled Dog Club
c/0 Cindy Molburg
Center Harbor, New Hampshire 03226

Northwest Sled Dog Club
Route 1
North Bend, Washington 98045

Alaska Sled Dog Racing Association
Fairbanks, Alaska 99701

North Star Sled Dog Club
Route 1, Box 562
Cambridge, Minnesota 55008

Rocky Mountain Sled Dog Club
Littleton, Colorado 80120

Aurora Dog Mushers Association
Wasilla, Alaska 99687

Tok Dog Mushers Association
Tok, Alaska 99780

CANADIAN DOG RACING CLUBS
Laurentian Sled Dog Club
Ste. Agathe Des Montes
Quebec, Canada

Trappers Festival Winter Carnival
The Pas, Manitoba, Canada

Sourdough Rendezvous
Whitehorse, Yukon, Canada

Correspondence to any of these groups will bring any desired information as to their functions and requirements for membership.

Highnoons Bannock Squaw. This lovely bitch is owned and was bred by Mrs. Janet Edmonds of Riding Hill House, Oxford, England. The sire was Kobuk Chancellor of Clebar *ex* Aninvak of Kananak.

7. THE ALASKAN MALAMUTE AS A PACK DOG

Strong and sure-footed, and steady in all kinds of weather, it is only natural that the Alaskan Malamute could be counted on as a first-rate pack dog. In the Far North Malamutes are used when there is not enough snow for sleds and are used also by fur trappers and hunters to bring pelts back in their packs rather than on the sleds when snow is scarce.

Pack trips are becoming very popular in this country, especially with the one-dog owner, and more and more Malamute owners are learning to enjoy mountain hikes after training their dogs themselves.

Dianne Ross and Len Miller co-owned American and Canadian Ch. Nikik Du Nordkyn. Whelped in 1965, Nikik was not only a pack dog but also a working, racing and sled dog, a sire of champions, a show dog with Group Placings and a delightful companion.

EARLY TRAINING

Training a dog to pack is relatively simple, with the main concern being the addition of the pack and the weight it carries. Start your early training with an empty pack, of course, and once the dog is used to the feel of it on his body, start filling it with something to get the dog used to the sensation of weight. Many packers suggest a light but bulky load right from the beginning to get the dog used to the feel and the "swing" of the pack. Naturally, you will not overload your dog, and especially not at the beginning of the training.

There are those who will pack almost one half the dog's weight; if the pack is packed properly and the dog properly conditioned, this is perfectly all right. You will find the dog will take to the pack quite easily and will eventually get rather protective of it, guarding it when you make camp and take the pack off!

During very cold weather in temperate climates, just as in the frozen North, if you are hiking it may become necessary to have moccasins for the dogs. At any rate, in cold weather and on very rough terrain, check out the dogs' feet for cut pads or ice balls between the toes. After you've made a few hikes their feet may toughen, but it is always best to be careful. It's a long way to carry them back home—if you can!

Since Alaskan Malamutes are such natural outdoor dogs, you will find they love to charge ahead of you along the trail. You must train your Malamute at a very early age to return promptly when called when they are off lead. Some packers use whistles, but in any case, make sure you and your dogs understand each other completely on this point before your first trip to avoid unfortunate disappearances. The reward system will really pay off on this point of training.

Alaskan Malamutes show a considerable amount of good sense when it comes to identifying trails on a pack trip.

FEEDING THE PACK DOG

It is not a good idea to feed the dog before starting on a trip. Feed at night before bedding down and when the dog can relax and properly rest while digesting his food. Water is essential for the pack dog and you will find they require much more water than they usually consume, and generally twice as much as a thirsty person. Since they do not drink out of canteens, remember to take along Sierra Club cups or aluminum dishes for them!

Dry foods, or semi-moist foods, carried in plastic bags are best and should be of the concentrated varieties which are high in protein for extra energy. Make sure everything is wrapped tightly in double plastic with wire twists so no water gets into the food in case you cross streams along the trail. You especially do not want water to get into the first aid kit! The first aid kit is something else that hikers are sure to want to take along.

Two of the chief worries when back-packing with the dogs are encounters with skunks and porcupines. You are wise to carry alligator-nose pliers along to remove porcupine quills if necessary. Tweezers are equally essential for the removal of ticks, and alcohol and swabs go hand in hand with both afflictions.

A past issue of *Field and Stream* magazine advocated the use of a solution of two teaspoonsful of common ordinary baking soda mixed with one cup of vinegar, patted on all exposed portions of each quill and then after a ten-minute wait, repeat the procedure. In another ten minutes you should be able to remove the quills painlessly, since the combined action of the soda and vinegar softens the quill to the point where it shrinks and can be removed. It is surely worth a try—but we sincerely hope the occasion will not arise! Death has been known to occur as a result of a dog's tangling with a porcupine, so do your best to steer clear of them.

Confrontations with skunks are less dangerous but certainly no more pleasant. A bath with strong soap and several rinses with tomato juice when you get home is about the only remedy for this.

A view from the top—Philip Lake and his ten-month-old pup on a packing trip in Acadia National Park.

AGE TO START PACK TRAINING

Training can start at about four months of age and should consist of the simple initial obedience training work for heel, sit, sit-stay, down, down-stay, and the extremely important recall! The recall can be either vocal or whistle; one whistle to mean return immediately and another whistle to mean for the dog merely to show itself on the trail to establish visual contact. A reward for a return is in order. Vocal commands can be taught in the backyard, whistle training on walks in the woods near home before starting on the longer hikes in the mountains.

It is best to take the puppies along with older dogs, which set an example and will help teach the puppies what trailing is all about. Make sure these first trips are not difficult or dangerous ones and *not too long*, which will tire the puppies and perhaps discourage them from future enjoyment. Start them off on the trail with empty packs on the home ground or on long walks. Then begin stuffing the packs with crumpled newspaper or magazines in increasing amounts until their capacity load has been attained. They they will be ready for the longer, rougher trails in the mountains.

THE PACK ITSELF

The pack is made of heavy canvas, leather and ripstop nylon. It is in several parts. There is a heavy canvas saddle with a leather cinch. Sewn to the saddle are two ripstop nylon bags. The bags have a breast strap and a belly strap, and are usually bright red in color to help hikers identify and spot their dogs at a distance.

The bag is placed on the dog as far forward as possible so that it rides over the withers. The cinch is secured firmly as far forward on the brisket as possible but not so tight that it in any way restricts the breathing or will be a discomfort to the dog. The breast and belly straps are loosely secured and help keep the bag in place, so that it does not shift too much when the dog is going up or down steep inclines.

There are eight D-rings sewn on the bags, one on top, one forward, one rear and one low on each bag. A wrap-around strap is passed through the D-rings to further hold the pack in place. The wrap-around is long, with an O-ring on one end. This passes over, under, in front of, and under the belly and back to the O-ring, where it is secured by a squaw hitch.

These packs come in three different sizes and styles and at the time of this writing can be obtained from Wenaha Dog Packs, 14421 Cascadian Way, Lynnwood, Washington, 98036. There are other sources of supply. Since one of the rules of backpacking is to try not to go alone, we assume you can ask the other party you will be hiking with for other places from which you can obtain any supplies.

PACKING THE PACK

Emphasize extreme consideration in the packing of the pack. Load sweaters and soft smooth items on the side of the pack that rests against the dog, and when packing shoes, for instance, pack one shoe on each side to balance the weight. With wise packing you can take along "extras" you would normally leave behind. The point is that even balance on either side of the dog is essential.

At times it might be necessary to unpack the dogs when hiking through rough streams to assure their safety. It is important that you plan ahead and not allow the dogs to plunge into a swift current with full pack if the current is too swift for them to handle.

BEDDING DOWN

When it comes time to bed down for the night it is common sense to let the dogs play for a bit without their packs and before feeding and watering. Make sure the dogs have their collars on and for added safety tie them to your sleeping bags so if an interesting sound or creature ambles by in the night the dogs aren't tempted into wandering off into the hills. Night running is dangerous for them, since they are even more likely to encounter deer, elk, bear, or porcupines and skunks!

8. THE STANDARD FOR THE BREED

OFFICIAL STANDARD FOR THE BREED

GENERAL APPEARANCE AND CHARACTERISTICS—The Alaskan Malamute is a powerful and substantially built dog with deep chest and strong, compact body, not too short coupled, with a thick, coarse guard coat of sufficient length to protect a dense, woolly undercoat, from 1 to 2 inches in depth when dog is in full coat. Stands well over pads, and this stance gives the appearance of much activity, showing interest and curiosity. The head is broad, ears wedge-shaped and erect when alerted. The muzzle is bulky with only slight diminishing in width and depth from root to nose, not pointed or long, but not stubby. The Malamute moves with a proud carriage, head erect and eyes alert. Face markings are a distinguishing feature. These consist of either cap over head and rest of face solid color, usually grayish white, or face marked with the appearance of a mask. Combinations of cap and mask are not unusual. The tail is plumed and carried over the back, not like a fox brush, or tightly curled, more like a plume waving.

Malamutes are of various colors, but are usually wolfish gray or black and white. Their feet are of the "snowshoe" type, tight and deep, with well-cushioned pads, giving a firm and compact appearance. Front legs are straight with big bone. Hind legs are broad and powerful, moderately bent at stifles, and without cowhocks. The back is straight, gently sloping from shoulders to hips. The loin should not be so short or tight as to interfere with easy, tireless movement. Endurance and intelligence are shown in body and expression. The eyes have a "wolf-like" appearance because of their position, but the expression is soft and indicates an affectionate disposition.

TEMPERAMENT—The Alaskan Malamute is an affectionate, friendly dog, not a "one-man" dog. He is a loyal, devoted companion, playful on invitation, but generally impressive by his dignity after maturity.

HEAD—The head should indicate a high degree of intelligence, and is broad and powerful as compared with other "natural" breeds, but should be in proportion to the size of the dog so as not to make the dog appear clumsy or coarse. *Skull*—The skull should be broad between the ears, gradually narrowing to eyes, moderately rounded between ears, rounding off to cheeks, which should be moderately flat. There should be a slight furrow between the eyes, the topline of skull and topline of the muzzle showing but little break downward from a straight line as they join. *Muzzle*—The muzzle should be large and bulky in proportion to size of skull, diminishing but little in width and depth from junction with skull to nose; lips close fitting; nose black; upper and lower jaws broad with large teeth, front teeth meeting with a scissors grip but never overshot or undershot.

EYES—Brown, almond shaped, moderately large for this shape of eye, set obliquely in skull. Dark eyes preferred. *Ears*—The ears should be of medium size, but small in proportion to head. The upper halves of the ears are triangular in shape, slightly rounded at tips, set wide apart on outside back edges of the skull with the lower part of the ear joining the skull on a line with the upper corner of the eye, giving the tips of the ears the appearance, when erect, of standing off from the skull. When erect, the ears point slightly forward, but when the dog is at work the ears are sometimes folded against the skull. High-set ears are a fault.

NECK—The neck should be strong and moderately arched.

BODY—The chest should be strong and deep; body should be strong and compactly built but not short coupled. The back should be straight and gently sloping to the hips. The loins should be well muscled and not so short as to interfere with easy, rhythmic movement with powerful drive from the hindquarters. A long loin which weakens the back is also a fault. No excess weight. *Shoulders, Legs and Feet*—Shoulders should be moderately sloping; forelegs heavily boned and muscles, straight to pasterns, which should be short and strong and almost vertical as viewed from the side. The feet should be large and compact, toes tight-fitting and well arched, pads thick and tough, toenails short and strong. There should be a protective growth of hair between toes. Hind legs must be broad and powerfully muscled through thighs; stifles moderately bent, hock joints broad and strong, moderately bent and well let down. As viewed from behind, the hind legs should not appear bowed in bone, but stand and move true in line with movement of the front legs, and not too close or too wide. The legs of the Malamute must indicate unusual strength and tremendous propelling power. Any indication of unsoundness in legs or feet, standing or moving, is to be considered a serious fault. Dewclaws on the hind legs are undesirable and should be removed shortly after pups are whelped.

Ch. Tigara's War Drum of Applehill pictured winning Best of Breed at the 1971 Elm City Kennel Club Show under judge Arnold Wolff. On the way to his championship, Barney was also Best of Winners at the New York-New Jersey Area Specialty Show held in conjunction with the Boardwalk Kennel Club in 1972 under judge Nelson Groh. Owner is Mary Ellen Narkis of New Preston, Connecticut.

TAIL—Moderately set and following the line of the spine at the start, well furred and carried over the back when not working—not tightly curled to rest on back—or short furred and carried like a fox brush, a waving plume appearance instead.

COAT—The Malamute should have a thick, coarse guard coat, not long and soft. The undercoat is dense, from 1 to 2 inches in depth, oily and woolly. The coarse guard coat stands out, and there is thick fur around the neck. The guard coat varies in length, as does the undercoat; however, in general, the coat is moderately short to medium along the sides of the body with the length of the coat increasing somewhat around the shoulders and neck, down the back and over the rump, as well as in the breeching and plume. Malamutes usually have shorter and less dense coats when shed out during the summer months.

COLOR AND MARKINGS—The usual colors range from light gray through the intermediate shadings to black, always with white on underbodies, parts of legs, feet, and part of mask markings. Markings should be either caplike and/or mask-like on face. A white blaze on forehead and/or collar or spot on nape is attractive and acceptable, but broken color extending over the body in spots or uneven splashings is undesirable. One should distinguish between mantled dogs and splash-coated dogs. The only solid color allowable is the all-white.

SIZE—There is a natural range in size in the breed. The desirable freighting sizes are: *Males:* 25 inches at the shoulders—85 pounds. *Females:* 23 inches at the shoulders—75 pounds. However, size consideration should not outweigh that of type, proportion, and functional attributes, such as shoulders, chest, legs, feet, and movement. When dogs are judged equal in type, proportion, and functional attributes, the dog nearest the desirable freighting size is to be preferred.

IMPORTANT—In judging Alaskan Malamutes their function as a sledge dog for heavy freighting must be given consideration above all else. The judge must bear in mind that this breed is designed primarily as the working sledge dog of the North for hauling heavy freight, and therefore he should be a heavy-boned, powerfully built, compact dog with sound legs, good feet, deep chest, powerful shoulders, steady, balanced, tireless gait, and the other physical equipment necessary for the efficient performance of his job. He isn't intended as a racing sled dog designed to compete in speed trials with the smaller Northern breeds. The Malamute as a sledge dog for heavy freighting is designed for strength and endurance and any characteristic of the individual specimen, including temperament, which interferes with the accomplishment of this purpose is to be considered the most serious of faults. Faults under this provision would be splayfoot-

Owner-handler Robert J. Zoller, of the Husky-Pak Kennels in Blue Ridge Summit, Pennsylvania, and his Ch. Apache Chief of Husky-Pak, voted Dog of the Year in 1955. First winner of the Wesson Seyburn Trophy, Chief is pictured at seven years of age, when he was 27 inches tall and weighed 100 pounds.

edness, any indication of unsoundness or weakness in legs, cowhocks, bad pasterns, straight shoulders, lack of angulation, stilted gait or any gait which isn't balanced, strong, and steady, ranginess, shallowness, ponderousness, lightness of bone, poor over-all proportion, and similar characteristics.

AKC REGISTRATIONS AND THE WORLD WAR II MASSACRE

In 1935, thanks to the years of preliminary work of Milton and Short Seeley, the Alaskan Malamute received its official recognition from the American Kennel Club. During that first year three Alaskan Malamutes were listed in the AKC Stud Book Register. They were Gripp of Yukon (the dog that also became the first AKC champion of record a year later), Rowdy of Nome and Taku of Kotzebue. When a reasonable time period had elapsed, during which time it was determined that an adequate base for pure foundation stock had been registered, the American Kennel Club according to its policy closed its Stud Book, and the breed was supposedly on its way and firmly established within the fancy. However, World War II was to play a role in the future of the breed.

During the combat many war dogs played a part. Among them were a number of Alaskan Malamutes, which naturally came from the foundation Kotzebue line. But following World War II a tragedy occurred which horrified dog lovers all over the world and nearly caused a mutiny in the United States Navy.

It seems that following one of the last Arctic missions the Navy chained the dogs to an ice floe and blew it up. The sailors on board the ship which carried out this horror were said to be on the verge of mutiny, and the story leaked out to the Malamute breeders. This dangerous loss to the Kotzebue line, which represented the breed in the Stud Book, was a near tragedy, and the owners of the M'Loot strain of Malamutes which originated in the Yukon country approached the American Kennel Club with the suggestion that they once again open the Stud Book Register to their M'Loot strain to sustain the breed.

The AKC agreed, but with a reservation. It was specified that in order to achieve registration one would have to prove at least three generations of pure breeding and the dogs would have to be shown on a "listed" rather than registered basis until 10 championship points were won. So it came about that the two types, or strains, of Alaskan Malamute were joined together to carry on the breed in the fancy. But so powerful were the "differences" between the two lines that even today fanciers read in kennel advertisements such phrases as "pure Kotzebue" or "concentrated M'Loot bloodlines" or sometimes even "a blending of both M'Loot and Kotzebue lines!"

So while the Arctic massacre lives on as a cruel act, the addition of the M'Loot line to the breed has had an influence on the breed as we know it today.

ALASKAN MALAMUTE COLOR, COAT AND MARKINGS

One of the keenest delights with this strikingly beautiful breed is the unusual colors and markings on the individual dogs. Each dog seems to have its very own individual pattern that sets it apart from every other Malamute.

Many admirers of the breed prefer the Alaskan Malamute when it most resembles the wolf. However, most breed enthusiasts will appreciate the Malamute that most closely adheres to the Standard for the breed and will take them in any color or pattern—which is the way it should be.

But there is no denying that the markings, especially the face markings, can be exotic, making the expression so appealing and bringing to mind the old saying that the dogs seem to be looking far off across endless miles of snow to the North Pole.

ALASKAN MALAMUTE COLORS

Several colors and combinations of colors are allowed in the breed, and while all of them are attractive, you may have a color preference. Here are the color descriptions:

BLACK AND WHITE: Black guard hair with black or dark undercoat.

ALASKAN SEAL AND WHITE: Black or black tipped guard hairs with white or cream undercoat. The dog appears black at a distance but is not a true black because of the light undercoat.

WOLF SABLE AND WHITE: Black or gray guard hairs with a reddish undercoat and red trimmings. Both black and red factors are evident.

WOLF GRAY AND WHITE: Gray guard hairs with light gray, cream, or white undercoat. Dog definitely appears gray even though there may be some black hairs on the topline. No red factor evident here.

SILVER AND WHITE: Light gray guard hairs with white undercoat.

RED AND WHITE: A definite shade of red. Either light or dark with light points (lip line and nose), and eye color. No black factor evident.

ALL WHITE: Both guard hairs and undercoat are white. Often evidence of a mask in cream color. White is the only solid color allowed.

TRIMMINGS: Shadings of gold, cream, buff, brown or reddish hues often found on legs, ears, tail and face between white areas of the underbody and the dark color above.

FACE MARKINGS

CAP: A cap of color covers the top of the head and ears, usually coming to a point in the center of the forehead.

GOGGLES: Dark areas under the eyes and extending sideways to the cap are referred to as goggles.

BAR: A dark area extending from the center point of the cap down the nose.

EYE SHADOW: Dark markings under the eyes but not extending out to the cap.

STAR: A small white spot in the center of the forehead.

BLAZE: A white mark extending from the center point of the cap back up the forehead. Width and length can vary.

CLOSED FACE: Dark coloring covering the face with no distinct markings on the face.

OPEN FACE: A cap covering the top of the head and no other markings on the face.

FULL MASK: The combination of cap, goggles and bar.

MASK: The combination of cap and goggles.

CHEST MARKINGS

NECKLACE: A curving band of dark color across the chest.

EAGLE: Two bands of dark color protruding partially across the chest, forming a pattern resembling an eagle emblem.

NECK AREA

COLLAR: A white band of color encircling the neck.

WITHERS SPOT: A white mark varying in size but centered on the withers or at the base of the neck.

MISMARKINGS

Mismarkings are those markings which are not symmetrical.

The above descriptions are from a descriptive color and marking code approved by the Alaskan Malamute Club of America. The purpose of this code is to supply prospective or new owners and breeders with a correct description of the breed and to provide a universally accepted set of color and marking definitions that can be utilized for breeders on pedigrees, registrations, etc., and to facilitate future studies and research in color genetics.

DIFFERENCES BETWEEN THE SIBERIAN HUSKY AND THE ALASKAN MALAMUTE

Many of those interested in the Northern breeds, and attracted to them because of the exotic facial and body markings, are inclined to

American and Canadian Ch. Zardal Baranof, bred and owned by Audrey Thomas, Zardal Kennels, Penfield, New York. Photo by Streeter.

think the Siberian Husky and the Alaskan Malamute are the same breed. It is only later when they delve into the writings on whichever breed it is they see first that they learn of the specific differences in these two breeds, which do resemble each other to the untrained eye.

The Alaskan Malamute and the Siberian Husky are the most alike in appearance of all the Northern breeds, and in photographs it is almost impossible to distinguish them without being familiar with the Standard for each breed. When one sees them in actuality the obvious difference in size is immediately apparent, and one soon learns that it is the Alaskan Malamute that is the larger and more powerful dog. As a matter of fact, the Standard for Siberians is quite specific as to the size of that breed, and while it has been discussed, nothing has yet been done about incorporating a size requirement for the Malamute as well. Many of today's Malamutes are reaching the 150-pound class, and many believe if the Standard is to be preserved an over-size disqualification might help. Others are equally quick to concede, however, that it is the larger, heavier dogs that are the best workers and can literally pull the most weight and keep the breed the freight dog capable of hauling great weights over long distances.

The height and weight limits of 23½ inches and 60 pounds for the Siberian Husky keep it well within the structure for a fast racing and sled dog, so important that exceeding this size range is a disqualification in the show ring. Perhaps it would also be advantageous to the breed to keep the Malamutes within their 25-inch, 85-pound suggested, or desirable, "natural" size.

Eye color is the next most noticeable difference. The Malamute has brown eyes—the darker the better—and the Siberian Husky has brown or blue, or both! Many believe the Husky with one blue and one brown eye to be the most fascinating attribute of the breed. But the Malamute has two almond-shaped brown eyes that are equally penetrating, especially when surrounded by interesting facial markings. Ear set is the next most obvious difference, with the Malamute ears being set much farther apart and standing off from the head as required in the Standard. Siberian Husky ears are larger and set high up on the head. The muzzle on the Malamute is also much heavier than the Siberian Husky's muzzle, which tapers slightly but is never snipey.

A very noticeable difference and an obvious one, especially when the dogs are in motion, is the tail, both in carriage and in appearance. The Siberian Husky tail is well-furred and carried over the back when in motion. The Malamute tail is not short-furred and gives a waving plume-like appearance.

Those of us interested in the breed are always eager to point out the appealing differences in the two Northern breeds in an effort to educate the public to the finer points.

9. ALASKAN MALAMUTE TEMPERAMENT AND BREED CHARACTERISTICS

You've decided you like the appearance and size of the Alaskan Malamute and you want to know a lot more about what the dog is really like. You have also decided that you probably won't want to race your dog or exhibit it as a show dog. . . you just want to enjoy the dog at home as a companion and member of your family. Now you want to know what you can expect in the way of temperament.

The Alaskan Malamute makes a fine house dog! He adores the companionship of people of all ages, he has an alert and charming personality, and he is top rated in all areas except when it comes to sharing either home or kennel with other male dogs. Males are highly competitive and highly argumentative with each other and cannot be housed together. This characteristic is one which is prevalent in many other breeds also, but it is particularly troublesome when their great size is considered. You can not risk having to try to separate two fighting males whenever they come in close contact with one another. While a fight to the death may not occur on every chance meeting, it is certainly not a condition to live with if you want to enjoy your dogs. Kennel owners are careful to see that males are always separated and kept as far from each other as possible. Males and females are of course another story.

Except for the semiannual shedding, the rest of the year the Alaskan Malamute loses very little hair. Aside from the shedding, the Alaskan Malamute makes an ideal indoor dog. He is not clumsy in the house, nor is he particularly given to jumping on the furniture, being content to remain on the floor.

It is almost useless, however, to try to designate a special bed for the dog. You will find that he will much prefer to sleep near a favorite member of the family. Alaskan Malamutes also are unusually clean eaters. They eat their food promptly and all at once and aren't known to play in their water dishes the way certain other breeds do, at least not after they have grown up!

The Alaskan Malamute is a particularly clean dog in other respects, too. At times they lick themselves clean in somewhat the same manner as a cat. This cleanliness most likely goes back to the North where they could always keep themselves clean by rolling in the snow. They have no typical "doggy odor" the way some of the other breeds have, except occasionally when they are soaking wet or have been exposed to special circumstances that might cause odors to cling to their coats. Occasional brushings will keep them clean and odor-free under normal circumstances.

For the dog that will be living in and will get its exercise in the form of walks each day, make sure that the dog is handled by a capable person. It is not considered "cute" to see a tiny child being pulled along by a dog that has just caught scent of a bitch in heat down the street, or suddenly gets the urge to chase some children flashing by on bicycles. If the dog has to defend itself in a fight, the child could end up in the middle of a canine scrap. Also, since the exotic appearance of the Alaskan Malamute sometimes inspires fear in those who don't understand its docile temperament, such persons often doubt the ability of the child to handle it when it is in their vicinity.

A dog that lives in must be exercised several times a day, and it should be done by an adult with sufficient strength to restrain the dog under any circumstances and sufficient walking speed to let the dog exercise at its normal gait. More and more people are seen on the roads and in the packs jogging with their dogs. Signs of the times!

STAKING OUT

One of the best ways to keep an Alaskan Malamute that you intend to use as a working dog is to stake it outside rather than allow it to live indoors. Here again, the workings of the Malamute mind can better tolerate the thoughts and conditions of a stake, because they generally find the confinement of four fence walls, no matter how large the enclosure, much less tolerable.

A soft, secure harness with a chain not more than ten feet long will give the dog a sufficiently large area to move in, with the only obstacle being the attachment to the harness. Shelter should be provided in some form, perhaps a simply constructed dog house made from plywood half an inch thick, with a flat though slightly tilted roof to allow the rain to run off, and for the dog to lie on if the ground is not to his liking.

It is a good idea to feed the dog on this roof also. The food is away from contact with the ground and the insect problem is therefore somewhat lessened; the roof also provides some protection against wandering animals which might stray onto the scene.

On the beach at Grayland, Washington, and a moment of confronta-
tion during sled racing practice. In the middle is American and Canadian Ch. Bearpaw Elk of Tote Um; on the left is Tote-Um's Muktuk, and
the child completes "the eternal triangle." This charming photograph
was published under that title in the November, 1967 *American Kennel
Gazette*. Owners of the dogs are Alice Jean and Phil Lucus of Seattle,
Washington.

The Call of the Wild!
One of Earl Norris's
team dogs protesting
his fate in Anchorage,
Alaska.

A snowy July and Inuit's Chinchilla of MacLean, owned by
Thelma and Robert MacLean, enjoys every minute of it!

There is nothing quite like the relationship between children and dogs
. . . especially Malamutes.

However, if you stake your dog outside and wish to campaign the
dog in the show ring, shade must be provided, since constant exposure to the sun can sunburn the coat, changing both the color and the
texture.

You must determine at the beginning whether your Alaskan Malamute is to be an indoor or outdoor dog. Depending on the severity of
the climate in the region where you live, your dog may be more comfortable living outdoors all year round. In the great snows which
occur in the North, the Northern breeds are able to take care of themselves under most any conditions. He sleeps in a hole he digs for him-

self in the snow, curled in a semi-circle with his furry tail as a cover for his face; this helps to prevent the frigid air from blasting into his face.

It is not to the dog's best interests to suddenly take pity on him during a blizzard and bring him inside to warm up. Once the ice and snow melt and wet the coat, it must be *completely* dry before the dog is put outside again, or the wet hair will freeze to it and either give the dog pneumonia or cause it to freeze to death.

A dog which lives outdoors must be given enough chain to be able to walk about and keep its circulation going or it will freeze. The chain must be long enough for it to move out of the way of the drifting snow so that it does not get buried and suffocate beneath the snow. The dog must be able to move about and shake off the snow periodically.

SPECIAL BREED CHARACTERISTICS

The legends of the hunting instincts and keen nose of the Alaskan Malamute are many! Drivers from the earliest times could recall countless stories of lead dogs finding the way home when the driver became hopelessly lost and of teams suddenly veering off course when they caught the scent of bear, moose or reindeer, leaving the driver hanging on desperately until he could manage to stop them and get back on course again.

Ch. Sena-Lak's Arctic Flash, for instance, saved his master's life on two different occasions by *refusing* to obey a command. This 95-pound, 28-inch dog was whelped in 1957 and was owned by Doug Rotach of Red Creek, New York. This directional "instinct" also played an important part in the Alaskan Serum Run as we recounted earlier, when the driver lost his way in a storm and the lead dog and the team brought the serum into Nome. This instinct is surely one of the most admirable characteristics of our wonderful Northern breed.

We must remember that our Northern breeds were hunting with their owners long before they were pulling sleds, but it must also be remembered that it is this hunting instinct that causes one of the major problems in our trying to get them used to living with domestic animals. With this strong inherent instinct to hunt it is difficult sometimes for them to discern which animals belong to the family and those which they were once meant to pursue and bring down. Everything from chickens, calves, sheep and even foals were within their territory, with cats their favorite victims today. All were chased, caught by the throat, and with a swiftness that almost could not be observed, finished off!

Waldemar Jochelson wrote in 1908 that on occasions when he had tried to domesticate dogs he had brought back from the wilds he

Ambara's Nuviya, left, an import owned by Mrs. B. Preston, pictured here playing with her daughter, Shadow. Shadow later became a Guide Dog in England.

found that they never lost this instinct to hunt and did all sorts of damage to local game and domestic animals while showing no hostility to strangers.

But Malamutes are no longer the aggressive hunters they were during the days when they were starving and had to hunt for food. It has been a long time since they have lived in the wilds where game was plentiful and they were expected to make a kill to keep their owners and themselves alive. Domestication has made stalking prey an exception—or a random thing—rather than a rule of life. But the instinct to capture anything that moves is inherent in many animals—especially in the cat family. So it is up to the owner to prevent the "law of the jungle" from causing a tragedy within the household if you harbor animals in addition to the Alaskan Malamute.

THE CALL OF THE WILD

All of us who love dogs and remember Clark Gable in the movie *The Call of the Wild*, whether you saw it when it was first produced or one of the countless times it has been re-run on television, will remember the distant howl of the Arctic wolves!

Shown here enjoying a swim is Berlin's Aneenak of Inuit. This bitch is a litter sister to the famous Wooly Bully.

Along the trail: two of Joan Kolman's dogs are on the trail of an interesting scent near their Lynn Kennels in Middlefield, Connecticut.

Gone fishin'! Two of Joan Kolman's Alaskans take to the water. True working dogs, Jamie Lynn and Jamie Lynn's Duncan are also used for sled work and are shown in the conformation classes at dog shows as well.

Alaskan Malamutes are also given more to howling than to barking. In the dead of night they are likely to lift their voices in "song," and there it remains at fever pitch for long periods of time and carrying over great distances. Just like in the movies!

The voices of these dogs have been described in earlier written records by men in the North as "long, melancholy howls of a wolf-like dog," and early commentators have remarked to the effect that you never hear these dogs bark—they are like wolves and only howl. Any dog, except perhaps the Basenji, can learn to bark, simply by observing other dogs. Anyone who has owned an Alaskan Malamute will also attest that they seldom make noise unnecessarily, but when they do it *is* reminiscent of the cry of the wolf.

Down through the centuries as man needed his dog to serve also as a guard for him it was trained to give voice and bark on certain occasions. However, the Malamute's inclination not to bark is one reason why Alaskan Malamutes do not make the very best watch dogs.

MALAMUTES AND THE BLIND

While the Alaskan Malamute is rather more difficult to train as a guide dog for the blind than some of the other breeds, there have been those which have distinguished themselves in this most worthy service to man. Coldfoot Princess Ponoka, C.D. was one of them. Whelped at the Coldfoot Kennels in 1964, Ponoka was also the dam of another leader for the blind. She finished her training three weeks faster than any other dog that had graduated from the training school in Rochester, Missouri, which she attended.

While completing her Companion Dog title, she became the first Alaskan Malamute to earn a Best in Obedience Trial win. Training can be said to come naturally to Ponoka when it is remembered that her sire was the famous obedience title-holder Ch. Coldfoot Minto, U.D.T.

Lady of the Morning Mist, C.D., bred by Andre and Monique Anctil in 1965, also became a leader dog for the blind and distinguished herself in this great work.

SKIJORRING

Alaskan Malamute owners also enjoy skijorring with their dogs on occasion. With either one dog or a team of three, skijorring can be exciting sport in the snow country.

Some of the racing clubs also feature skijorring events along with weight-pulling contests at their sledding meets, especially while waiting for the racing teams to return from some of the longer races.

10. THE BREED IN JEOPARDY

The Alaskan Malamute—just like every other breed in the canine world—has from time to time been threatened by certain devastating diseases.

Most of these diseases are hereditary and therefore of alarming consequences in a time of ever-increasing breeding and popularity. Prior to the 1970's the Alaskan Malamute was often referred to as a rare and unusual breed. But recent enormous leaps in popularity have caused the perpetuation of many of the faults that are a direct result of demand breeding and selling in the dog world.

The Alaskan Malamute, along with just about every other breed, has suffered from the severe malady of hip dysplasia. It also has been subjected to the toll exacted by progressive retinal atrophy, or PRA; by the time we entered the 1970's there were a few other dangers threatening the soundness of this largest and most powerful of all the Northern breeds.

Hemeralopia, or day blindness, was one of the hereditary eye diseases that came along. However, thanks to modern research and the efforts of a Canadian medical doctor and work at the University of Pennsylvania, it has almost been erased from the scene.

But chondrodysplasia is something else again. . .

Chondrodysplasia, or dwarfism, is also hereditary—and heart-breaking. Originally diagnosed as a form of rickets, chondrodysplasia now has been determined to be an hereditary ailment involved with a simple recessive gene; both sire and dam must carry this gene in order to produce a chondrodysplastic puppy.

The condition is detectable only by x-ray before the age of six weeks. As the puppies grow it becomes more and more obvious that something is seriously wrong, because the legs become more and more deformed and seem not to grow in length.

Unfortunately, this disease can be passed on without the more obvious condition of warped limbs. Dogs can be perfectly normal looking in their appearance and still be carriers of the defect. Naturally dogs which show the defect as well as those who carry it without showing it should not be used for breeding. But when the dogs appear to be normal it is sometimes difficult to determine the carriers. Puppies bred from one normal (non-carrier) parent and a carrier will not appear to have the disease and will show no deformity. But some puppies from such breedings will be carriers through the genetic inheritance of the gene from the carrier parent. And that number will remain unknown unless all the puppies out of the carrier and the clear dog breeding are themselves test-bred.

The continued breeding of possible carriers obviously increases the number of carriers circulating in the breed, and it is this unfortunate situation that has allowed the malady to get such a foothold in the breed. Far too many breeders, knowing their stock carries this gene, breed anyway for commerical reasons, and they are responsible for the spread it has reached today.

WHAT THE PARENT CLUB IS DOING ABOUT IT

In an effort to wipe out chondrodysplasia from the breed the parent club is requesting that owners of Alaskan Malamutes send a copy of their dog's pedigree to the American Malamute Club of America Master Plan Committee for study. The committee is, of course, in no position to determine from the pedigree alone whether

The heartbreaking telltale signs of dwarfism. . . litter brothers, one normal and one with this horrendous defect, clearly display the crippling effects and stunted growth that is characteristic of chondrodysplasia. The dog on the right, Lynx, is featured on the cover of the Alaskan Malamute Club of America's descriptive booklet on the disease and has been a test dog at the Washington State University research project since March, 1969. Owned and donated to the University by Alice Jean Lucus of Seattle.

Bearpaw Lynx, resident king of the chondrodysplasia research colony since March 13, 1969. Bearpaw was donated to the colony by Phil and Alice Jean Lucus.

or not the dog is a carrier, but will on the basis of the number of ancestors known to have produced chondrodysplastic offspring calculate the probability that the dog in question is or is not itself a carrier. The reliability of the mathematical computation depends absolutely upon the accuracy of the pedigree and the honesty of the breeders.

Through the efforts of this committee a substantial amount of information has been gathered to date to aid in determining the probability rating of Malamutes suspected of carrying the gene. The club advocates that a Malamute with a rating of 6.25% or less need not be

John F. Cummings, Ph.D., a veterinarian at New York State Veterinary College at Cornell University with one of the Alaskan Malamutes used in the frontal lobotomy technique for uncontrollable dogs.

test-bred, whereas testing is indicated if the rating is higher than that.

It must be pointed out that not every bloodline has been found to carry chondrodysplasia. In order to differentiate between those that don't and those that do the AMCA issues a certificate stating that a particular line is genetically uninvolved with the disease.

TEST BREEDING

Everyone will agree that test breeding is a rather costly and sometimes unfortunate way to prove a case. There is considerable effort being made to develop a better method of testing a suspected Malamute, especially when it is often necessary to breed more than one litter to prove the presence of the disease. Also, the disposal of the test puppies has been a very controversial subject. The Master Plan Committee has given it considerable thought, you can be sure.

THE CERTIFICATION SYSTEM

The AMCA has adopted a certification system so that each dog will have a series of letters and numbers following its name to indicate its status with the club, and it is essential that all prospective buyers of the breed request puppies from breeders whose stock has been certified and is declared free of the disease.

CHONDRODYSPLASIA INFORMATION

The Alaskan Malamute Club of America has published a bulletin on chondrodysplasia and it is advised that any prospective buyer obtain the booklet for a full explanation of both the disease and the complete explanation of the certification numbers, as well as the latest developments in the attempt to stamp it out.

THE MASTER PLAN COMMITTEE

Linda M. Dowdy is chairman of the Master Plan Committee, and Dorothy Pearson, Henry M. Dodd, Jr., Reid Saunders, Dr. Kenneth Bourns, Warren Rice and Robert Carsten are members representing all sections of the United States and Canada.

Dwarfism in Alaskan Malamutes can—and will be—wiped out now that the disease is out in the open and its existence is no longer denied or covered up by breeders. In fact, the breeders have realized at last how widespread and how serious the problem is and now are cooperating remarkably well with the various veterinary research programs that are determined also to do something about it.

LOBOTOMY AND THE VICIOUS DOG

While all the talk about the Malamute's being the perfect family dog, working dog, sled dog, etc., is perfectly true, those that are

Brave, a dwarf Malamute bred by Alice Lucus and donated by her to the project for research in chondrodysplasia.

actively breeding Malamutes will be the first to tell you that male Alaskan Malamutes do not get along too well with other male Alaskan Malamutes. As mentioned previously, this holds true in many of the other breeds as well, but along with other revelations about the breed has come the truth about male Malamutes and their relationships with each other.

A prefrontal lobotomy was performed early in the 1970's at Cornell University on two Alaskan Malamutes used as sled dogs that had become so viciously aggressive toward each other that their owner could no longer hitch them to a sled. The operation was conducted as part of a study to determine the effect of prefrontal lobotomy on aggressive dogs. Following surgery, the dogs could be walked side by side on leashes.

Dr. John F. Cummings, a veterinarian at New York State Veterinary College, Cornell University, was able to rehabilitate the dogs by

Future Canadian Ch. Bearpaw Lobo and his dwarf litter brother, Lynx. This photograph was taken just before Alice Jean Lucus donated this chondrodysplastic puppy to Washington State University for research in 1969.

Jock as a puppy; Jock grew up to be Ch. Kotzebue Jock of Chinook, owned by Sy and Ann Goldberg, Cinnaminson Kennels, Cream Ridge, New Jersey.

surgically removing the prefrontal part of their brains. Dr. Cummings and Mr. Bruce Allen made a study of the possibilities of using surgical procedures on the frontal lobes of aggressive dogs as an alternative to their destruction. The work was sponsored by a grant from the Morris Animal Foundation, which backs studies of animal health problems.

The lobotomy seemed to have had no adverse effect on the dogs and must be considered as an alternative to the destruction of overly aggressive military or guard dogs and dogs that become fear biters or are aggressive with other dogs and people. Such a modification of their behavior might mean the difference between life and death for them.

The operation is moderately hazardous, and Dr. Cummings does not suggest its use except as a last resort—in other words, when an animal would otherwise have to be destroyed. Eventually the experimenters hope to have it perfected to the point where it can be performed by a method familiar to the average practitioner.

11. THE ALASKAN MALAMUTE IN FAR OFF LANDS

THE ALASKAN MALAMUTE IN ALASKA

While Alaska has since January 3, 1959 been a part of the United States as the 49th state, many of us still tend to think of it by its nickname of "The Last Frontier." Its climate is so different from ours that we can almost say that much of Alaska belongs more to the North Pole than to the United States. However, the breed we have come to know and love does bear the name of the state that undeniably denotes the land of its origin, confirming its ancestry!

Alaskan Malamute history was first recorded in Alaska in reports from the early explorers, expeditions, fur-trading and gold-mining companies that were the first to penetrate these northern regions during the partial conquest of Alaska's huge land area. Therefore, it is only natural that even today several important people in the breed still live in "The Land of the Midnight Sun" and are involved in the Alaskan Malamute breed.

Among the first, and still active in the mid-1970's, are Earl and Natalie Norris, active in all phases of the breed in Alaska for many years. Mrs. Norris is a judge and officiated in the Siberian Husky ring at the 1973 Bronx County Kennel Club show in New York, which had an entry of 98.

In 1971 Linton and Kay Moustakis of Anchorage went Best in Show at the Alaska Kennel Club Show under judge Dr. Frank Booth. It was the first time in 22 years of Alaskan dog shows that a Malamute won the top award. Bred, owned and handled by the Moustakises, 4-year-old Ch. Kougarok also won the *Kennel Review* magazine Top Alaskan Show Dog award for that year. Kougarok, along with his dam, is lead dog on a working sled dog team and is a delightful companion as well. . . a true all-around Malamute excelling in the land of the breed's origin!

Alaskan Malamutes are being seen more and more in the show rings in Alaska, with the Earl Norrises and Judy Burlingham show-

Ch. Wolfpak's K'Loot photographed at a show in Anchorage, Alaska in May, 1969. K'Loot is co-owned by Earl Norris and Judy Burlingham.

ing their co-owned Ch. Wolfpak's M'Loot in 1969 and Barbara Litwin with her Aleuts Kanuck of Inuit. In 1968 Al and Carol Crook were active in the breed with their Ch. Tote-Ums Snowmiss of Valsun, the dam of two Canadian champions. They followed the 1965 appearances of Ch. Tote-Ums Littlest Hobo, a weight-pulling freight dog, owned by Roger and Malle Burggraf of College, Alaska.

Today we are aware of fanciers such as Linda Lovejoy, George Will, Jr., Joanne Munger, Constance Le Van and Judith Wise, all of whom show interest in the breed through their membership in the Alaskan Malamute Club of America.

ALASKAN MALAMUTES IN ENGLAND

The Alaskan Malamute was introduced into Great Britain in 1959 by Mr. and Mrs. William Preston. While in the United States the Prestons used the name Ambara as their kennel prefix. Once in England, however, they changed it to Kananak. The Prestons began showing in England in 1960. The original imports they had were Pawnee Flash of North Wind, Preston's Cheechako and Ambara's Nuviya. Flash and Cheechako later returned to America with the Prestons. The first breeding of Pawnee Flash and Nuviya (in England) managed to have a wide effect on the breed.

In 1964 an Alaskan Malamute Club was formed in England as interest in the breed began to spread. Other imports were purchased to

Alaskan's Issuk of Kubak, bred by Earl Norris and Judy Burlingham, pictured winning at an Alaskan Kennel club show. Owned by Joanne Munger of Anchorage, Alaska.

Tote Um's Tamahine of Seacourt photographed in quarantine kennel upon his arrival in England. Bred by Dianne Ross of Cle Elum, Washington, he was imported to England by Mrs. J.S. Parkyns of Seacourt Kennels, Buckingham, England.

help establish the breed starting in 1964, when Mrs. B. Cook obtained Kobuk Chancellor of Clebar. In 1966 Mrs. J.S. Parkyns of Buckingham and Mrs. Janet Edmonds of Oxford imported Tote-Um's Arctic Hawk. He was to become the sire of many fine show puppies. Hawk was bred by Dianne Ross of the Tote-Um Kennels in Cle Elum, Washington, U.S.A., and was so well admired that in 1969 Mrs. Parkyns imported from Mrs. Ross Tote-Um's Tamahine of Seacourt for her Seacourt Kennels.

Other Alaskan Malamutes were imported by Americans residing in the United Kingdom but not used in any particular breeding program in that country.

Unfortunately, hip dysplasia was discovered in the breed, and all breeding almost came to a halt until the arrival of the Tote-Um dogs,

Tote Um's Tamahine of Seacourt, top Malamute in England for 1974. Bred by Mrs. Dianne Ross of Cle Elum Washington, the sire was Am. Ch. Pak N Pull's Kaltag *ex* Bearpaw Egavik of Tote Um. Imported to England by owner J.S. Parkyns, Seacourt Kennels, Buckingham, England.

Highnoons Dakota, Best of Breed in 1972 and bred and owned by Janet Edmonds of Oxford, England. The bitch's sire was Tote-Um's Arctic Hawk *ex* Aninvak of Kananak.

Highnoons Dakota, bred and owned by Mrs. Janet Edmonds, Oxford, England. The sire was Tote-Um's Arctic Hawk *ex* Aninvak of Kananak. Dakota was a Best of Breed winner during the 1972 show season.

Isola of Clebar, owned by J.S. Parkyns, Buckingham, England. Zibe was sired by Tote-Um's Arctic Hawk *ex* Uttholtz Guidewell Halkett. The breeder was Mrs. B. Cook. The lovely bitch was a winner at the 1971 Crufts show.

Boomerang of Clebar photographed in December, 1968. Bred by Mrs. Cook, this lovely bitch is owned by Miss A. Thurley of England. Boomerang has also represented the breed in the obedience ring in England.

which appear to have set the breed back up on its feet again. It has now been several years since a severe case has come to light.

By the mid-1970's there were about two hundred Alaskan Malamutes in Britain, with the two major breeders being two of the early keen supporters of the breed: Mrs. Janet Edmonds of the Highnoon Kennels, who has been in the breed since the very beginning, and Mrs. Janetta Parkyns of the Seacourt Kennels, who became interested in the breed in 1964. Private breeders or those who breed only an occasional litter are not active in the show rings, which is one of the reasons why the breed still does not qualify to compete for Challenge Certificates with an eye toward championships.

Actually, too few are ever shown to qualify for the C.C.'s, and most competition is in the "Any Variety Not Separately Classified Classes," which are comparable to the American Miscellaneous Class.

146

At some shows there are breed classes, such as the Nordic Open Show, Guildford Open and National Working Breed Championship shows. Some other shows schedule "Any Variety Sled Dog" classes in which the Alaskan Malamutes compete against the Siberian Huskies and other traditional sledding breeds.

Another drawback against the breed's really "catching on" in Britain is the fact that owners are not allowed to work dogs in harness. Since one of the outstanding abilities of the Alaskan Malamute is his tremendous power and desire to pull, there is a serious handicap for the dog to do the work he was really intended by nature to do. And this, of course, also eliminates racing.

Interested parties have turned to obedience training for their Malamutes, but the breed proved to be only moderately successful. The Guide Dogs for the Blind Association also tried to use the breed successfully over a period of years for this work but found the Malamute required too specialized training to make it desirable in that role.

They also came up against the fact that the breed seemed to prove aggressive with other breeds of dogs and therefore could not be housed too successfully with more than one dog in the house, and that they also presented a problem when turned loose for proper exercise in cities or suburbia. In the country, they were found to be completely unsafe with sheep, and when you bear in mind the English countryside with fields full of sheep. . . coupled with a law which allows farmers to shoot dogs threatening their flocks. . . it is easy to see why the Alaskan Malamute did not fare well as a country dog either.

There has been no alternative but for the dedicated fanciers to enjoy the Alaskan Malamute as a very specialized breed, with limited numbers of owners, exhibitors and breeders.

Mrs. Janet Edmonds, who is the 1975 Honorable Secretary of the Alaskan Malamute Club in England, states that the owners of the Malamutes fully realize the place of the breed in that country and when they do breed and sell puppies they are sure to alert the prospective owners of their responsibilities to the dogs and to society.

ALASKAN MALAMUTES IN CANADA

The first name which comes to mind when thinking of the Alaskan Malamute in Canada is that of Lorna Jackson of Ontario, owner of the Lorn-Hall Kennels. Lorna Jackson had many fine dogs and was active in the breed for many years. She also owned Ch. Lorn-Hall Iigiriij M'Loot, a police-trained dog who helped locate victims of the devastating Hurricane Hazel.

Minnie Graham of Vancouver has been active in the breed for several decades. She owned American and Canadian Ch. Bearpaw Geena and one of the first Canadian C.D. dogs, Ch. Husky Pak Forecast by Cliquot, C.D.

Inuit's Warrior of Skagway, photographed at his Canada home with owner Nancy Windover.

Litter of Canadian puppies sired by Inuit's Warrior of Skagway. Bred and owned by Nancy Windover.

Ch. Oak's Kudlooktoo winning the Breed in 1973 under judge Dr. Frank Booth at the Canadian Sportsmens' Show in Canada. Handled by B. Taylor for owner Mrs. Anita Murphy, Wilinda Kennels, Ontario, Canada. Whelped in July, 1969, his sire was Oomalikbuk of Oak *ex* Oak's Tuk Tuk.

Mickey and Frances Bakos of Ontario own Canadian Ch. Wobiskas Teddy of Nekanesu, bred by Harold Oakes and whelped in 1968.

Larry Erickson was owner of Sena-Lak's Alaskan Blizzard, a 24½-inch, 80-pound white Malamute which was a leader of a team of dogs consisting of both wolves and Malamutes; the dog worked a trap line for his young master and worked in the movie *Nikki, Wild Dog of the North*.

D.J. Macwatt does not show his Malamutes, but his Koroks Siskiyou of Tote-Um is a hard working freight dog.

Names like Joan White and Mrs. A. Murphy of Ontario, and her Ch. Oaks Otonabee of Wilenda also figure in the Canadian scene.

Illanak, bred by Joanne Munger and owned by Betsey Correy Ketclaar-Triller of Holland.

SPAIN

In 1957 Sena-Lak's Lady Llano was sent to her new owner in Madrid, Spain. Her new owner was Maria Tordesillas, and Lady was the first Alaskan Malamute sent to Europe for show purposes.

CUBA

Lois and Bill Dawson bred the first champion in Cuba. Their Ch. Kobuk's Erkluk was also the first Alaskan Malamute in that country to place in a Group; it won Second in 1957 under judge Lloyd Brackett. Erkluk also became a Mexican champion in 1959. He was owned by Mary de Labadie. Ms. de Labadie also finished Kobuk's Dido to a Mexican championship in 1958.

NORWAY

J.B. Kionig, while not active in the breed in Norway, is a member of the parent club and thereby keeps up with the breed's activities.

MEXICO

The same applies to Victor DeLeon of Mexico City: not active but a member of the parent club and in touch with the breed.

In 1958 Mr. R. Newman finished Yukon Wolf of Yakatat to a championship.

HOLLAND

In the Netherlands the breed is represented by several Malamute owners. Betsey Corry Ketclaar-Triller, for example, owns Shamrocks Atataq Taku and Anernak. Anita Haas Andela and Marge Broekhuizen were known as owners of Ch. Tigara's Matanuska U-Chee. Whelped in 1966, U-Chee was bred by Dorothy Dillingham and Gloria Schwalbe. Dr. Bertha Van Dantzig imported a Tigara dog also, Ch. Tigara's Matanushka Magic, which became one of Europe's top-winning show dogs with Group Placements to his credit. Magic was bred by Darlene Martin. Dr. Dantzig also imported Tigara's Matanushka Laska.

Elizabeth Urlis is also interested in the breed and a member of the Alaskan Malamute Club of America.

SWITZERLAND

Helly Vogt of Blauen, Switzerland, owned International Ch. Coldfoot Wagnark, bred by M. and J. Pokrefsky.

In 1973 Roman Beier and his wife imported Inuits Honkita of Silanouk, and David Lynch (of Geneva, Switzerland) owns Alaskaland's Wolfgang Inuit.

Inuit's Honkita of Sillanouk, owned by Roman Beier in Geneva, Switzerland.

THE SWISS CLUB FOR NORTHERN BREEDS

It was only after 1963, when the Swiss Club for Northern Dogs was established, that cross-breeds were frowned upon and Northern breed owners began once again to have interest in promoting pure-bred dogs.

Upon this breakthrough in 1963 the Alaskan Malamute, the Samoyed, the Greenland Dog, the Norwegian Elkhound, the Karelian

Bear Hound, the Akita Inu and the Siberian Husky came under the protection of the Swiss Club for Northern Dogs. This organization maintained a firm hold on the breed, much more so even than any breed club in this country.

Annually, or semi-annually, the official breed clubs hold a meeting for a selection of dogs worthy of breeding. No dog receives papers unless his parents have also passed this breeding selection and abilities test.

First of all they maintained that the dog must be one year of age or older, must be x-rayed and declared by a veterinarian to be free of hip dysplasia. The dog is weighed and measured and examined thoroughly by a judge and the president of the breeding committee for any and all breed disorders or major faults. Even character defects are duly noted on the record for their registry.

The club has a record of every dog and bitch in the country to record which are and which are not eligible to be bred, thereby giving them complete control of any breeding programs. They further declare that no dog under 18 months of age is eligible to be bred and only six or fewer puppies per litter are allowed. Furthermore, breeders must put their dogs through this judging every three years, and even non-members of the Swiss Club for Northern Dogs must have the club approval of their dogs if they wish to breed.

THE FEDERATION CYNOLOGIQUE INTERNATIONALE

The FCI is the top European organization in the world of dogs and was formed in the early 1930's. It is the central governing body and is composed of a few selected representatives and delegates of each of the national kennel clubs whose purpose it is to standardize breeds and shows. They establish the rules for the shows, select the recognized breeds and put them in their groupings and settle all disagreements which might arise within the establishing of International Championship titles. Their group consists of 21 member countries and 13 associate member countries. They issue points toward the title called the Certificate of Beauty and Aptitude.

The International Champion title is the highest award a dog can achieve. Before a dog can be called an International Champion, he must have received the CACIB certificate four times, at four different shows in three different countries (including his home country) and under three different judges. The CACIB certificate stands for Certificate of Ability to Compete for the Title of National Champion and can be compared to the United States Winners Dog or Winners Bitch wins in that they are receiving points toward their titles. CACIB wins are earned from the Open Classes.

While there is a Youth Class for dogs from 10 to 15 months, the minimum age for Open Class is 15 months, so most European dogs

Shamrock's Atataq Taku, owned by Betsey Correy Ketclaar-Triller in Holland.

are entered in the Open Class starting with their very first show at exactly 15 months of age. They are working toward their championship from their very first ring appearance. There are at times classes for braces or groups of the same breed, but there are no Specials Classes as we know them in this country. Champions also compete from Open Class, and there is no Best of Breed, Best of Winners, or Group judging, nor is there any Best in Show award in Europe.

In Switzerland, the title is awarded for one year's duration only! If a dog competes and wins again he is said to be a Plural Swiss champion.

Other countries give CAC's as well. Three of these certificates give the right for the dog to be called Champion of France, or Champion of Italy, etc., for a lifetime. These hard-won multiple titles and championships keep the Europeans entering dog shows on a fairly regular basis.

The Alaskan Malamute is judged in Europe by those judges qualified to judge all the Northern dog breeds, or by an all-breed judge.

12. THE ALASKAN MALAMUTE CLUBS

The Alaskan Malamute Club of America is, of course, the parent club for the breed and a member of the American Kennel Club. The club secretary changes periodically, so those wishing to get in touch with the club secretary should telephone or write to the American Kennel Club for the name and address of the current secretary.

As we discuss elsewhere in this book, it is wise for anyone owning an Alaskan Malamute to join both the parent club and also a regional specialty club if there is one in your area. This information can be obtained by writing to the secretary of the parent club, who will supply you with the information you desire.

SPECIALTY CLUBS

Some of the regional clubs devoted exclusively to the breeding and advancement of the Alaskan Malamute are:

Golden State Alaskan Malamute Club of California
Alaskan Malamute Sledge Dog Association (California)
Nutmeg Malamute Fanciers (Connecticut)
Yankee Alaskan Malamute Club (New England)
Empire Alaskan Malamute Club (New York-New Jersey)
Alaskan Malamute Club of Greater Detroit
Alaskan Malamute Club of North Eastern New York
Alaskan Malamute Association of Long Island
Chicagoland Alaskan Malamute Club
Snow King Alaskan Malamute Fanciers (Northwestern U.S.)
Iroquois Malamute Club (New York)
Alaskan Malamute Club of San Diego
Northern California Alaskan Malamute Association
Alaskan Malamute Club of Wisconsin
Alaskan Malamute Club of Greater St. Louis

HISTORY OF THE ALASKAN MALAMUTE CLUB

Actually the parent club got its start as a local New England club initiated and guided by Mrs. Milton Seeley. With the ever-increasing interest in the breed at the time, the club quite naturally began to grow, and by 1953 it was ready for full status as the official national breed club. From the first few members that "Short" Seeley gathered together in the beginning, the membership in the Alaskan Malamute Club of America by the mid-1970's had reached a membership roster containing over 700 names.

ALASKAN MALAMUTE CLUB AWARDS

In 1968 an award, the first to be presented on an annual basis, was given. Called the Navarro Award, in honor of its creators, Leon and Val Navarro, it was given to those who had contributed to the breed through an act of exceptional humanitarianism. Later the award was given by the club itself and no longer carried the Navarro name. The winners were:

    1968 — Brenda Malesa
    1969 — Dr. and Mrs. John Schmidt
    1970 — Mr. and Mrs. Richard Schwalbe
    1971 — Ralph and Marchetta Schmitt
    1971 — Linda Dowdy

Since 1973 no award in this category has been made.

"DOG WORLD" MAGAZINE AWARDS

Beginning in 1953, *Dog World* magazine allowed for an award (through a vote from the club) to someone for outstanding service to dogs. This award was called the *Dog World* Award for Service To Dogs and was presented as follows:

    1953 — Mrs. Eva B. Seeley
    1956 — Mr. and Mrs. W.R. Gormley
    1957 — Mr. and Mrs. J.W. Dawson
    1959 — Mr. and Mrs. H.B. Pearson
    1960 — Mr. and Mrs. Roy Truchon
    1962 — Mr. and Mrs. D.C. Dillingham
    1964 — Mr. Robert Zoller
    1965 — Mr. Melvin Pokrefky
    1967 — Mr. Roger Burggraf
    1968 — Mrs. Dorothy Dillingham
    1969 — Mrs. Alice Jean Lucus

Dog World magazine has not presented this award since the 1969 presentation.

THE GAINES MEDAL

Over the years the Gaines Dog Food Company has through cooperation with the members of the breed clubs presented after a vote tally held by the clubs the Gaines Medal for Good Sportsmanship. The first award voted on by the Alaskan Malamute Club was awarded in

1954. The recipients of this award have been:

1954 — Mr. J.J. Lynn, Jr.
1957 — Mrs. Alice Spawn
1959 — Mrs. Merry Stockburger
1960 — Mrs. Delta Wilson
1962 — Mr. Kim Johnson
1964 — Mr. Walter Corcelius
1967 — Mrs. Joan Byrne
1968 — Mr. John McCartney
1969 — Mrs. Nancy Russell
1970 — Mrs. Mary Ellen Narkis
1971 — Mr. Wayne Zimmerman
1972 — Mrs. Sue Sprenkle
1973 — Mrs. Millie Land

1973 was the last award presented.

ALASKAN MALAMUTE CLUB OF AMERICA'S NATIONAL SPECIALTY BEST OF BREED WINNERS

1952 — Ch. Toro of Bras Clupe
1953 — Ch. Arctic Storm of Husky Pak
1954 — Ch. Mulpus Brooks The Bear
1959 — Ch. Aabara of Redhorse
1960 — Ch. Rogue of Tigara
1961 — Ch. Spawn's Hot-Shot of Roy-El
1963 — Ch. Eldor's Little Bo
1964 — Ch. Spawn's T'Domar's Panda
1965 — Ch. Sno Crest's Mukluk
1966 — Ch. Tigara's Eskimo Eddy of Kaiyuh
1967 — Ch. Kodara Kodiak of Erowah
1968 — Ch. T'Domar's Ghengis Kim Shadow
1969 — Ch. Glacier's Burbon King
1970 — Ch. Glaciers Storm Kloud
1971 — Ch. Burbon's Aristocrat of Brenmar
1972 — Ch. J Len's Captain Koriak
1973 — Ch. Lobito's Cougar Cub
1974 — Ch. Inuit's Sweet Lucifer

EVA B. SEELEY HONORARY TROPHY

All winners of the Best of Breed award at the National Specialty receive the Eva B. Seeley Memorial Trophy Bowl; 1971 was the first year it was awarded, and the following dogs have had possession:

1971 — Burbon's Aristocrat of Brenmar
1972 — J'Len's Captain Koriak

1973 — Lobito's Cougar Cub
1974 — Inuit's Sweet Lucifer

AMCA FIRST INDEPENDENT SPECIALTY

The first Independent Alaskan Malamute Club of American National Specialty show was held on October 6, 1973 at McCambridge Park in Burbank, California. There was an entry of 161 dogs for the competition.

Charles Berger, D.V.M. judged the Puppy Sweepstakes, and Dorothy Dillingham's puppy Tigara's Same Space was awarded Best Sweepstakes Puppy award from the 12-to-18-month dog class. Mr. Noah Bloomer judged the breed classes, and his choice for Best of Breed was Ch. Lobito's Cougar Cub, owned and bred by Dr. Richard and Dawn Woods. The Best of Opposite Sex win went to the winner of the Veteran and Brood Bitch class, named Ch. Sena-Lak's Beowulf Tawechi; this bitch also holds a Canadian C.D. title. She also happened to be the granddam of the Best of Breed winner—a lovely win for this prestigious show! Her owner, Beth Harris, was thrilled.

Bernadette Russo's dog Ch. Tigara's Jo-Dan of Arctica at 10 years of age won the Veteran Dog Class. A 15-year-old dog, Ch. May-Glen's Shaman, owned by Robert and Louise Webster, was the oldest dog at the show and responded admirably to his standing ovation and let everyone know that he remembered the good old days when he was competing in the show ring.

One of the outstanding features of the show was an expedition staged by the Golden State Alaskan Malamute Club. This group presented carting demonstrations with relay, sourdough and weight-pulling competitions. Top pull was made by Keith and Lynne Hurrell's Shadak's Arctic Sunrise, C.D.X. when he pulled a car weighing over 3,000 pounds.

The extra-curricular activities supervised by Tracy Young ended with judge Noah Bloomer being ridden in a cart behind a team of Malamutes from the sledding area back to the bench show ring!

The show festivities were climaxed by a banquet. Chairlady Kathy Frick acted as Mistress of Ceremonies and club president Lawson Williams introduced the guest speaker, Duncan Wright, president of the American Dog Owners Association.

AMCA ANNUAL MEETINGS

Each June the Alaskan Malamute Club of America holds its annual meeting to discuss all business and tend to the election of officers.

At this meeting members also elect an editor for the club newsletter. The editor not only tends to the publication of the Newsletter but also compiles annual statistics in the breed, i.e., names of Best in Show, Group and Obedience Title winners, etc.

Short Seeley presenting her "Eva B. Seeley Memorial Trophy" for Best of Breed at the Alaskan Malamute Club of America National Specialty Show. The 1974 winner was Ch. Inuit's Sweet Lucifer, owned by Sheila Balch, Inuit Kennels, Valley Cottage, New York.

ALASKAN MALAMUTE CLUB JOURNALS

In the spring of 1971 the Alaskan Malamute Club of America published *The Alaskan Malamute Reference Journal*. This was a three-ring loose leaf notebook type of publication with a dual value to Alaskan Malamute owners. First, it was a collection of pictorial pedigrees for the breed, and secondly it provided a valuable and useful reference to the sincere breeder by supplying all necessary information on any future breeding programs.

However, with such an enormous endeavor, there had to be certain limitations to the listings, since it was obvious not everyone could be included. Therefore, certain qualifications were necessary to have a pictorial presentation of a dog or bitch in the Journal. All champions were permitted, or the sires and dams of champions; obedience title holders, working or sled dogs of note, or dogs that held weight-pulling records.

The book also included a chronological listing of those included in the volume as well as an alphabetical listing. Volume II was published in 1972, and future volumes are expected.

THE ALASKAN MALAMUTE NEWSLETTER

The Alaskan Malamute Club of America publishes a monthly newsletter for all members. Robert Zoller was the founder back in the 1950's when the AMCA was founded. Its purpose is to keep members informed about all that is going on in the breed under the club's jurisdiction.

THE AMCA MEDALLION

The Alaskan Malamute Club of America has an official emblem which was rendered by Drew Dasher. This emblem is also issued in the forms of stickers and on stationery and club newsletters, etc. The dog representing the breed is Ch. Cliquot of Husky Pak, C.D.X.

ALASKAN MALAMUTE CLUBS IN OTHER COUNTRIES

There is an Alaskan Malamute Club in Canada, and for information regarding this organization it is suggested that contact be made with Mary Ann Breen, 78 Willowpoint Road, Winnipeg, Manitoba, Canada.

For information on The Alaskan Malamute Club in England, the Honorable Secretary is Mrs. Janet Edmonds, Riding Hill House, Finstock, Oxford, England.

Kemo Spartacus at the age of 3 months winning his first blue ribbon at his first match show. Owners are 13-year-old Marie Markiewicz (pictured handling Kemo) and Paula Markiewicz of Plantsville, Connecticut.

Ch. Icefloe's Knave of Hearts, better known as Juneau, is a lead dog on the sled team of Icefloe Kennels. Sire was Ch. Glacier's Burbon King *ex* Ch. Icefloe's North Star, top-producing bitch for 1972, with six champions to her credit. Owned by Jeri Lea Hooks, Los Lunas, New Mexico.

13. THE ALASKAN MALAMUTE IN LITERATURE

Explorers who ventured into the great wastes of the North and South Pole regions have always held a special interest to those of us with adventure in our souls. From the earliest accounts of Admiral Byrd and the rest of those brave men and their famous expeditions, we have all enjoyed reading about their voyages.

Many books have been written about their discoveries and the trials and tribulations of those early journeys, and almost all of them have to some degree included accounts of the Northern dogs. Dogs of North regions have always been popular with young and old readers alike, and we present here a list of books which deal with the Northern breeds in general and Alaskan Malamutes in particular:

I, Nuligak; Maurice Metayer
People of the Deer; Farley Mowat
Never Cry Wolf; Farley Mowat
Wild Voice of the North; Sally Carighar
My Friends the Huskies; Robert Dovers
Baldy of Nome and Navarre of the North; Esther Birdsall Darling
On Arctic Ice; Fred Machetanz
A Puppy Named Gih; Fred Machetanz
The Snow People; Marie Herbert
Toilers of the Trails; George Marsh
The Central Eskimo; Franz Boas
The Top of the World and *Back to the Top of the World*; Hans Ruesch
A Dog Named Wolf; Erik Munsterhjelm
My Life With the Eskimos; Vilhjalmur Stefanson
Dark Companion; Bradley Robinson
Toyon: Dog of the North; Nicholas Kalashnikoff
Snow Dog; Jim Kjelgaard
Howl of the Malamute; Sara Machetanz
Kazan the Wolf Dog and *Baree, Son of Kazan*; James O. Curwood
Alaska Trail Dogs; Elsie Caldwell

American and Canadian Ch. Zardal Cotati, bred, owned and handled by Audrey I. Thomas, Zardal Kennels, Penfield, New York, winning Veteran Bitch Class at a recent show at 10 years of age. Photo by Stephen Klein.

Ch. Frostfield Kemosabe winning Best of Winners at the 1974 Northshore Kennel Club show on the way to his championship; bred by David Manning. The sire was Ch. Yukon King's Arctic Prince of Frostfield *ex* Chonga's Aleutia. Kemosabe is handled here by Thomas L. Jones, who co-owns the dog with Jerry and Wendy Wisefield, Frostfield Kennels, Avon, Massachusetts.

Eskimo Dogs, Forgotten Heroes; W. Elmer Ekblau
Sledge Dogs; Helmer Hanssen
Mush, You Malamutes!; Bernard R. Hubbard
Ten Thousand Miles with a Dog Sled; Hudson Struck
Alone Across the Top of the World; Jack O'Brien
Arctic Adventure—My Life in the Frozen North; Peter Freuchen
Peter Freuchen's Book of the Eskimos; Peter Freuchen
Chinook and His Family; Eva Seeley and Martha Lane
Discovery, the Second Byrd Antarctic Expedition; Richard Evelyn
 Byrd
A Dog Puncher on the Yukon; Arthur Treadwell Walden
Farthest North Voyage of the Fram; Dr. Fridtjof Nansen
Little America—The First Byrd Antarctic Expedition; Richard
 Evelyn Byrd
The Long Whip; Jane Brevoort Walden and Stuart D.L. Paine
Minstel of the Yukon; Jack Hines
Nearest the Pole; Robert E. Peary
Ninety Degrees South; Dr. Paul Siple
The North Pole; Robert E. Peary
Sir John Franklin and the Arctic Regions; P.L. Simmond
Travels in Alaska and on the Yukon; Frederick Whymper
Nùnaga—Ten Years of Eskimo Life; Duncan Pryde
The People of the Twilight; Diamond Janess
Polaris, The Story of an Eskimo Dog; Ernest H. Baynes
Gold, Men and Dogs; A.A. Allen
Dogs from Disko; Greeley
Stikine; John Muir
Harness and Pack; Arthur T. Walden
Album of Northern Dogs; Prince Andrew Shirinsky-Shihmatoff
The Wolf King; Joseph W. Lippincott
The Last of the Few; Kaare Rodahl, M.D.
Antarctica—the Worst Place in the World; Allyn Baum
How To Raise and Train an Alaskan Malamute; Charles Berger,
 D.V.M.
Alone; Richard E. Byrd
Arctic Wild; Lois Chrisler
Eskimo Adventure; Edward Keithan
The Sledge Patrol; David Howarth
Togo's Fireside Reflections (Siberian Husky); Elizabeth M. Ricker
Winner Lose All—Dr. Cook and the Theft of the North Pole; Hugh
 Eames

Other titles such as Jack London's *Call of the Wild, Nanook of the North*, and *Sgt. Preston and the Mounties* also come to mind, also from the happy reading hours of our childhood. However, we must also add that many of these are out of print, rare editions found only in private collections, but worth tracking down if you enjoy reading about the dogs of the North. Even if they can be found they are likely to be expensive, but worth having if only to let the parent club historian make a record of its existence, or to donate to the American Kennel Club Library.

THE ALASKAN MALAMUTE IN POETRY

Poems about dogs—even those confined to the Northern breeds—are too numerous to mention here, but one we especially like, since it mentions the Malamute specifically, reads like this:

A MALAMUTE DOG
by Pat O'Cotter

You can't tell me God would have Heaven
So a man couldn't mix with his friends—
That we are doomed to meet disappointment
When we come to the place the trail ends.

That would be a low-grade sort of Heaven
And I'd never regret a damned sin
If I rush up to the gates white and pearly
And they don't let my Malamute in.

For I know it would never be homelike
No matter how golden the strand,
If I lose out that pal-loving feeling
Of a Malamute's nose on my hand.

The above poem was taken from a book titled *Best Loved Poems of the American People*, edited by Hazel Tellman—Garden City Publishing Co., 1936.

THE ALASKAN MALAMUTE IN THE MOVIES

Sena-Lak's Alaskan Blizzard, whelped in 1957, and owned by Larry Erickson of Alberta, Canada, played a part in the movie *Nikki, Wild Dog of the North*. Blitz, as she was called, weighed 80 pounds and was lead dog on a team of dogs and wolves by the time she was 8 months old, and also worked a trap line for her young owner.

American and Canadian Champion Kodara El Toro played a part in the Walt Disney movie *Lefty, the Ding-A-Ling Lynx*. Toro is mentioned elsewhere in this book as a top weight-pulling Malamute and show dog.

SGT. PRESTON OF THE YUKON!

In the late 1950's Stuart Mace, who provided the Alaskan Malamutes for the television series *Sgt. Preston of the Yukon* called Eleanor Du Buis of the Sena-Lak Kennels and requested additional dogs to be trained for this series. A virus had wiped out the majority

Grand Puppy Sweepstakes winner at the New England area trophy show under judge Eva Short Seeley was Kaila's Wicked Witch of Inuit, co-owned by Eileen and Chris Gabriel of Golden Bridge, New York, and handled by Mr. Gabriel.

At 9 years of age, the fabulous American, Canadian and Bermudian Ch. Inuit's Wooly Bully wins Best of Breed (and Group Second) at the 1974 North East Area Alaskan Malamute Specialty Show from the Veteran's Class! This grand old gentleman took this sensational win under judge J. Roy Kibler. Breeder-owner Sheila Balch, Inuit Kennels, Valley Cottage, New York.

Sena-Lak's Rock of Alaska, one of Eleanore DuBuis's most famous Alaskan Malamutes. This classic head study has appeared in many books and is featured on her Sena-Lak Kennel stationery. The Sena-Lak Kennels are situated in Valois, New York.

of those he had been using in the series up to that date, and he needed more. Five were sold to him after the proper waiting period to be sure the disease contamination on the premises had passed.

Perhaps the most famous of all of them was Sena-Lak's Rock of Alaska, whose photograph as Sgt. Preston's dog King became well-known over the years in connection with this series. As late as the 1970's the series is still being distributed by Jack Wrather Productions and being viewed in foreign countries. In other words, the famous Sergeant Preston is still spreading the word about our marvelous working breed and the part it played in the Canadian North over the years.

CANADIAN POLICE DOGS

In addition to the Royal Canadian Mounted Police and Sgt. Preston, the Alaskan Malamute has been used on occasion by the Canadian police for rescue work. In Toronto, Ch. Lorn-Hall Oogorook M'Loot, bred in 1945 by Lorna Jackson, was used by their police force to locate people both living and dead which had become victims of the disastrous hurricane named Hazel.

ALASKAN MALAMUTE TOUR GUIDE

Ch. Sena-Lak's Purgha, whelped in 1965, and her owner, Mary Pearson, have conducted tourists on vacation excursions through Russia and Poland, this after Purgha had helped her owner learn to walk again after a serious impairment.

NO LANGUAGE BARRIER

Ch. Sena-Lak's Miss Tardy, owned by the Richard L. Sassamans of Driftwood, Pennsylvania, was the first dog trained by Harris Dunlap, 1970-1971 Musher of the Year. Miss Tardy learned all her commands in German and has logged over 1500 miles of sledding experience.

WHAT'S IN A NAME?

The most unusual name for an Alaskan Malamute we came across was Ch. Alaskaland's Liger. Liger was named after Shasta, the only "Liger" in the world. Shasta's father was a lion and her mother was a tiger. Hence, "Liger." The Alaskan Malamute Liger finished for his championship in just 12 shows before he was one year of age. He was owned and bred by Sheila Land, Holladay, Utah.

CAJOLING THE JUDGES

Anyone who has ever entered a dog show knows that some handlers and exhibitors are capable of the most unusual ploys for attracting the attention of the judge in the ring, in the hopes of drawing special consideration for their dogs.

Captions for reverse page:

Top left: American and Canadian Ch. Bearpaw Elk of Tote-Um welcoming a friend to the Pinetop Kennels owned by Alice Jean and Philip Lucus of Seattle, Washington. This charming photograph has been used in the past in connection with Alaskan Malamute Club of America brochures on the breed.

Center left: American and Canadian Ch. Kodara El Toro, show dog, lead dog, weight-puller and friend, the epitome of the all-around Alaskan Malamute. Owned by Dick and Dianne Ross, Tote-Um Kennels, Cle Elum, Washington.

Bottom left: Inuit's Mischevious Muffin, owned by James and Marie Miller of Michigan. Muffie is shown at her first show at exactly 6 months of age, going Best of Winners for her first three Canadian points from the Puppy Class. The sire was Ch. Inuit's Sweet Lucifer *ex* Inuit's Zanna of Aleut. Brauer photograph.

Top right: Kotzebue Chandlar of Chinook pictured winning at 15 months under judge James Trullinger at the 1975 Cape Cod Kennel Club show. Bred by Eva B. Seeley, Kusko is owned by Mr. and Mrs. Philip Lake, Aurora Kennels, Holbrook, Massachusetts. The sire was Ch. Kotzebue Bering of Chinook *ex* Kotzebue Muffin Chinook.

Bottom right: American and Canadian Ch. Bernard pictured finishing for his championship with a three-point major under judge John Honig. Sire was Ch. Inuit's Wooly Bully *ex* Kotzebue of Chinook. Owners are Judith and Philip Lake, Aurora Kennels, Holbrook, Massachusetts.

The Wizard of Inuit pictured winning under breeder-judge Jo Brand when he was 6 months old. Nicknamed "Noony Brown," he is shown exclusively for owner Sheila Balch by Shannon Sollinger. The sire was Ch. Inuit's Sweet Lucifer *ex* Ch. Cordova's Tasha.

Ch. Kiche's Past Is Prologue, youngest champion in breed history in Canada. She finished at 7 months and 24 days old from the Junior Puppy Class. Bred and owned by Gail Corning, Kiche Kennels, St. Agatha, Ontario, Canada.

Well, it is perfectly understandable then for owners of Alaskan Malamutes to know that it is also perfectly possible for some of the dogs to draw attention to themselves in the show ring.

Ch. Sena-Lak's Gigante Grande Toro, owned by Mr. and Mrs. William Brown III of McFarland, Wisconsin, had a habit of acting as if he were chewing gum in the show ring. He would work his tongue and jaws in such a way that caused a few judges to actually inquire if he was chewing gum.

In the obedience ring, Frostwind Ooga Looga Luska, C.D. never made his C.D.X. degree because he died after being kicked by a horse, but he had caused his handler considerable doubt about it anyway, since he had an unusual way of rolling the dumbbell around in his mouth while wiggling his ears at the same time. Whelped in 1968 by Jan Shelton, Mike was owned by Margaret D. Goin of Norco, California.

TOURIST ATTRACTION

Dog sled races and other outdoor events held for the Northern breeds have become so popular in this country that travel columns in the better magazines are making their readers aware of the fact that dog sled rides are available for tourists.

A 1975 issue of *Better Homes and Gardens*, for instance, featured an article on winter fun at Lake Placid. Along with other outdoor winter sport attractions at that popular vacation resort there was a picture of a driver and an 11-dog team in a beautiful snow setting, and the paragraph headed "Dogsled rides" told of a 30-minute ride on the lake itself.

They announced that the sled rides are run during daylight hours when the lake is frozen over, usually from New Year's to the end of February, and the price is ten dollars. There is supposedly room for mom and dad and three or four kids on these five- to seven-dog sleds.

MALAMUTE LONGEVITY

While this healthy, hearty breed manages to live a good long life, the record for old age that has been touted was Ch. Daku of Husky Pak, whelped in 1952, bred by the Robert Zollers and owned by Franklin Martin of Albion, Pennsylvania. Daku lived to be 15½ years old.

14. GROOMING YOUR ALASKAN MALAMUTE

It goes without saying that a clean dog requires some special care and grooming to be at its best, whether it is a show dog or just a member of the family. If your dog is a true working dog, he is going to look and smell like one. Even though the Alaskan Malamute is basically a clean, odor-free dog in its natural habitat, in today's cities and towns they do manage to pick up dirt, especially if they are working dogs. When this odor becomes noticeable a bath is generally in order, especially if he is a show dog or if he lives in the house.

DRY BATHS

It is not always necessary to give the dog a complete wet bath. There are many "dry shampoo" products available at pet shops which will keep your dog relatively clean and odor-free for indoor living. These are usually pleasant-smelling powders which are sprinkled thoroughly into the coat and then brushed right out again. There are also chalks and powders which also serve the same purpose, and corn starch is also used for the dry shampoo process. The proper brush for the Malamute coat can be obtained at the store where you purchase your dry shampoo products.

THE BATHING AREA

A bath the day before a dog show is usually in order. Bathing will help remove any dead hair and put the desired sheen on the coat. And with young dogs, a bath also helps to stimulate the growth of new hair.

Before you even reach for the shampoo and towels, be sure that you have a space set aside to confine the dog until he is completely dry. Otherwise the coat will pick up dust and dirt right from the moment he gets out of the tub. Have all your implements ready also, and make sure you have a rubber mat for the dog to stand on so he can be secure with his footing. Nothing makes a dog more restless than to be on a slippery surface. Fill the tub with the first water before picking the dog up and lifting it (if you need someone to help,

Eleven-month-old Aurora's Northern Princess pictured winning at the 1975 Providence Kennel Club show. Sired by American and Canadian Ch. Bernard *ex* Aurora's Kantishna Meadow, Princess was bred by Judith Lake and Edward J. Juengst and is owned by Judith Lake and Edward and Marcia Juengst.

Ch. Alaskaland's American Pie pictured winning Best of Winners award and championship at the 1974 Alaskan Malamute Club of America's Specialty Show under judge J. Roy Kibler. This dog is a full brother to the Best of Breed dog at this Specialty, Ch. Inuit's Sweet Lucifer. Sired by American, Canadian and Bermudian Ch. Inuit's Wooly Bully ex Ch. Voyageurs Elke. Owner is Patti Colcord.

The striking Mrs. Cleveland Amory of New York City and her equally striking Alaskan Malamutes Ivan and Peter patiently await their turn in line to have the dogs tattooed.

make sure that person is going to be there if you need help lifting the dog out of the tub also). The water should be very warm, but not hot. The dryer or vacuum attachment with blower should be ready and near the grooming table along with plenty of towels.

THE ACTUAL BATH

The water in the tub should be, if possible, high enough to touch the dog's stomach so that the heaviest concentrations of dirt on the legs and stomach, which constantly touch the ground, can be soaking in the water and getting through to the skin.

Using a pan, pour water over the dog, or use a hose and wet the dog until he is saturated to the skin all over. Save the head until last. You might want to put oil in the dog's eyes to prevent the shampoo from burning should a bit get into the eyes, and perhaps cotton in the ears for the same reason. Using a wet wash cloth to do the face will usually prevent this from happening.

Once the dog is thoroughly wet to the skin on all parts of the body, use the shampoo. Give the dog two complete latherings and thorough rinsings. Then give a *third* rinsing just to be sure there is no shampoo left in the coat! Special attention should be given to make sure that the vent area and the elbows and hocks have been cleaned thoroughly.

THE DRYING PROCESS

After allowing the dog to "drip dry" for a few minutes after the final rinsing, use turkish towels to gently squeeze dry to get off the excess water. Place the dog on the grooming table; after the dryer has warmed up a bit you are ready to start the drying process.

Direct the current of air from the dryer slowly all over the body, brushing back the coat while drying and seeing to it that the warm air gets all the way down to the skin. The dryer should be held anywhere from six to twelve inches from the body, or at least far enough away for you to be able to brush the coat in the proper direction.

If done properly and leisurely, the dog will actually enjoy the warmth and stimulation and attention that accompanies a bath. If he is fretful or restless, you are not doing it right. If the dog pants excessively, offer a drink of water now and then, since either nervousness or too much air around the face from the dryer will dry out his mouth, and a drink will prevent this discomfort.

Keep up the drying process until the dog is completely dry. If there is even a hint of dampness confine the dog to an area that is completely free of drafts.

THE DAY OF THE DOG SHOW

While the bath the day before the show should be sufficient to present your dog at his very best, sometimes weather conditions are

Kemo Spartacus, pictured winning Best of Winners and Best of Breed at the Philadelphia Kennel Club show under judge Vincent Buoniello, Jr.; 13-year-old Marie Markiewicz handled Kemo to this three-point major. Kemo's sire was Jamie Lynn *ex* Duchess von Mark. He is co-owned by Marie and Paula Markiewicz of Plantsville, Connecticut.

Best of Breed at the 1974 N.E. Area Specialty Show from Veterans Class, "Floyd" is pictured with the trophy sled he won donated by A.M.C.A. member Toby Sprague, right. Owner Sheila Balch completes the picture. Ashbey photo.

Canadian Champion Bearpaw Lobo pulling 1,350 pounds in 1973. He has pulled this weight once on ice and snow and again on a gravel road. Lobo is owned by Philip and Alice Jean Lucus of the Elk's Pinetop Kennels, Seattle, Washington.

Left is Inuit's Chinchilla of McLean and on the right her daughter, McLean's Teeka of Nunamiut, C.D., owned by Diana Wittich. The dam is owned by the Robert McLeans.

Mrs. Amory whispers reassurance to one of her dogs during the completely painless process of having the owner's Social Security number tattooed on the dog's groin.

such that the dog gets a little soiled on the way to the show grounds. Be prepared to wash down the legs and feet in a bucket and towel dry, or powder clean the legs at the show. There is usually water available and you can carry a small pail and a small amount of shampoo or a dry shampoo with you in your tack box. The wet face cloth can clean up the face if necessary, and in warm weather a smear of Vaseline on the nose will erase any trace of white "salt" that might have accumulated on the nose as the dog panted.

In addition to the general foot care mentioned later in this chapter, it is proper to trim the feet to the shape of the foot and to trim the whiskers for the show ring. This is done with blunt or curved tipped scissors (or baby scissors) and always with the points of the scissors pointing *away* from the dog's face. If the dog is restless about the scissors, get someone to hold the dog steady for you rather than risk cutting the dog.

There are also last minute sprays which can be purchased to put on the dog's coat for a little extra shine, but if your dog is healthy and in good coat they are superfluous. Dog owners are sometimes known to have what they consider "secret" preparations to enhance the beauty of the coat, but if you find it necessary to experiment with such things, it is wise to do it at home and not on the day of the show!

GROOMING THE PUPPY

All of the preceding rules of order also apply to your Alaskan Malamute puppy. However, it is not advisable, or usually necessary, to bathe a puppy. . . especially not in winter, or before six months of age. However, this makes periodic grooming more important than ever. Occasional brushings will prevent the coat from getting so dirty it will need a bath. Soft baby brushes will do the trick for the very young puppy. Getting used to grooming at an early age will pay off for you in later years, especially if you intend to show your dog. And your dog will be a happier dog if he is clean.

FOOT CARE

Every dog should have particular attention paid to his feet. Nails should be trimmed short enough so that they cannot be heard clicking on bare floors. They should be cut just in front of the vein. The vein can be judged in white nails by holding the nail up to the light. In black nails the vein cannot be seen in this way and extra care must be taken to cut back slowly and repeatedly so that too much isn't taken off. A veterinarian is the best teacher the first time you wish to attempt it. Later on, instinct will tell you. If you cut the vein, bleeding (and mess) will be excessive and will require smearing the end with Vaseline after pressing wet cotton to the end, or the application of a styptic pencil. Any repeated or painful experience like this is very likely to make a dog foot shy, which may go against him in the show ring.

Winner of the Stud Dog Class at the 1974 North East Area Specialty Show under judge Roy Kibler was American, Canadian and Bermudian Ch. Inuit's Wooly Bully. Far left is "Floyd," then Ch. Kaila's Wicked Witch of Inuit, owned by Chris and Eileen Gabriel; Ch. Bernard, owned by Phil and Judy Lake; Kaila's the Iron Horse, owned by the Gabriels; and Sweet Lucifer, also owned by Sheila Balch. Floyd also won the Stud Dog Class at the 1974 National Specialty, but his get were too numerous to fit into one picture.

Ch. Alaskaland's Inuit Elke Angle, owned by Carol Kearns of Fords, New Jersey. "Swiss Miss" is pictured winning Best of Opposite Sex over Specials bitches at the Mid-East area Malamute Specialty Show held in conjunction with the Harrisburg Kennel Club event in March, 1974. She was BOS to her Best of Breed brother, Ch. Inuit's Sweet Lucifer. She was also BOW and BOS over other bitch Specials at the 1974 Westminster Kennel Club show.

Hair should be cut out from between the toes with blunt end scissors until it is even with the pads on the underside of the foot.

EYE CARE

Any dog requires special care for the area around the eyes. Excessive watering or tearing will stain the area under the eyes and detract from the beauty and expression on the dog's face. Desitin ointment, commercial creams, sticks, and the like are available from veterinarians and pet shops. Prolonged tearing or watering should merit a visit to the vet for a more serious cause of the condition.

The Alaskan Malamute Club of America Specialty Show held at the Western Pennsylvania show on May 21, 1955 saw the late judge Alva Rosenberg awarding Best of Breed to Ch. Cherokee of Husky-Pak. Dog owned and handled by Robert J. Zoller. Brown photograph.

EAR CARE

All breeds of dogs seem prone to picking up dirt in their ears. With the Alaskan Malamute it is particularly important for the ears to stand erect, and there is nothing more certain to make a dog hold down his ears than an ear problem, perhaps from mites or an infection. Even scratching from excess wax or dirt can ruin the coat around the ear as well as make the dog miserable.

Start ear cleaning when the dog is still a puppy, using cotton tips or swabs. Clean the outside of the ear gently first rather than by digging right in. But when you clean down in the ear canal remember to keep the swab in a straight line with the dog's nose since that is the direction the ear canal runs. Be gentle and slow; use a twirling motion rather than a scraping motion. Do not try to probe deeper or "to go around corners." If this simple care is not enough, it is time to see the veterinarian.

TEETH

If you are feeding your dog the proper diet there will be little work for you to do on his teeth. If drinking water in your area is bad, or if a particular health problem with your dog presents somewhat of a problem by discoloring his teeth, a toothbrush and baking soda are advised for brushing. Any tartar that forms should be removed by a veterinarian, since scaling the teeth with the scaler held at an improper angle can permanently damage the enamel on the teeth and lead to all sorts of problems. Care of the teeth is especially important with the old dog. Teeth are essential to proper digestion and therefore must be in good condition for the older dog to digest and benefit fully from the food he eats.

SHEDDING

All dogs shed. . . yet the question of just how much is always asked by anyone thinking seriously about buying a dog, especially if it is a new breed to them.

The Alaskan Malamute generally sheds twice a year, and it is usually exactly when he feels like it! There has been no positive proof that a full shedding has to do with whether or not they race of pull, little to do with extreme heat or cold weather conditions, little or nothing to do with diet or the part of the world in which they live! Generally speaking, they shed twice a year—spring and fall.

Some Malamutes shed completely and all at once. One day they are magnificent in the show ring, the next day they are naked! Others shed in clumps, and still others just lose varying amounts of the loose hair. Many Malamutes go through no more than a sort of thinning out process and merely lose hair evenly all over.

For those who exhibit their Malamutes in the show ring, this uncertainty can be frustrating. But if you see the shedding coming on,

Nishlik, a sled dog used by owner Donald Brooks when he gives talks to local children's groups in the Philadelphia area to further acquaint people with this magnificent breed.

Ch. Zardal Faro King, owned by Dr. Howard Axelrod of Rochester, New York. Handling for Dr. Axelrod is Shirley Hubbell. Breeder was Audrey I. Thomas. Photo by Stephen Klein.

you can help speed the process along by helping to remove the dead hair with extra brushing or combing or with the use of a stripper. A bath can also aid in the removal of this dead hair.

Once a dog "blows his coat" or sheds unevenly or to any great degree, you can count on a good two or three months' lapse of time before you make any more show entries! It will probably take that much time before the dog comes into full bloom once again. Some exhibitors add a coat conditioner to their dogs' diet to help encourage the growth of the new hair. But there are just as many exhibitors who will tell you after years of experience that the new coat comes in no faster than the general good health of the dog will allow.

Between shedding periods you can count on your Alaskan Malamute coat causing you little concern. The coat's texture being what it is, it does not mat, and regular daily brushings are not necessary. An occasional going-over with a rubber-base wire brush will be sufficient to keep your dog in well groomed condition and will present him in his natural beauty.

SHOWING DURING THE SHEDDING PERIOD

If you have a few important shows coming up and you have already sent in your entries, there are a few things to remember that might help your chances of winning in spite of the loss of hair. One is *not* to give a hot bath if shedding has started. There are dry shampoos to use on legs and face and tail or other places where dirt has gathered so that a regular brushing dry will not take out most of the coat. There are also sprays that can be used to give a little extra gloss to the coat without having to wet down the dog or submerge it entirely in water.

Lack of undercoat during the shedding season is normal, and most judges will allow for it. But trimming the dog to make it look more even is not allowable! Trimming toes and whiskers is one thing . . . scissoring a dog to even it out, or trimming guard hairs to level off a body line, is not permissible. And if you use chalk or cornstarch or powder of any kind on the white areas, we caution once again to be sure to get it all out before entering the show ring!

15. THE POWER IN PEDIGREES

Someone in the dog fancy once remarked that the definition of a show prospect puppy is one third the pedigree, one third what you see, and one third what you *hope* it will be! Well, no matter how you break down your qualifying fractions, we all quite agree that good breeding is essential if you have any plans at all for a show career for your dog! Many breeders will buy on pedigree alone, counting largely on what they can do with the puppy themselves by way of feeding, conditioning and training. Needless to say, that very important piece of paper commonly referred to as "the pedigree" is mighty reassuring to a breeder or buyer new at the game or to one who has a breeding program in mind and is trying to establish his own bloodline.

One of the most fascinating aspects of tracing pedigrees is the way the names of the really great dogs of the past keep appearing in the pedigrees of the great dogs of today. . . positive proof of the strong influence of heredity, and witness to a great deal of truth in the statement that great dogs frequently reproduce themselves, though not necessarily in appearance only. A pedigree represents something of value when one is dedicated to breeding better dogs.

To the novice buyer or one who is perhaps merely switching to another breed and sees only a frolicking, leggy, squirming bundle of energy in a fur coat, a pedigree can mean *everything*! To those of us who believe in heredity, a pedigree is more like an insurance policy . . . so read them carefully and take heed!

FIRST ALASKAN MALAMUTE CHAMPION

Ch. Gripp of Yukon was bred by Mrs. Milton Seeley and whelped on August 24, 1929. The sire was Yukon Jad, and the dam was a bitch named Bessie. Gripp's championship was recorded by the American Kennel Club in 1936. Gripp was a gray and white dog; he was 21½ inches at the withers and weighed 75 pounds.

Gripp was also the first Alaskan Malamute to gain national recognition for the breed, when he was acclaimed for being the lead dog in a team of all A.K.C.-registered Malamutes which competed at the 1932 Winter Olympics at Lake Placid, New York. The team's dri-

Inuit's Arctic Thunder pictured winning Best of Breed from the Puppy Class at 7 months of age under judge Arnold Wolff with his owner, junior handler Pamela Ihrig of California. The sire was Ch. Tigara's Karluk of Roy-El ex Ch. Inuit's Mehitabel. Klein photo.

Cordova's Brave Bruin won Best of Winners under judge Seekins at the 1974 Kenilworth Kennel Club Show on the way to his championship. The sire was Ch. Sittiak Kosak Warrior of Mesa ex Ch. Cordova's Tasha. Shown is owner-handler Carol Perham, Cordova Kennels, Lakeside, Connecticut.

ver, Mrs. Seeley, competed with this great team against ten male drivers. This team was one of the two teams considered best conditioned and most uniform among the entries. It was good going, since the other teams had drivers of renown, among them Leonard Seppala, Emmet St. Goddard and Shorty Russick, all ardent racers during that time.

ANOTHER EARLY "GREAT"

Another early all-around Malamute which did much to establish the popularity of the breed, bred by Mrs. Milton Seeley in 1945 and owned by Earl and Natalie Norris of Anchorage, Alaska, was Ch. Toro of Bras Coupe. Toro, a light wolf gray and white dog, was working in harness in Alaska for 7 years before he ever entered the show ring. Not only was he one of the many foundation dogs at the Norrises' kennel, but he managed to win Best of Breed honors at the 1952 Westminster Kennel Club show in New York City at 7 years of age!

Toro was 24 inches at the withers and weighed 90 pounds. His ancestors went back to the Admiral Byrd expedition dogs, and his grandsire was the famous Ch. Gripp of Yukon.

OFFICIAL PEDIGREES

Pedigree of CH. TORO OF BRAS COUPE, bred by Eva B. Seeley. Sex: male; whelped: 1945; color: light wolf gray & white.

Sire: Ch. Kim of Kotzebue.
Dam: Kotzebue Cleopatra.

Grandsire on Sire's Side: Navarre of Kotzebue (Ch. Gripp of Yukon *ex* Taku of Kotzebue).

Granddam on Sire's Side: Pandora of Kotzebue (Ch. Gripp of Yukon *ex* Wray of Antarctica).

Grandsire on Dam's Side: Yukon Blizzard (Yukon Jad *ex* Bessie).

Granddam on Dam's Side: Antarctica Cleo (Antarctica Taku Milt *ex* Taku of Antarctica).

Pedigree of CH. MULPUS BROOK'S MASTER OTTER, bred by Paul Voelker & Ralph Schmitt.
Sex; male; whelped: 2-27-46; color: Alaskan seal & white.

Sire: Mikiuk.
Dam: Noma.

Grandsire on Sire's Side: Tobuk (Oomik *ex* Nanook).

Granddam on Sire's Side: Kapuk (Peluk *ex* Oolik).

Grandsire on Dam's Side: Silver King (Baree, Son of Kazan *ex* Tosha).

Granddam on Dam's Side: Silver Girl (Tarko *ex* Hoonah).

Ch. Tigara's Arctic Explorer, owned by Dorothy Dillingham of California and photographed by Joan Ludwig.

American and Canadian Ch. Bernard is ready for the race! Owned by Philip and Judith Lake, Aurora Kennels, Holbrook, Massachusetts.

Sittiak Passion of Aurora at 2½ months of age. Passion was bred by Gloria Royal of the Sittiak Kennels and is owned by Philip and Judith Lake, Aurora Kennels, Holbrook, Massachusetts.

The young Duchess von Mark, owned by Ed and Marie Markiewicz of Plantsville, Connecticut.

Aleut's Kanuck of Inuit with owner Barbara Litwin in Anchorage, Alaska.

Ch. Arctic Storm of Husky-Pak (formerly Wilton's Black Takoma), photographed at three years of age. This beautiful bitch was 25 inches at the shoulder and weighed 80 pounds. Sire was Wilton's Alaska, the 1950 Best of Breed winner at Westminster. She herself was Best Opposite Sex at Westminster in 1951 and Best of Breed at many shows while being campaigned in the east.

Pedigree of CH. SPAWN'S ALASKA, bred by Robert McCorkle.
Sex: male; whelped: 9-7-46.

Sire: Koyak.
Dam: Kiska.

Grandsire on Sire's Side: Silver King (Baree, Son of Kazan *ex* Tosha).

Granddam on Sire's Side: Tosha (Happy *ex* Laska).

Grandsire on Dam's Side: Gemo (Igloo *ex* Lynx).

Granddam on Dam's Side: Sitka (Cree *ex* Fox).

Pedigree of CH. ARCTIC STORM OF HUSKY-PAK, bred by Hazel Wilton.
Sex: female; whelped: 6-7-48; color: black & white.

Sire: Ch. Spawn's Alaska.
Dam: Chitina.

Grandsire on Sire's Side: Koyuk (Silver King *ex* Tosha).

Granddam on Sire's Side: Kiska (Gemo *ex* Sitka).

Grandsire on Dam's Side: Schmoo's M'Loot (Mikiuk *ex* Vixen).

Granddam on Dam's Side: Tora M'Loot (Gentleman Jim *ex* Lucky).

Pedigree of CH. SHUYAK CARO OF COLD FOOT, C.D., bred by Earl & Natalie Norris.

Sex: male; whelped: 7-26-56; color: Alaskan seal & white.

Sire: Sno Pak Kaghis Tugg.

Dam: Alaskan Agnishuk of Kuvak.

Grandsire on Sire's Side: Kaghi of Kobuk (Ch. Toro of Bras Coupe *ex* Helen of Bras Coupe).

Granddam on Sire's Side: Musher Lane Kila (Igloo Paks Gripp *ex* Musher Lanes Taku of Chinook).

Grandsire on Dam's Side: Ch. Keowuk of Kobuk (Ch. Toro of Bras Coupe *ex* Helen of Bras Coupe).

Granddam on Dam's Side: Helen of Bras Coupe (Ch. Kim of Kotzebue *ex* Kotzebue Cleopatra).

Ch. Spawn's Alaska, black and white male photographed from a painting made of him at seven years of age. Owned by the W. Robert Gormleys of the Barb-Far Kennels, Barberton, Ohio.

Ch. Inuit's Sweet Lucifer pictured winning Best of Breed at a 1974 dog show; this win came under judge Robert Salomon, who also placed him Third in the Working Group at the same show. Owner, Sheila Balch.

OF
ED

ASHBEY PHOTO

Lovely headstudy of two of Joan Kolman's Alaskan Malamutes, taken at their Lynn Kennels, Middlefield, Connecticut.

Photographed in Geneva, Switzerland in 1974: left to right, Alaskaland's Wolfgang Inuit, owned by David and Leslie Lynch, a Siberian Husky bitch, and the Roman Beiers' Malamute Inuit's Honkita of Sillanouk.

Pedigree of CH. TIGARA'S ARCTIC EXPLORER, bred by D.C. Dillingham.

Sex: male; whelped: 9-1-55; color: wolf gray & white.

Sire: Ch. Toro of Bras Coupe.

Dam: Sno-Pak Kavik's Oonalik.

Grandsire on Sire's Side: Ch. Kim of Kotzebue (Navarre of Kotzebue *ex* Pandora of Kotzebue).

Granddam on Sire's Side: Kotzebue Cleopatra (Yukon Blizzard *ex* Antarctica Cleo).

Grandsire on Dam's Side: Ch. Chinook Kotzebue Gripp (Ch. Kim of Kotzebue *ex* Taku's Mascara of Chinook).

Granddam on Dam's Side: Kavik of Sno-Pak (Ch. Toro of Bras Coupe *ex* Musher Lane Kila).

Pedigree of INT. CH. COLDFOOT OONANIK, U.D.T., bred by Coldfoot Kennel Reg.

Sex: male; whelped: 5-20-64; color: wolf gray & white.

Sire: Ch. Cold Foots Lucky Strike Mine, C.D.

Dam: Cold Foots Kareok.

Grandsire on Sire's Side: Sue Rons Ringo (Ch. Midnight Shadow of Kuvak *ex* Ch. Misty of Northwind, C.D.).

Granddam on Sire's Side: Hoonah of Cold Foot (Ch. Shuyak Caro of Coldfoot, C.D. *ex* Ch. Coldfoots Chevak).

Grandsire on Dam's Side: Bruno Shean (Ch. Shuyak Caro of Coldfoot *ex* Nahanie of Laird).

Granddam on Dam's Side: Ch. Cold Foots Chevak (Ch. Shuyak of Coldfoot, C.D. *ex* Kiska Queen of Coldfoot).

Pedigree of CH. ALYESKA SU SON, bred by Dr. O.T. Needles.

Sex: male; whelped: 12-13-64; color: black and white cap with bar & eyeshadow.

Sire: Tigara's Kipnuk of Arctica.

Dam: Sena-Lak's Kiska.

Grandsire on Sire's Side: Ch. Tigara's Justin Morgan (Ch. Tigara's Arctic Explorer *ex* Brite Star's Tanana).

Granddam on Sire's Side: Tigara's Tomisha of Mar Venus (Ch. Tigara's Arctic Explorer *ex* Tigara's Winsome Witch).

Grandsire on Dam's Side: Ch. Sena-Lak's Thor II (Sena-Lak's Thor *ex* Ch. Aurora of Sena-Lak).

Granddam on Dam's Side: Red Flash Mischief (Ch. Sena-Lak's Arctic Flash *ex* Malanor's Tonto).

Balch's Lil Spook of Roy-El at eight weeks of age, owned by Sheila Balch. This photograph was taken in May, 1963.

Captions for reverse page:

Top left: Inuit's Hannah of My-T-Fine pictured winning under judge Robert Salomon; she finished for her championship the next day at the Westchester show. Hannah, or Coco as she is called, finished in 8 shows, including a Winners Bitch award at the 1974 National Specialty Show. Sired by Ch. Inuit's Sweet Lucifer *ex* Inuit's Can-De Aleut, Coco is co-owned by Sheila Balch and Wilma Boar of Ascutney, Vermont.

Top right: Kaila's Wicked Witch of Inuit pictured winning the Best of Winners Award at the Farmington Valley Kennel Club Show in 1974. Co-owned by Chris and Eileen Gabriel of Golden Bridge, New York, and handled by Mr. Gabriel.

Bottom: Yunaska's Sweet Lara is pictured winning Reserve Winners Bitch at the 1974 Alaskan Malamute Club of America Specialty Show under judge J. Roy Kibler. Lara has both majors and is always owner-handled by junior handler Mary Susan Matus. Sire was Ch. Inuits Sweet Lucifer *ex* Holly. Gilbert photo.

Bottom right: Alaskalands Arctic Cat pictured winning the Bred By Exhibitor class at the 1st Independent Alaskan Malamute Club of America National Specialty Show, held in California in 1973. Arctic Cat is a full brother to the 1974 National Specialty Best of Breed dog and littermate to the 1974 National Specialty Best of Winners winner. Owner-breeder-handler Sheila Land, Holliday, Utah. Sire was Am., Can. and Ber. Ch. Inuit's Wooly Bully *ex* Ch. Voyageur's Elke. Missy Yuhl photo.

Ch. Inuit's Sweet Lucifer, owned by Sheila Balch, Best of Breed at the 1974 Alaskan Malamute Club of America Specialty. Photo by Alton Anderson.

Pedigree of CH. GLACIERS' STORM KLOUD, C.D., bred by Lois Olmen.

Sex: male; whelped: 4-1-65; color: Alaskan seal and white.

Sire: Kadluk of North Wind.

Dam: Ch. Glacier Lady of the Arctic.

Grandsire on Sire's Side: Ch. Midnight Shadow of Kuvak (Alaskan Kakolik of Kuvak *ex* Alaskan Ooowuk of Kuvak).

Granddam on Sire's Side: Ch. Nome of North Wind (Lobo of North Wind *ex* Klondike Kate of North Wind).

Grandsire on Dam's Side: Kodiak of North Star (Midwest's Moosecat Jack *ex* Shuli Brooke of North Wind).

Granddam on Dam's Side: Princess Rose of North Star (Midwest's Moosecat Jack *ex* Princess Kina of North Star).

Pedigree of AM., CAN., & BER. CH. INUIT'S WOOLY BULLY, bred by Sheila Balch.

Sex: male; whelped: 11-15-65; color: dark wolf gray.

Sire: Ch. Spawn's Hot-Shot of Roy-El.

Dam: Ch. Balch's Ingrid of Brenmar.

Grandsire on Sire's Side: Ch. Fakir of Roy-El (Erik of Roy-El *ex* Marclars Una).

Granddam on Sire's Side: Snowmasque White Diamond (Musher Lane Erebus of Chinook *ex* Musher Lane Pandora).

Grandsire on Dam's Side: Ch. Tigaras Karluk of Roy-El (Ch. Tigaras Dortic Shagluck *ex* Ch. Tigaras Arctica Eve).

Granddam on Dam's Side: Ch. Sno Pak Nashoba (Ch. Kim of Sno Pak *ex* Musher Lane Pandora).

Pedigree of CH. T'DOMAR'S VOODOO KING, bred by Thomas Baxter.

Sex: male; whelped: 12-10-60; color: Alaskan seal & white.

Sire: Ch. Spawn's Kulak.

Dam: Ch. Husky-Pak Gazelle.

Grandsire on Sire's Side: Ch. Barb-Far Lootok (Ch. Daku of Husky-Pak *ex* Ch. Koonah of Silver Sled).

Granddam on Sire's Side: Ch. Spawn's Chee Chee (Polar *ex* Arrow of Husky-Pak).

Grandsire on Dam's Side: Ch. Husky-Pak Eagle (Ch. Apache Chief of Husky-Pak *ex* Ch. Kelerak of Kobuk).

Granddam on Dam's Side: Arctic Dawn of Husky-Pak (Ch. Apache Chief of Husky-Pak *ex* Ch. Husky-Pak Mikya of Sequin).

Am., Can. and Bermudian Ch. Inuit's Wooly Bully being set up for judging at the 1968 Westminster Kennel Club Show. Owner Sheila Balch, Valley Cottage, New York.

With Lake Geneva, Switzerland in the background, Inuit's Honkita of Sillanok and owner Roman Beier are shown. The sire was Ch. Sittiak Barron *ex* Ch. Inuits Sitkabone of Cordova.

This magnificent team of Alaskan Malamutes was featured in the Walt Disney TV movie *Lefty the Ding-A-Ling Lynx*. Driver is Dick Ross; the lead dog is Ch. Kodara El Toro. Owned by Dick and Dianne Ross of Cle Elum, Washington.

Pedigree of AM. CAN. CH. TOTE-UMS KOOTEEYAK, bred by Marlene Vangemert.

Sex: female; whelped: 9-24-61; color: Alaskan seal & white.

Sire: Am. Can. Ch. Kodara El Toro
Dam: Erowah Mountain Mist.

Grandsire on Sire's Side: Ch. Husky-Pak Erok (Ch. Apache Chief of Husky-Pak *ex* Ch. Kelerak of Kobuk).

Granddam on Sire's Side: Kobuks Dark Beauty (Ch. Mulpus Brooks the Bear *ex* Ch. Baloo).

Grandsire on Dam's Side: Ch. Amarok (Ch. Husky-Pak Forecast by Cliquot, C.D. *ex* Barb Far Marclars Marook).

Granddam on Dam's Side: Feather Dance of Erowah (Ch. Husky-Pak Erok *ex* Barb Far Marclars Mikwah).

Pedigree of CH. BALCH'S INGRID OF BRENMAR, bred by Sheila Balch.

Sex: female; whelped: 11-9-63; color: light gray—open face.

Sire: Ch. Tigaras Karluk of Roy-El.
Dam: Ch. Sno Pak Nashoba.

Grandsire on Sire's Side: Ch. Tigaras Dortic Shagluck (Ch. Tongass of Tigara *ex* Sno Pak Kaviks Oonalik).

Granddam on Sire's Side: Ch. Tigaras Arctica Eve (Ch. Toro of Bras Coupe *ex* Ch. Alaskan Kuvak's Nasota).

Grandsire on Dam's Side: Ch. Kim of Sno Pak (Ch. Toro of Bras Coupe *ex* Musher Lane Kila).

Granddam on Dam's Side: Musher Lane Pandora (Igloo Pak's Gripp *ex* Musher Lane Ring òf Chinook).

Captions for reverse page:

Top left: Indian Warlord of Seacourt, bred and owned by Mrs. J. Parkyns of Buckingham, England. This magnificent dog was sired by Tote-Um's Arctic Hawk **ex** Highnoons Bella Loola.

Top right: Magnificent headstudy of Ch. Erowah Cinnaman, C.D., owned by the Tote-Um Kennels of Dick and Dianne Ross, Cle Elum, Washington.

Bottom left: Future Ch. Icefloe's Yukon Jake, photographed in the snow at three months of age. Owned by Jeri Lea Hooks, licensed handler of the Icefloe Kennels, Los Lunas, New Mexico.

Bottom right: Inuit's Sweet Lucille, co-owned by Sheila Balch and Elinore Hannah. Sired by Ch. Inuit's Sweet Lucifer *ex* Inuit's Can-De Aleut.

Ch. Tigara's Torch of Arctica is shown being handled by breeder-owner Mrs. Dorothy Dillingham. Sire was Ch. Tigara's Arctic Explorer *ex* Tigara's Winsome Witch. Joan Ludwig photograph.

Ch. Kimbra's King Notak, bred by Dorothy Dillingham and owned by Mary Wiebe of Anaheim, California, was the first Alaskan Malamute to be portrayed on the cover of a modern book devoted exclusively to the Alaskan Malamute breed.

Pedigree of CH. COLDFOOT MINTO, U.D.T., bred by Coldfoot Kennel, Reg.

Sex: male; whelped: 5-7-63; color: wolf gray & white.

Sire: Stikeen of Tyee.

Dam: Ch. Coldfoot Chevak.

Grandsire on Sire's Side: Alaskan Knik of Koyukuk (Ch. Toro of Bras Coupe *ex* Helen of Bras Coupe).

Granddam on Sire's Side: Atausik of Tyee (Sno Pak Kaghis Tugg *ex* Kiana of Kuvak).

Grandsire on Dam's Side: Ch. Shuyak Caro of Coldfoot, C.D. (Sno Pak Kaghis Tugg *ex* Alaskan Agnishuk of Kuvak).

Granddam on Dam's Side: Kiska Queen of Coldfoot (Ch. Keowuk of Kobuk *ex* Alaskan Muhko-Kih of Kuvak).

Pedigree of TAARALASTE NAKI NEIU, bred by Roger & Malle Burggraf.

Sex: female; whelped: 12-6-66; color: wolf gray & white.

Sire: Ch. Tote-Um's Littlest Hobo.

Dam: Night Frost's Kikan Queen.

Grandsire on Sire's Side: Ch. Kodara El Toro (Ch. Husky-Pak Erok *ex* Kobuks Dark Beauty).

Granddam on Sire's Side: Ch. Tote-Um's Alaskan Parka (Ch. Erowah Cinnaman *ex* Siska of Erowah).

Grandsire on Dam's Side: Ch. Night Frost's De Mr. Christian (Au Sable of Night Frost *ex* Thunder Talla of Erowah).

Granddam on Dam's Side: Ch. Night Frost's Crown Jewel (Au Salbe of Night Frost *ex* Thunder Talla of Erowah).

Captions for reverse page:

Top left: Sy Goldberg handles "Piggy" to Best of Winners under judge Marie Moore on the way to championship, at the 1973 Carroll County Kennel Club Show. The 16-month-old Malamute is co-owned by Sy and Ann Goldberg, Cinnaminson Kennels, Cream Ridge, New Jersey.

Top right: Inuit's Chinchilla of McLean, photographed in January, 1969. Bred by Sheila Balch, Chinchilla is owned by Thelma and Bob McLean. The sire was Ch. Kotzebue Bering of Chinook *ex* Ch. Balch's Ingrid of Brenmar.

Bottom left: Ch. Oak's Otonabee of Wilinda pictured winning the Breed at a Canadian show under judge Harry Thomas. Owned by Mrs. A. Murphy of Ontario, Canada. Handler for Mrs. Murphy is B. Taylor.

Bottom right: Ch. Inuit's Sitka Bone of Cordova pictured taking Best of Breed from the classes over champions at the 1972 Queensboro Kennel Club Show under judge Arnold Woolf. This lovely bitch is owned by Carol Perham, Lakeside, Connecticut.

16. BUYING YOUR MALAMUTE PUPPY

There are several paths that will lead you to a litter of puppies where you can find the puppy of your choice. Write to the parent club and ask for the names and addresses of members who have puppies for sale. The addresses of breed clubs can be obtained by writing the American Kennel Club, 51 Madison Avenue, New York, N.Y. 10010. They keep an accurate, up-to-date list of reputable breeders from whom you can seek information on obtaining a good healthy puppy. You might also check listings in the classified ads of major newspapers. The various dog magazines also carry listings and usually a column each month which features information and news on the breed.

It is to your advantage to attend a few dog shows in the area where purebred dogs of just about every breed are being exhibited in the show ring. Even if you do not wish to buy a show dog, you should be familiar with what the better specimens look like so that you may at least get a decent looking representative of the breed for your money. You will learn a lot by observing the dogs in action in the show ring, or in a public place where their personalities come to the fore. The dog show catalogue will list the dogs and their owners with local kennel names and breeders whom you can visit to see the types and colors they are breeding and winning with at the shows. Exhibitors at these shows are usually delighted to talk to people about their dogs and the specific characteristics of their particular breed.

Once you have chosen your breed above all others because you admire its exceptional beauty, intelligence and personality, and because you feel the breed will fit in with your family's way of life, it is wise to do a little research on it. The American Kennel Club library, your local library, bookshops, and the breed clubs can usually supply you with a list of reading matter or written material on the breed, past and present. Then, once you have drenched yourself in the breed's illustrious history and have definitely decided that this is the breed for you, it is time to start writing letters and making phone calls to set up appointments to see litters of puppies.

A word of caution here: don't let your choice of a kennel be determined by its nearness to your home, and then buy the first cute puppy

Jamie Lynn's Duncan, pictured in a woodland setting near the Lynn Kennels in Middlefield, Connecticut. Owner is Joan Kolman.

The prey has been sighted, and Jamie Lynn's Duncan is off on the chase.

Ch. Pak N Pull's Kaltag with Dick Ross preparing to pull some wood blocks near Tote-Um Kennels in Cle Elum, Washington.

Ch. Sena-Lak's Eric the Red owned by Eleanore DuBuis, Valois, New York.

Sno-Pak Cougar of Aurora and Philip Lake pause for a rest while climbing Kadillac Mountain in Acadia National Park in 1972.

Inuit's Oopik Chinook photographed in June, 1968 at the age of three months.

Seven-week-old puppy bitch of Kotzebue breeding. MacLean's Teeka of Nunamiut, owned by Diana Wittich.

that races up to you or licks the end of your nose. All puppies are cute, and naturally you will have a preference among those you see. But don't let preferences sway you into buying the wrong puppy.

If you are buying your dog as a family pet, a preference might not be a serious offense. But if you have had, say, an age preference since you first considered this breed, you would be wise to stick to it. If you are buying a show dog, all physical features must meet with the Standard for the breed. In considering your purchase you must think clearly, choose carefully, and make the very best possible choice. You will, of course, learn to love whichever puppy you finally decide upon, but a case of "love at first sight" can be disappointing and expensive later on if a show career was your primary objective.

To get the broadest possible concept of what is for sale and the current market prices, it is recommended that you visit as many kennels and private breeders as you can. With today's reasonably safe, inexpensive and rapid non-stop flights on the major airlines, it is possible to secure dogs from far-off places at nominal additional charges, allowing you to buy the valuable bloodlines of your choice if you have a thought toward a breeding program in the future.

While it is always safest to actually *see* the dog you are buying, there are enough reputable breeders and kennels to be found for you to buy a dog with a minimum of risk once you have made up your mind what you want, and when you have decided whether you will buy in your own country or import to satisfy your concept of the breed Standard. If you are going to breed dogs, breeding Standard type can be a moral obligation, and your concern should be with buying the best bloodlines and individual animals obtainable, in spite of cost or distance.

It is customary for the purchaser to pay the shipping charges, and the airlines are most willing to supply flight information and prices upon request. Rental on the shipping crate, if the owner does not provide one for the dog, is nominal. While unfortunate incidents have occurred on the airlines in the transporting of animals by air, the major airlines are making improvements in safety measures and have reached the point of reasonable safety and cost. Barring unforeseen circumstances, the safe arrival of a dog you might buy can pretty much be assured if both seller and purchaser adhere to and follow up on even the most minute details from both ends.

Mrs. W. Lane and her Ch. Mulpus Brooks Master Otter, Best of Breed winner at the 1950 Alaskan Malamute Specialty Show, held August 19 in conjunction with the North Shore Kennel Club Show. Otter went on to Third in the Working Group that same day.

A 5-month-old puppy owned by Sy and Ann Goldberg of Cream Ridge, New Jersey.

Tote-Um's Dark Shadows poses near a river bank near kennels of Dick and Dianne Ross in Cle Elum, Washington.

Patti Colcord of New York with Ch. Chistochina's Oona Poona and her 3-week-old puppy.

Marliese Beier in Geneva, Switzerland with a Husky bitch and her pure-bred Alaskan Malamute imported from Sheila Balch's Inuit Kennels in New York.

Ch. Tigara's Dortic Shag-Luck, bred and owned by Dorothy Dilling-
ham, is pictured winning at a show a few years ago under judge Lorna
Demidoff. The sire was Ch. Tongass of Tigara *ex* Sno-Pak Kavik's
Oonalik. Joan Ludwig photo.

THE PUPPY YOU BUY

Let us assume you want to enjoy all the cute antics of a young puppy and decide to buy a six-to-eight-week-old puppy. This is about the age when a puppy is weaned, wormed and ready to go out into the world with a responsible new owner. It is better not to buy a puppy under six weeks of age; it simply is not yet ready to leave the mother or the security of the other puppies. At eight to twelve weeks of age you will be able to notice much about the appearance and the behavior. Puppies, as they are recalled in our fondest childhood memories, are gay and active and bouncy, as well they should be! The normal puppy should be interested, alert, and curious, especially about a stranger. If a puppy acts a little reserved or distant, however, such

Ten-week-old Alaskan Malamute puppies photographed in a relaxed moment by Alton Anderson.

Above left: A darling quartet of Sena-Lak Alaskan Malamute puppies owned by Eleanore, Gigi and A.J. DuBuis of Valois, New York. *Above, right:* Ch. Kotzebue Panuck of Chinook, owned and bred by Eva B. Seeley, Chinook Kennels, Wonalancet, New Hampshire.

American, Canadian and Bermudian Ch. Inuit's Wooly Bully, owned and bred by Sheila Balch of Valley Cottage, New York; an excellent example of the ideal Alaskan Malamute head and expression. Photo by A.M.C.A. member Warren Rice.

One-month-old Alaskan Malamute puppies owned by Mrs. Lorna Jackson of Ontario, Canada. Photo by Evelyn Shafer.

act need not be misconstrued as shyness or fear. It merely indicates he hasn't made up his mind whether he likes you as yet! By the same token, he should not be fearful or terrified by a stranger—and especially should not show any fear of his owner!

In direct contrast, the puppy should not be ridiculously over-active either. The puppy that frantically bounds around the room and is never still is not especially desirable. And beware of the "spinners"! Spinners are the puppies or dogs that have become neurotic from being kept in cramped quarters or in crates and behave in an emotionally unstable manner when let loose in adequate space. When let out they run in circles and seemingly "go wild." Puppies with this kind of traumatic background seldom ever regain full composure or adjust to the big outside world. The puppy which has had the proper exercise and appropriate living quarters will have a normal, though spirited, outlook on life and will do his utmost to win you over without having to go into a tailspin.

Eight-week-old puppies owned by A.M.C.A. members. At right is the male The Devil's Disciple of Inuit, owned by Don and Kathy Thayer of Winterport, Maine; the bitch is Inuit's Miss Muffet, owned by Jim and Marie Miller of Michigan. Sire was Ch. Inuit's Sweet Lucifer *ex* Inuit's Zanna of Aleut.

If the general behavior and appearance of the dog thus far appeal to you, it is time for you to observe him more closely for additional physical requirements. First of all, you cannot expect to find in the puppy all the coat he will bear upon maturity. That will come with time and good food, and will be additionally enhanced by the many wonderful grooming aids which can be found on the market today. Needless to say, the healthy puppy's coat should have a nice shine to it, and the more dense at this age, the better the coat will be when the dog reaches adulthood.

Look for clear, dark, sparkling eyes, free of discharge. Dark eye rims and lids are indications of good pigmentation, which is important in a breeding program, and even for generally pleasing good looks.

When the time comes to select your puppy, take an experienced breeder along with you if this is possible. If it is not possible, take the Standard for the breed with you. Try to interpret the Standard as best you can by making comparisons between the puppies you see.

Check the bite completely and carefully. While the first set of teeth can be misleading, even the placement of teeth at this young age can be a fairly accurate indication of what the bite will be in the grown dog. The gums should be a good healthy pink in color, and the teeth should be clear, clean and white. Any brown cast to them could mean a past case of distemper and would assuredly count against the dog in the show ring and against the dog's general appearance at maturity.

Puppies take anything and everything into their mouths to chew on while they are teething, and a lot of infectious diseases are transmitted this way. The aforementioned distemper is one, and the brown teeth as a result of this disease never clear. The puppy's breath should not be sour or even unpleasant or strong. Any acrid odor could indicate a poor mixture of food, or low quality of meat, especially if it is being fed raw. Many breeders have compared the breath of a healthy puppy to that of fresh toast, or as being vaguely like garlic. At any rate, a puppy should never be fed just table scraps, but should have a well-balanced diet containing a good dry puppy chow and a good grade of fresh meat. Poor meat and too much cereal or fillers tend to make the puppy too fat. We like puppies to be in good flesh, but not fat from the wrong kind of food.

It goes without saying that we want to find clean puppies. The breeder or owners who shows you a dirty puppy is one from whom to

Inuit's Murook photographed at ten months of age. Owned by William Iffert.

steer away! Look closely at the skin. Rub the fur the wrong way or against the grain; make sure it is not spotted with insect bites or red, blotchy sores or dry scales. The vent area around the tail should not show evidences of diarrhea or inflammation. By the same token, the puppy's fur should not be matted with dry excrement or smell of urine.

True enough, you can wipe dirty eyes, clean dirty ears and give the puppy a bath when you get it home, but these things are all indications of how the puppy has been cared for during the important formative first months of its life, and can vitally influence its future health and development. There are many reputable breeders raising healthy puppies that have been reared in proper places and under the proper conditions in clean housing, so why take a chance on a series of veterinary bills and a questionable constitution?

MALE OR FEMALE?

The choice of sex in your puppy is also something that must be given serious thought before you buy. For the pet owner, the sex that would best suit the family life you enjoy would be the paramount

Scout, a Skagway puppy owned by Nancy Windover of Ontario, Canada. Scout's sire was Inuit's Warrior of Skagway.

Inuit's Honkita of Sillanouk with Marliese Beier and her son, photographed at their home in Geneva, Switzerland.

choice to consider. For the breeder or exhibitor, there are other vital considerations. If you are looking for a stud to establish a kennel, it is essential that you select a dog with both testicles evident, even at a tender age, and verified by a veterinarian before the sale is finalized if there is any doubt.

The visibility of only one testicle, known as monorchidism, automatically disqualifies the dog from the show ring or from a breeding program, though monorchids are capable of siring. Additionally, it must be noted that monorchids frequently sire dogs with the same deficiency, and to introduce this into a bloodline knowingly is an unwritten sin in the fancy. Also, a monorchid can sire dogs that are completely sterile. Such dogs are referred to as cryptorchids and have no testicles.

If you want the dog to be a member of the family, the best selection would probably be a female. You can always go out for stud service if you should decide to breed. You can choose the bloodlines doing the most winning because they should be bred true to type, and you will not have to foot the bill for the financing of a show career. You can always keep a male from your first litter that will bear your own "kennel name" if you have decided to proceed in the kennel "business."

The Alaskan Malamute makes an excellent house dog and family pet. Malamutes' remarkable personal cleanliness and "no doggy odor" are just part of their charm. Mrs. Robert Zoller of the Husky-Pak Kennels is pictured here with her bitch Mikya of Sequin in the living room of their home.

An additional consideration in the male versus female decision for the private owners is that with males there might be the problem of leg-lifting and with females there is the inconvenience while they are in season. However, this need not be the problem it used to be— pet shops sell "pants" for both sexes, which help to control the situation.

THE PLANNED PARENTHOOD BEHIND YOUR PUPPY

Never be afraid to ask pertinent questions about the puppy, as well as questions about the sire and dam. Feel free to ask the breeder if you might see the dam, the purpose of your visit to determine her general health and her appearance as a representative of the breed. Ask also to see the sire if the breeder is the owner. Ask what the puppy has been fed and should be fed after weaning. Ask to see the pedigree, and inquire if the litter or the individual puppies have been registered with the American Kennel Club, how many of the temporary and/or permanent inoculations the puppy has had, when and if the puppy has been wormed and whether it has had any illness, disease or infection.

You need not ask if the puppy is housebroken. . . it won't mean much. He may have gotten the idea as to where "the place" is where he lives now, but he will need new training to learn where "the place" is in his new home! And you can't really expect too much from puppies at this age anyway. Housebreaking is entirely up to the new owner. We know puppies always eliminate when they first awaken and sometimes dribble when they get excited. If friends and relatives are coming over to see the new puppy, make sure he is walked just before he greets them at the front door. This will help.

The normal time period for puppies around three months of age to eliminate is about every two or three hours. As the time draws near, either take the puppy out or indicate the newspapers for the same purpose. Housebreaking is never easy, but anticipation is about 90 per cent of solving the problem. The schools that offer to house-break your dog are virtually useless. Here again the puppy will learn the "place" at the schoolhouse, but coming home he will need special training for the new location.

A reputable breeder will welcome any and all questions you might ask and will voluntarily offer additional information, if only to

Well-known Alaskan Malamute Club of America junior handler Mitchell Gatz and his eight-month-old puppy friend "Lewis."

Indian Wigwam of Seacourt. "Cherokee" was bred by Mrs. J. Parkyns and is owned by Stella Gouding. Sire was Tote-Um's Arctic Hawk *ex* Highnoons Bella Koda. Photographed in England in January, 1971.

brag about the tedious and loving care he has given the litter. He will also sell a puppy on a 24-hour veterinary approval. This means you have a full day to get the puppy to a veterinarian of your choice to get his opinion on the general health of the puppy before you make a final decision. There should also be veterinary certificates and full particulars on the dates and types of inoculations the puppy has been given up to that time.

PUPPIES AND WORMS

Let us give further attention to the unhappy and very unpleasant subject of worms. Generally speaking, most all puppies—even those raised in clean quarters—come into contact with worms early in life. The worms can be passed down from the mother before birth or picked up during the puppies' first encounters with the earth or their kennel facilities. To say that you must not buy a puppy because of an infestation of worms is nonsensical. You might be passing up a fine animal that can be freed of worms in one short treatment, although a heavy infestation of worms of any kind in a young dog is dangerous and debilitating.

The extent of the infection can be readily determined by a veterinarian, and you might take his word as to whether the future health and conformation of the dog has been damaged. He can prescribe the dosage and supply the medication at the time and you will already have one of your problems solved. The kinds and varieties of worms and how to detect them is described in detail elsewhere in this book and we advise you to check the matter out further if there is any doubt in your mind as to the problems of worms in dogs.

VETERINARY INSPECTION

While your veterinarian is going over the puppy you have selected to purchase, you might just as well ask him for his opinion of it as a breed as well as the facts about its general health. While few veterinarins can claim to be breed conformation experts, they usually have a good eye for a worthy specimen and can advise you where to go for further information. Perhaps your veterinarian could also recommend other breeders if you should want another opinion. The veterinarian can point out structural faults or organic problems that affect all breeds and can usually judge whether an animal has been abused or mishandled and whether it is oversized or undersized.

I would like to emphasize here that it is only through this type of close cooperation between owners and veterinarians that we can expect to reap the harvest of modern research in the veterinary field.

Five-week-old Barb-Far Patrick photographed several years ago with six-year-old Susan Gormley. Parents of this darling little girl are the W. Robert Gormleys of the Barb-Far Kennels in Barberton, Ohio.

Tyuni's Misty Morn, owned by Virginia Russik, at four months of age. The sire was Ch. Inuit's Wooly Bully *ex* Brandy's Nugget of Polar Den. Photograph taken in December, 1974.

Most reliable veterinarians are more than eager to learn about various breeds of purebred dogs, and we in turn must acknowledge and apply what they have proved through experience and research in their field. We can buy and breed the best dog in the world, but when disease strikes we are only as safe as our veterinarian is capable—so let's keep them informed breed by breed, and dog by dog. The veterinarian represents the difference between life and death!

THE CONDITIONS OF SALE

While it is customary to pay for the puppy before you take it away with you, you should be able to give the breeder a deposit if there is any doubt about the puppy's health. You might also (depending on local laws) postdate a check to cover the 24-hour veterinary approval. If you decide to take the puppy, the breeder is required to supply you with a pedigree, along with the puppy's registration paper. He is also obliged to supply you with complete information about the inoculations and American Kennel Club instructions on how to transfer ownership of the puppy into your name.

A sailor on leave in Bermuda stops by the Botanical Gardens long enough to visit with this Alaskan Malamute at a Kennel Club of Bermuda show. Photo courtesy of the Bermuda News Bureau.

Ch. Sena-Lak's Tenana on the bench at a show with an admirer. Tenana is owned by Eleanore DuBuis of Valois, New York.

Some breeders will offer buyers time payment plans for convenience if the price on a show dog is very high or if deferred payments are the only way you can purchase the dog. However, any such terms must be worked out between buyer and breeder and should be put in writing to avoid later complications.

You will find most breeders cooperative if they believe you are sincere in your love for the puppy and that you will give it the proper home and the show ring career it deserves (if it is sold as a show quality specimen of the breed). Remember, when buying a show dog, it is impossible to guarantee nature. A breeder can only tell you what he *believes* will develop into a show dog. . . so be sure your breeder is an honest one.

Also, if you purchase a show prospect and promise to show the dog, you definitely should show it! It is a waste to have a beautiful dog that deserves recognition in the show ring sitting at home as a family pet, and it is unfair to the breeder. This is especially true if the breeder offered you a reduced price because of the advertising his kennel and bloodlines would receive by your showing the dog in the ring. If you want a pet, buy a pet. Be honest about it, and let the breeder decide on this basis which is the best dog for you. Your conscience will be clear and you'll both be doing a real service to the breed.

BUYING A SHOW PUPPY

If you are positive about breeding and showing your dog, make it clear that you intend to do so so that the breeder will sell you the best possible puppy. If you are dealing with an established kennel, you will have to rely partially if not entirely on their choice, since they know their bloodlines and what they can expect from the breeding. They know how their stock develops, and it would be foolish of them to sell you a puppy that could not stand up as a show specimen representing their stock in the ring.

However, you must also realize that the breeder may be keeping the best puppy in the litter to show and breed himself. If this is the case, you might be wise to select the best puppy of the opposite sex so that the dogs will not be competing against one another in the show rings for their championship title.

THE PURCHASE PRICE

Prices vary on all puppies, of course, but a good show prospect at six weeks to six months of age will sell for several hundred dollars. If the puppy is really outstanding, and the pedigree and parentage is

Ch. Kotzebue's Kunek of Seegoo with owner Judith Lake of Aurora Kennels.

Mrs. Lou Ihrig displays her three-week-old Malamute puppies, sired by American, Canadian and Bermudian Ch. Inuit's Wooly Bully *ex* Inuit's Trouble and Strife.

also outstanding, the price will be even higher. Honest breeders, however, will be around the same figure, so price should not be a deciding factor in your choice. If there is any question as to the current price range, a few telephone calls to different kennels will give you a good average. Breeders will usually stand behind their puppies; should something drastically wrong develop, such as hip dysplasia, etc., their obligation to make an adjustment is usually honored. Therefore, your cost is covered.

THE COST OF BUYING ADULT STOCK

Prices for adult dogs fluctuate greatly. Some grown dogs are offered free of charge to good homes; others are put out with owners on breeders' terms. But don't count on getting a "bargain" if it doesn't cost you anything! Good dogs are always in demand, and worthy studs or brood bitches are expensive. Prices for them can easily go up into the four-figure range. Take an expert with you if you intend to make this sort of investment. Just make sure the "expert" is free of professional jealousy and will offer an unprejudiced opinion. If you are reasonably familiar with the Standard, and get the expert's opinion, between the two you can usually come up with a proper decision.

Buying grown stock does remove some of the risk if you are planning a kennel. You will know exactly what you are getting for your foundation stock and will also save time on getting your kennel started.

17. GENETICS

No one can guarantee the workings of nature. But, with facts and theories as guides, you can plan, at least on paper, a litter of puppies that should fulfill your fondest expectations. Since the ultimate purpose of breeding is to try to improve the breed, or maintain it at the highest possible standard, such planning should be earnestly done, no matter how uncertain particular elements may be.

There are a few terms with which you should become familiar to help you understand the breeding procedure and the workings of genetics. The first thing that comes to mind is a set of formulae known as Mendelian Laws. Gregor Mendel was an Austrian cleric and botanist born July 22, 1822 in what is now named Hyncice and is in Czechoslovakia. He developed his theories on heredity by working for several years with garden peas. A paper on his work was published in a scientific journal in 1866, but for many years it went unnoticed. Today the laws derived from these experiments are basic to all studies of genetics and are employed by horticulturists and animal breeders.

To use these laws as applicable to the breeding of dogs, it is necessary to understand the physical aspects of reproduction. First, dogs possess reproductive glands called gonads. The male gonads are the testicles and there are produced the sperms (spermatozoa) that impregnate the female. Eggs (ova) are produced in the female gonads (ovaries). When whelped, the bitch possesses in rudimentary form all the eggs that will develop throughout her life, whereas spermatozoa are in continual production within the male gonads. When a bitch is mature enough to reproduce, she periodically comes in heat (estrus). Then a number of eggs descend from the ovaries via the fallopian tubes and enter the two horns of the uterus. There they are fertilized by male sperm deposited in semen while mating, or they pass out if not fertilized.

In the mating of dogs, there is what is referred to as a tie, a period during which anatomical features bind the male and female together and about 600 million spermatozoa are ejected into the female to fertilize the ripened eggs. When sperm and ripe eggs meet, zygotes are created and these one-celled future puppies descend from the fallopian tubes, attach themselves to the walls of the uterus, and begin the developmental process of cell production known as mitosis. With all inherited characteristics determined as the zygote was formed, the dam then assumes her role as an incubator for the developing organisms. She has been bred and is in whelp; in these circumstances she also serves in the exchange of gases and in furnishing nourishment for the puppies forming within.

Let us take a closer look at what is happening during the breeding process. We know that the male deposits millions of sperms within the female and that the number of ripe eggs released by the female will determine the number of puppies in the litter. Therefore, those breeders who advertise a stud as a "producer of large litters" do not know the facts or are not sticking to them. The bitch determines the size of the litter; the male sperm determines the sex of the puppies. Half of the millions of sperm involved in a mating carry the characteristic that determines development of a male and the other half carry the factor which triggers development of a female, and distribution of sex is thus decided according to random pairings of sperms and eggs.

Each dog and bitch possesses 39 pairs of chromosomes in each body cell; these pairs are split up in the formation of germ cells so that each one carries half of the hereditary complement. The chromosomes carry the genes, approximately 150,000 like peas in a pod in each chromosome, and these are the actual factors that determine inherited characteristics. As the chromosomes are split apart and rearranged as to genic pairings in the production of ova and spermatozoa, every zygote formed by the joining of an egg and a sperm receives 39 chromosomes from each to form the pattern of 78 chromosomes inherited from dam and sire which will be reproduced in every cell of the developing individual and determine what sort of animal it will be.

To understand the procedure more clearly, we must know that there are two kinds of genes—dominant and recessive. A dominant gene is one of a pair whose influence is expressed to the exclusion of the effects of the other. A recessive gene is one of a pair whose influence is subdued by the effects of the other, and characteristics determined by recessive genes become manifest only when both genes of a pairing are recessive. Most of the important qualities we wish to perpetuate in our breeding programs are carried by the dominant genes. It is the successful breeder who becomes expert at eliminating undesirable genes and building up the desirable gene patterns.

We have merely touched upon genetics here to point out the importance of planned mating. Any librarian can help you find further information, or books may be purchased offering the very latest findings on canine genetics. It is a fascinating and rewarding program toward creating better dogs.

18. BREEDING YOUR ALASKAN MALAMUTE

Let us assume the time has come for your dog to be bred, and you have decided you are in a position to enjoy producing a litter of puppies that you hope will make a contribution to the breed. The bitch you purchased is sound, her temperament is excellent and she is a most worthy representative of the breed.

You have taken a calendar and counted off the ten days since the first day of red staining and have determined the tenth to fourteenth day, which will more than likely be the best days for the actual mating. You have additionally counted off 65 to 63 days before the puppies are likely to be born to make sure everything necessary for their arrival will be in good order by that time.

From the moment the idea of having a litter occurred to you, your thoughts should have been given to the correct selection of a proper stud. Here again the novice would do well to seek advice on analyzing pedigrees and tracing bloodlines for your best breedings. As soon as the bitch is in season and you see color (or staining) and a swelling of the vulva, it is time to notify the owner of the stud you selected and make appointments for the breedings. There are several pertinent questions you will want to ask the stud owners after having decided upon the pedigree. The owners, naturally, will also have a few questions they wish to ask you. These questions will concern your bitch's bloodlines, health, age, how many previous litters if any, etc.

THE HEALTH OF THE BREEDING STOCK

Some of your first questions should concern whether or not the stud has already proved himself by siring a normal healthy litter. Also inquire as to whether or not the owners have had a sperm count made to determine just exactly how fertile or potent the stud is. Also ask whether he has been X-rayed for hip dysplasia and found to be clear. Determine for yourself whether the dog has two normal testicles.

When considering your bitch for this mating, you must take into consideration a few important points that lead to a successful breeding. You and the owner of the stud will want to recall whether she has had normal heat cycles, whether there were too many runts in the lit-

Alaska of Komatik at three months of age.

Ch. Balch's Ingrid of Brenmar and her four-week-old son.

ter, and whether Caesarean section was ever necessary. Has she ever had a vaginal infection? Could she take care of her puppies by herself, or was there a milk shortage? How many surviving puppies were there from the litter, and what did they grow up to be in comparison to the requirements of the breed Standard?

Don't buy a bitch that has problem heats and has never had a litter. But don't be afraid to buy a healthy maiden bitch, since chances are, if she is healthy and from good stock, she will be a healthy producer. Don't buy a monorchid male, and certainly not a cryptorchid. If there is any doubt in your mind about his potency, get a sperm count from the veterinarian. Older dogs that have been good producers and are for sale are usually not too hard to find at good established kennels. If they are not too old and have sired quality show puppies, they can give you some excellent show stock from which to establish your own breeding lines.

THE DAY OF THE MATING

Now that you have decided upon the proper male and female combination to produce what you hope will be—according to the pedigrees—a fine litter of puppies, it is time to set the date. You have selected the two days (with a one day lapse in between) that you feel

242

are best for the breeding, and you call the owner of the stud. The bitch always goes to the stud, unless, of course, there are extenuating circumstances. You set the date and the time and arrive with the bitch *and* the money.

Standard procedure is payment of a stud fee at the time of the first breeding, if there is a tie. For the stud fee, you are entitled to two breedings with ties. Contracts may be written up with specific conditions on breeding terms, of course, but this is general procedure. Often a breeder will take the pick of a litter to protect and maintain his bloodlines. This can be especially desirable if he needs an outcross for his breeding program or if he wishes to continue his own bloodlines if he sold you the bitch to start with, and this mating will continue his line-breeding program. This should all be worked out ahead of time and written and signed before the two dogs are bred. Remember that the payment of the stud fee is for the services of the stud—not for a guarantee of a litter of puppies. This is why it is so important to

Two six-week-old puppies bred by the Aurora Kennels in Holbrook, Massachusetts.

Ch. Inuit's Mehitabel, litter sister to Ch. Inuit's Wooly Bully, owned by Sheila Balch and Georgia Brand. The dam of many champions, Mehitabel was Winners Bitch at Westminster in 1969. Photo by William Gilbert.

Four-week-old puppies sired by Frostfield Kotzebue Kayak and Frostfield Kotzebue Klyde. Owners are Jerry and Wendy Wisefield, Frostfield Kennels, Avon, Massachusetts.

make sure you are using a proven stud. Bear in mind also that the American Kennel Club will not register a litter of puppies sired by a male that is under eight months of age. In the case of an older dog, they will not register a litter sired by a dog over 12 years of age, unless there is a witness to the breeding in the form of a veterinarian or other responsible person.

Many studs over 12 years of age are still fertile and capable of producing puppies, but if you do not witness the breeding there is always the danger of a "substitute" stud being used to produce a litter. This brings up the subject of sending your bitch away to be bred if you cannot accompany her.

The disadvantages of sending a bitch away to be bred are numerous. First of all, she will not be herself in a strange place, so she'll be difficult to handle. Transportation if she goes by air, while reasonably safe, is still a traumatic experience, and there is the danger of her being put off at the wrong airport, not being fed or watered properly, etc. Some bitches get so upset that they go out of season and the trip, which may prove expensive, especially on top of a substantial stud fee, will have been for nothing.

If at all possible, accompany your bitch so that the experience is as comfortable for her as it can be. In other words, make sure before setting this kind of schedule for a breeding that there is no stud in the area that might be as good for her as the one that is far away. Don't sacrifice the proper breeding for convenience, since bloodlines are so important, but put the safety of the bitch above all else. There is always a risk in traveling, since dogs are considered cargo on a plane.

HOW MUCH DOES THE STUD FEE COST?

The stud fee will vary considerably—the better the bloodlines, the more winning the dog does at shows, the higher the fee. Stud service from a top winning dog could run up to $500.00. Here again, there may be exceptions. Some breeders will take part cash and then, say, third pick of the litter. The fee can be arranged by a private contract rather than the traditional procedure we have described.

Here again, it is wise to get the details of the payment of the stud fee in writing to avoid trouble.

THE ACTUAL MATING

It is always advisable to muzzle the bitch. A terrified bitch may fear-bite the stud, or even one of the people involved, and the wild bitch may snap or attack the stud, to the point where he may become discouraged and lose interest in the breeding. Muzzling can be done with a lady's stocking tied around the muzzle with a half knot, crossed under the chin and knotted at the back of the neck. There is enough "give" in the stocking for her to breathe or salivate freely and yet not open her jaws far enough to bite. Place her in front of her own-

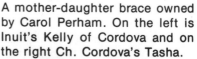

Ch. Sena-Lak's Tenana in show pose with owner Eleanore Du-Buis, Sena-Lak Kennels, Valois, New York.

A mother-daughter brace owned by Carol Perham. On the left is Inuit's Kelly of Cordova and on the right Ch. Cordova's Tasha.

er, who holds onto her collar and talks to her and calms her as much as possible.

If the male will not mount on his own initiative, it may be necessary for the owner to assist in lifting him onto the bitch, perhaps even in guiding him to the proper place. But usually, the tie is accomplished once the male gets the idea. The owner should remain close at hand, however, to make sure the tie is not broken before an adequate breeding has been completed. After a while the stud may get bored and try to break away. This could prove injurious. It may be necessary to hold him in place until the tie is broken.

A trio of Tote-Um puppies, owned and bred by Dick and Dianne Ross of Cle Elum, Washington.

We must stress at this point that while some bitches carry on physically, and vocally, during the tie, there is no way the bitch can be hurt. However, a stud can be seriously or even permanently damaged by a bad breeding. Therefore the owner of the bitch must be reminded that she must not be alarmed by any commotion. All concentration should be devoted to the stud and a successful and properly executed service.

Many people believe that breeding dogs is simply a matter of placing two dogs, a male and a female, in close proximity, and letting nature take its course. While often this is true, you cannot count on it. Sometimes it is hard work, and in the case of valuable stock it is essential to supervise to be sure of the safety factor, especially if one or both of the dogs are inexperienced. If the owners are also inexperienced it may not take place at all!

ARTIFICIAL INSEMINATION

Breeding by means of artificial insemination is usually unsuccessful, unless under a veterinarian's supervision, and can lead to an infection for the bitch and discomfort for the dog. The American Kennel Club requires a veterinarian's certificate to register puppies from such a breeding. Although the practice has been used for over two decades, it now offers new promise, since research has been conducted to make it a more feasible procedure for the future.

Great dogs may eventually look forward to reproducing themselves years after they have left this earth. There now exists a frozen semen concept that has been tested and found successful. The study, headed by Dr. Stephen W.J. Seager, M.V.B., an instructor at the University of Oregon Medical School, has the financial support of the American Kennel Club, indicating that organization's interest in the work. The study is being monitored by the Morris Animal Foundation of Denver, Colorado.

Dr. Seager announced in 1970 that he had been able to preserve dog semen and to produce litters with the stored semen. The possibilities of selective world-wide breedings by this method are exciting. Imagine simply mailing a vial of semen to the bitch! The perfection of line-breeding by storing semen without the threat of death interrupting the breeding program is exciting, also.

As it stands today, the technique for artificial insemination requires the depositing of semen (taken directly from the dog) into the bitch's vagina, past the cervix and into the uterus by syringe. The correct temperature of the semen is vital, and there is no guarantee of success. The storage method, if successfully adopted, will present a new era in the field of purebred dogs.

THE GESTATION PERIOD

Once the breeding has taken place successfully, the seemingly endless waiting period of about 63 days begins. For the first ten days after the breeding, you do absolutely nothing for the bitch—just spin dreams about the delights you will share with the family when the puppies arrive.

Around the tenth day it is time to begin supplementing the diet of the bitch with vitamins and calcium. We strongly recommend that you take her to your veterinarian for a list of the proper or perhaps necessary supplements and the correct amounts of each for your particular bitch. Guesses, which may lead to excesses or insufficiencies, can ruin a litter. For the price of a visit to your veterinarian, you will be confident that you are feeding properly.

The bitch should be free of worms, of course, and if there is any doubt in your mind, she should be wormed now, before the third week of pregnancy. Your veterinarian will advise you on the necessity of this and proper dosage as well.

Ch. Chargi's Buckeye, owned by Jerry and Shannon Sollinger, Kunoe
Alaskan Malamutes, Newburgh, New York.

PROBING FOR PUPPIES

Far too many breeders are overanxious about whether the breeding "took" and are inclined to feel for puppies or persuade a veterinarian to radiograph or X-ray their bitches to confirm it. Unless there is reason to doubt the normalcy of a pregnancy, this is risky. Certainly 63 days are not too long to wait, and why risk endangering the litter by probing with your inexperienced hands? Few bitches give no evidence of being in whelp, and there is no need to prove it for yourself by trying to count puppies.

ALERTING YOUR VETERINARIAN

At least a week before the puppies are due, you should telephone your veterinarian and notify him that you expect the litter and give him the date. This way he can make sure that there will be someone available to help, should there be any problems during the whelping. Most veterinarians today have answering services and alternate vets on call when they are not available themselves. Some veterinarians suggest that you call them when the bitch starts labor so that they may further plan their time, should they be needed. Discuss this matter with your veterinarian when you first take the bitch to him for her diet instructions, etc., and establish the method which will best fit in with his schedule.

DO YOU NEED A VETERINARIAN IN ATTENDANCE?

Even if this is your first litter, I would advise that you go through the experience of whelping without panicking and calling desperately for the veterinarian. Most animal births are accomplished without complications, and you should call for assistance only if you run into trouble.

When having her puppies, your bitch will appreciate as little interference and as few strangers around as possible. A quiet place, with her nest, a single familiar face and her own instincts are all that is necessary for nature to take its course. An audience of curious children squealing and questioning, other family pets nosing around, or strange adults should be avoided. Many a bitch which has been distracted in this way has been known to devour her young. This can be

Ch. Great Barrington Geronimo, owned by Mr. and Mrs. Robert J. Zoller of the Husky-Pak Kennels in Blue Ridge Summit, Pennsylvania. Geronimo finished at the National Capitol Show several years ago. Geronimo stood 26 inches at the shoulder and weighed 85 pounds. He was two-and-a-half years of age when this photograph was taken.

Buccaneer of Husky-Pak, son of Ch. Arctic Storm, photographed at twelve months of age. Owners: Mr. and Mrs. Robert J. Zoller of Blue Ridge Summit, Pennsylvania.

the horrible result of intrusion into the bitch's privacy. There are other ways of teaching children the miracle of birth, and there will be plenty of time later for the whole family to enjoy the puppies. Let them be born under proper and considerate circumstances.

LABOR

Some litters—many first litters—do not run the full term of 63 days. So, at least a week before the puppies are actually due, and at the time you alert your veterinarian as to their arrival, start observing the bitch for signs of the commencement of labor. This will manifest itself in the form of ripples running down the sides of her body, which will come as a revelation to her as well. It is most noticeable when she is lying on her side—and she will be sleeping a great deal as the arrival date comes closer. If she is sitting or walking about, she will perhaps sit down quickly or squat peculiarly. As the ripples become more frequent, birth time is drawing near; you will be wise not to leave her. Usually within 24 hours before whelping, she will stop eating, and as much as a week before she will begin digging a nest. The bitch should be given something resembling a whelping box with layers of newspaper (black and white only) to make her nest. She will dig more and more as birth approaches, and this is the time to begin making your promise to stop interfering unless your help is specifically required. Some bitches whimper and others are silent, but whimpering does not necessarily indicate trouble.

THE ARRIVAL OF THE PUPPIES

The sudden gush of green fluid from the bitch indicates that the water or fluid surrounding the puppies has "broken" and they are about to start down the canal and come into the world. When the

Best of Breed at the prestigious Trenton Kennel Club Show in May, 1974 was Ch. Inuit's Sweet Lucifer, handled by Philip Marsman. Judge was Robert Salomon. Owner Sheila Balch, Inuit Kennels, Valley Cottage, New York.

water breaks, birth of the first puppy is imminent. The first puppies are usually born within minutes to a half hour of each other, but a couple of hours between the later ones is not uncommon. If you notice the bitch straining constantly without producing a puppy, or if a puppy remains partially in and partially out for too long, it is cause for concern. Breech births (puppies born feet first instead of head first) can often cause delay or hold things up, and this is often a problem which requires veterinarian assistance.

FEEDING THE BITCH BETWEEN BIRTHS

Usually the bitch will not be interested in food for about 24 hours before the arrival of the puppies, and perhaps as long as two or three days after their arrival. The placenta which she cleans up after each puppy is high in food value and will be more than ample to sustain her. This is nature's way of allowing the mother to feed herself and her babies without having to leave the nest and hunt for food during the first crucial days. The mother always cleans up all traces of birth in the wilds so as not to attract other animals to her newborn babies.

However, there are those of us who believe in making food available should the mother feel the need to restore her strength during or after delivery—especially if she whelps a large litter. Raw chopmeat, beef boullion, and milk are all acceptable and may be placed near the whelping box during the first two or three days. After that, the mother will begin to put the babies on a sort of schedule. She will leave the whelping box at frequent intervals, take longer exercise periods, and begin to take interest in other things. This is where the fun begins for you. Now the babies are no longer soggy little pinkish blobs. They begin to crawl around and squeal and hum and grow before your very eyes!

It is at this time, if all has gone normally, that the family can be introduced gradually and great praise and affection given to the mother.

BREECH BIRTHS

Puppies normally are delivered head first. However, some are presented feet first, or in other abnormal positions, and this is referred to as a "breech birth." Assistance is often necessary to get the puppy out of the canal, and great care must be taken not to injure the puppy or the dam.

Aid can be given by grasping the puppy with a piece of turkish toweling and pulling gently during the dam's contractions. Be careful not to squeeze the puppy too hard; merely try to ease it out by moving it gently back and forth. Because even this much delay in delivery may mean the puppy is drowning, do not wait for the bitch to remove the sac. Do it yourself by tearing the sac open to expose the face and head. Then cut the cord anywhere from one-half to three-quarters of

Pictured winning at an Alaskan Malamute Club of America Specialty·
Show in the 1950's was Ch. Cherokee of Husky-Pak, Best of Breed,
and (on the left) Best of Opposite Sex, Husky-Pak Marclar's Sioux;
both owned by the Robert J. Zollers of Blue Ridge Summit, Pennsylvania. Mr. Zoller is shown handling Cherokee; Miss Merry Stockburger
is handling the bitch.

an inch away from the navel. If the cord bleeds excessively, pinch the
end of it with your fingers and count five. Repeat if necessary. Then
pry open the mouth with your finger and hold the puppy upside-down
for a moment to drain any fluids from the lungs. Next, rub the puppy
briskly with turkish or paper toweling. You should get it wriggling
and whimpering by this time.

If the litter is large, this assistance will help conserve the
strength of the bitch and will probably be welcomed by her. However,
it is best to allow her to take care of at least the first few herself to
preserve the natural instinct and to provide the nutritive values obtained by her consumption of the afterbirths.

DRY BIRTHS

Occasionally the sac will break before the delivery of a puppy
and will be expelled while the puppy remains inside, thereby depriv-
ing the dam of the necessary lubrication to expel the puppy normally.

Inserting vaseline or mineral oil via your finger will help the puppy pass down the birth canal. This is why it is essential that you be present during the whelping so that you can count puppies and afterbirths and determine when and if assistance is needed.

THE TWENTY-FOUR-HOUR CHECKUP

It is smart to have a veterinarian check the mother and her puppies within 24 hours after the last puppy is born. The vet can check the puppies for cleft palates or umbilical hernia and may wish to give the dam—particularly if she is a show dog—an injection of Pituitin to make sure of the expulsion of all afterbirths and to tighten up the uterus. This can prevent a sagging belly after the puppies are weaned and the bitch is being readied for the show ring.

FALSE PREGNANCY

The disappointment of a false pregnancy is almost as bad for the owner as it is for the bitch. She goes through the gestation period with all the symptoms—swollen stomach, increased appetite, swollen nipples—even makes a nest when the time comes. You may even take an oath that you noticed the ripples on her body from the labor pains. Then, just as suddenly as you made up your mind that she was definitely going to have puppies, you will know that she definitely is not! She may walk around carrying a toy as if it were a puppy for a few days, but she will soon be back to normal and acting just as if nothing happened—and nothing did!

CAESAREAN SECTION

Should the whelping reach the point where there is complication, such as the bitch's not being capable of whelping the puppies herself, the "moment of truth" is upon you and a Caesarean section may be necessary. The bitch may be too small or too immature to expel the puppies herself; or her cervix may fail to dilate enough to allow the young to come down the birth canal; or there may be torsion of the uterus, a dead or monster puppy, a sideways puppy blocking the canal, or perhaps toxemia. A Caesarean section will be the only solution. No matter what the cause, get the bitch to the veterinarian immediately to insure your chances of saving the mother and/or puppies.

The Caesarean section operation (the name derived from the idea that Julius Caesar was delivered by this method) involves the removal of the unborn young from the uterus of the dam by surgical incision into the walls through the abdomen. The operation is performed when it has been determined that for some reason the puppies cannot be delivered normally. While modern surgical methods have made the operation itself reasonably safe, with the dam being perfectly capable of nursing the puppies shortly after the completion of the surgery, the chief danger lies in the ability to spark life into the puppies immediately upon their removal .from the womb. If the mother dies, the time element is even more important in saving the young, since the oxygen supply ceases upon the death of the dam, and the difference between life and death is measured in seconds.

After surgery, when the bitch is home in her whelping box with the babies, she will probably nurse the young without distress. You must be sure that the sutures are kept clean and that no redness or swelling or ooze appears in the wound. Healing will take place naturally, and no salves or ointments should be applied unless prescribed by the veterinarian, for fear the puppies will get it into their systems. If there is any doubt, check the bitch for fever, restlessness (other than the natural concern for her young) or a lack of appetite, but do not anticipate trouble.

EPISIOTOMY

Even though large dogs are generally easy whelpers, any number of reasons might occur to cause the bitch to have a difficult birth. Before automatically resorting to Caesarean section, many veterinarians are now trying the technique known as episiotomy.

Used rather frequently in human deliveries, episiotomy (pronounced A-PEASE-E-*OTT*-O-ME) is the cutting of the membrane between the rear opening of the vagina back almost to the opening of the anus. After delivery it is stitched together, and barring complications, heals easily, presenting no problem in future births.

SOCIALIZING YOUR PUPPY

The need for puppies to get out among other animals and people cannot be stressed enough. Kennel-reared dogs are subject to all sorts of idiosyncrasies and seldom make good house dogs or normal members of the world around them when they grow up.

The crucial age, which determines the personality and general behavior patterns which will predominate during the rest of the dog's life, are formed between the ages of three and ten weeks. This is particularly true during the 21st to 28th day. It is essential that the puppy be socialized during this time by bringing him into family life as much as possible. Floor surfaces, indoor and outdoor, should be experienced; handling by all members of the family and visitors is important; preliminary grooming gets him used to a lifelong necessity; light training, such as setting him up on tables and cleaning teeth and ears and cutting nails, etc., has to be started early if he is to become a show dog. The puppy should be exposed to car riding, shopping tours, a leash around its neck, children—your own and others—and in all possible ways develop relationships with humans.

It is up to the breeder, of course, to protect the puppy from harm or injury during this initiation into the outside world. The benefits

Ch. Fakir of Roy-El is owned by Walter A. and Sylvia M. Corcelius. Bred by Elsie A. Truchon, Fakir was sired by Erik of Roy-El *ex* Marclar's Una. Mr. Corcelius is pictured handling Fakir under the late judge Albert E. Van Court. Evelyn Shafer photo.

reaped from proper attention will pay off in the long run with a well-behaved, well-adjusted grown dog capable of becoming an integral part of a happy family.

REARING THE FAMILY

Needless to say, even with a small litter there will be certain considerations which must be adhered to in order to insure successful rearing of the puppies. For instance, the diet for the mother should be appropriately increased as the puppies grow and take more and more nourishment from her. During the first few days of rest while the bitch just looks over her puppies and regains her strength, she should be left pretty much alone. It is during these first days that she begins to put the puppies on a feeding schedule and feels safe enough about them to leave the whelping box long enough to take a little extended exercise.

It is cruel, however, to try and keep the mother away from the puppies any longer than she wants to be because you feel she is being too attentive or to give the neighbors a chance to peek in at the puppies. The mother should not have to worry about harm coming to her puppies for the first few weeks. The veterinary checkup will be enough of an experience for her to have to endure until she is more like herself once again.

Judge Sheila Balch selects Ch. Storm Kloud's Ilitkusik, owned by Robert Lundstrom of Minnesota, as Best in Sweepstakes at the November, 1974 Great Lakes Area Independent Specialty Show. Booth photograph.

Ch. Kotzebue's Kunek of Seegoo with her three-week-old puppies. Owner, Judith Lake, Aurora Kennels, Holbrook, Massachusetts.

As the puppies continue to thrive and grow, you will notice that they take on individual characteristics. If you are going to keep and show one of the puppies, this is the time to start observing them for various outstanding characteristics.

EVALUATING THE LITTER

A show puppy prospect should be outgoing, (probably the first one to fall out of the whelping box!) and all efforts should be made to socialize the puppy which appears to be the most shy. Once the puppies are about three weeks old, they can and should be handled a great deal by friends and members of the family.

During the third week they begin to try to walk instead of crawl, but they are unsteady on their feet. Tails are used for balancing, and they begin to make sounds.

The crucial period in a puppy's life occurs when the puppy is from 21 to 28 days old, so all the time you can devote to them at this time will reap rewards later on in life. This is the age when several other important steps must be taken in a puppy's life. Weaning should start if it hasn't already, and it is the time to check for worms. Do not worm unnecessarily. A veterinarian should advise on worming and appropriate dosage and can also discuss with you at this time the schedule for serum or vaccination, which will depend on the size of the puppies as well as their age.

Exercise and grooming should be started at this time, with special care and consideration given to the diet. You will find that the dam will help you wean the puppies, leaving them alone more and more as she notices that they are eating well on their own. Begin by leaving them with her during the night for comfort and warmth; eventually, when she shows less interest, keep them separated entirely.

By the time the fifth week of their lives arrives you will already be in love with every one of them and desperately searching for reasons to keep them all. They recognize you—which really gets to you!—and they box and chew on each other and try to eat your finger and a million other captivating antics which are special with puppies. Their stomachs seem to be bottomless pits, and their weight will rise. At eight to ten weeks, the puppies will be weaned and ready to go.

SPAYING AND CASTRATING

A wise old philosopher once said, "Timing in life is everything!" No statement could apply more readily to the age-old question which every dog owner is faced with sooner or later. . . to spay or not to spay.

For the one-bitch pet owner, spaying is the most logical answer, for it solves many problems. The pet is usually not of top breeding quality, and therefore there is no great loss to the bloodline; it takes the pressure off the family if the dog runs free with children and certainly eliminates the problem of repeated litters of unwanted puppies or a backyard full of eager males twice a year.

But for the owner or breeder, the extra time and protection which must be afforded a purebred quality bitch can be most worthwhile—even if it is only until a single litter is produced after the first heat. It is then not too late to spay, the progeny can perpetuate the bloodline, the bitch will have been fulfilled—though it is merely an old wives' tale that bitches should have at least one litter to be "normal"—and she may then be retired to her deserved role as family pet once again.

With spaying the problem of staining and unusual behavior around the house is eliminated without the necessity of having to keep her in "pants" or administering pills, sprays, or shots. . . which most veterinarians do not approve of anyway.

In the case of males, castration is seldom contemplated, which to me is highly regrettable. The owner of the male dog merely overlooks the dog's ability to populate an entire neighborhood, since they do not have the responsibility of rearing and disposing of the puppies. But when you take into consideration all the many females the male dog can impregnate it is almost more essential that the males be taken out of circulation than that the female be. The male dog will still be inclined to roam but will be less frantic about leaving the grounds, and you will find that a lot of the wanderlust has left him.

Highnoons Eskimo Shaman and Highnoons Eno Chief at five weeks of age. Hank and Snoopy were bred and are owned by Mrs. Janet Edmonds of Oxford, England. The sire was Tote-Um's Tamahine of Seacourt *ex* Highnoons Dakota.

STERILIZING FOR HEALTH

When considering the problem of spaying or castrating, the first consideration after the population explosion should actually be the health of the dog or bitch. Males are frequently subject to urinary diseases, and sometimes castration is a help. Your veterinarian can best advise you on this problem. Another aspect to consider is the kennel dog which is no longer being used at stud. It is unfair to keep him in a kennel with females in heat when there is no chance for him to be used. There are other more personal considerations for both kennel and one-dog owners, but when making the decision remember that it is final. You can always spay or castrate, but once the deed is done there is no return!

Seven-month-old puppy bitch Frostfields Alyeska Kotzebue Koona, bred by Wendy Wisefield, is shown going Best of Opposite Sex from Puppy Class handled by owner Frederick Schramm at the 1975 Mobile Kennel Club Show.

Indian Chief of Seacourt, bred and owned by Mrs. J.S. Parkyns, Seacourt Kennels, Oxford, England, pictured on the bench at a recent dog show. Silver Moon of Seacourt is pictured in the background. Sire was Tote-Um's Arctic Hawk *ex* Highnoons Bella Koola.

Ch. Yukon King's Arctic Prince of Frostfield pictured winning Best of Breed under judge Velma Hiser at the 1973 Providence County Kennel Club Show. This example of the Hinman type Malamute, with the extra-heavy coat, was bred by Robert Kohls and was sired by Whispering Pines Yukon King; the dam was Shinook's Arctic Princess. He is shown handled here by Jerry Wisefield, who co-owns Prince with Wendy Wisefield, Frostfield Kennels, Avon, Massachusetts.

Here going Best of Breed from Open Dog Class on the way to his championship is Burbon's Aristocrat of Brenmar. Judge Eva Seeley awarded breed win, and Aristocrat went on to Group Second under judge Donald Booxbaum at the 1969 Sussex Hills Kennel Club show. Handled by Phillip Marsman for owner Frank Bongarzone of New Shrewsbury, New Jersey. William Gilbert photograph.

19. TRAINING YOUR ALASKAN MALAMUTE

There are few things in the world a dog would rather do than please his master. Therefore, obedience training, or even the initial basic training, will be a pleasure for your dog, if taught correctly, and will make him a much nicer animal to live with for the rest of his life.

WHEN TO START TRAINING

The most frequently asked question by those who consider training their dog is, naturally, "What is the best age to begin training?" The answer is "not before six months."A dog simply cannot be sufficiently or permanently trained before this age and be expected to retain all he has been taught. If too much is expected of him, he can become frustrated and it may ruin him completely for any serious training later on, or even jeopardize his disposition. Most things a puppy learns and repeats before he is six months of age should be considered habit rather than training.

THE REWARD METHOD

The only proper and acceptable kind of training is the kindness and reward method which will build a strong bond between dog and owner. A dog must have confidence in and respect for his teacher. The most important thing to remember in training any dog is that the quickest way to teach, especially the young dog, is through repetition. Praise him when he does well, and scold him when he does wrong. This will suffice. There is no need or excuse for swinging at a dog with rolled up newspapers, or flailing hands which will only tend to make the dog hand shy the rest of his life. Also, make every word count. Do not give a command unless you intend to see it through. Pronounce distinctly with the fewest possible words, and use the same words for the same command every time.

Include the dog's name every time to make sure you have his undivided attention at the beginning of each command. Do not go on to another command until he has successfully completed the previous one and is praised for it. Of course, you should not mix play with the serious training time. Make sure the dog knows the difference between the two.

In the beginning, it is best to train without any distractions whatsoever. After he has learned to concentrate and is older and more proficient, he should perform the exercises with interference, so that the dog learns absolute obedience in the face of all distractions. Needless to say, whatever the distractions, you never lose control. You must be in command at all times to earn the respect and attention of your dog.

HOW LONG SHOULD THE LESSONS BE?

The lessons should be brief with a young dog, starting at five minutes, and as the dog ages and becomes adept in the first lessons, increase the time all the way up to one-half hour. Public training classes are usually set for one hour, and this is acceptable since the full hour of concentration is not placed on your dog alone. Working under these conditions with other dogs, you will find that he will not be as intent as he would be with a private lesson where the commands are directed to him alone for the entire thirty minutes.

If you should notice that your dog is not doing well, or not keeping up with the class, consider putting off training for awhile. Animals, like children, are not always ready for schooling at exactly the same age. It would be a shame to ruin a good obedience dog because you insist on starting his training at six months rather than at, say, nine months, when he would be more apt to be receptive both physically and mentally. If he has particular difficulty in learning one exercise, you might do well to skip to a different one and come back to it again at another session. There are no set rules in this basic training, except, "don't push!"

WHAT YOU NEED TO START TRAINING

From three to six months of age, use the soft nylon show leads, which are the best and safest. When you get ready for the basic training at six months of age, you will require one of the special metal-link choke chains sold for exactly this purpose. Do not let the word "choke" scare you. It is a soft, smooth chain and should be held slack whenever you are not actually using it to correct the dog. This chain should be put over the dog's head so that the lead can be attached over the dog's neck rather than underneath against his throat. It is wise when you buy your choke collar to ask the sales person to show you how it is put on. Those of you who will be taking your dog to a training class will have an instructor who can show you.

To avoid undue stress on the dog, use both hands on the lead. The dog will be taught to obey commands at your left side, and therefore, your left hand will guide the dog close to his collar on a six-foot train-

Ch. Zardal Cliquot, owned by Lois and James Williams of Penfield, New York. Cliquot is pictured with his handler, Parker Harris, taking Best of Breed at the Chicago International Show in 1966 his first time shown as a Special. Breeder was Audrey I. Thomas.

ing lead. The balance of the lead will be held in your right hand. Learn at the very beginning to handle your choke collar and lead correctly. It is as important in training a dog as is the proper equipment for riding a horse.

WHAT TO TEACH FIRST

The first training actually should be to teach the dog to know his name. This, of course, he can learn at an earlier age than six months, just as he can learn to walk nicely on a leash or lead. Many puppies will at first probably want to walk around with the leash in their mouths. There is no objection to this if the dog will walk while doing it. Rather than cultivating this as a habit, you will find that if you don't make an issue of it, the dog will soon realize that carrying the lead in his mouth is not rewarding and he'll let it fall to his side where it belongs.

Judge Sheila Balch awards first place to future Ch. Alaskaland's American Pie at the 1972 Alaskan Malamute Association of Long Island Match Show. Chris Gabriel handled for owner Patti Colcord of Pound Ridge, New York.

Ten-day-old all-white litter bred in 1972 by Jerry and Wendy Wisefield of Frostfield Kennels in Avon, Massachusetts. The only allowable solid color for Malamutes is the all-white, and this litter was bred from two white parents; sire was Polar Trails Nanook *ex* Virgo's Star Mist.

We also let the puppy walk around by himself for a while with the lead around his neck. If he wishes to chew on it a little, that's all right too. In other words, let it be something he recognizes and associates with at first. Do not let the lead start out being a harness.

If the dog is at all bright, chances are he has learned to come on command when you call him by name. This is relatively simple with sweet talk and a reward. On lead, without a reward, and on command without a lead is something else again. If there has been, or is now, a problem, the best way to correct it is to put on the choke collar and the six-foot lead. Then walk away from the dog, and call him, "Pirate, come!" and gently start reeling him in until the dog is in front of you. Give him a pat on the head and/or reward.

Walking, or heeling, next to you is also one of the first and most important things for him to learn. With the soft lead training starting very early, he should soon take up your pace at your left side. At the command to "heel" he should start off with you and continue alongside until you stop. Give the command, "Pirate, sit!" This is taught by leaning over and pushing down on his hindquarters until he sits next to you, while pulling up gently on the collar. When you have this down pat on the straightaway, then start practicing it in circles, with turns and figure eights. When he is an advanced student, you can look forward to the heels and sits being done neatly, spontaneously, and off lead as well.

THE "DOWN" COMMAND

One of the most valuable lessons or commands you can teach your dog is to lie down on command. Some day it may save his life, and is invaluable when traveling with a dog or visiting, if behavior and manners are required even beyond obedience. While repeating the words, "Pirate, down!" lower the dog from a sitting position in front of you by gently pulling his front legs out in front of him. Place your full hand on him while repeating the command, "Pirate, down!" and hold him down to let him know you want him to *stay* down. After he gets the general idea, this can be done from a short distance away on a lead along with the command, by pulling the lead down to the floor. Or perhaps you can slip the lead under your shoe (between the heel and sole) and pull it directly to the floor. As the dog progresses in training, a hand signal with or without verbal command, or with or without lead, can be given from a considerable distance by raising your arm and extending the hand palm down.

THE "STAY" COMMAND

The stay command eventually can be taught from both a sit and a down position. Start with the sit. With the dog on your left side in the sitting position give the command, "Pirate, stay!" Reach down with the left hand open and palm side to the dog and sweep it in close to his nose. Then walk a short distance away and face him. He will at first, having learned to heel immediately as you start off, more than likely start off with you. The trick in teaching this is to make sure he hears "stay" before you start off. It will take practice. If he breaks, sit him down again, stand next to him, and give the command all over again. As he masters the command, let the distance between you and your dog increase while the dog remains seated. Once the command is learned, advance to the stay command from the down position.

THE STAND FOR EXAMINATION

If you have any intention of going on to advanced training in obedience with your dog, or if you have a show dog which you feel you will enjoy showing yourself, a most important command which should be mastered at six months of age is the stand command. This is essential for a show dog since it is the position used when the show judge goes over your dog. This is taught in the same manner as the stay command, but this time with the dog remaining up on all four feet. He should learn to stand still, without moving his feet and without flinching or breaking when approached by either you or strangers. The hand with palm open wide and facing him should be firmly placed in front of his nose with the command, "Pirate, stand!" After he learns the basic rules and knows the difference between stand and stay, ask friends, relatives, and strangers to assist you with this exercise by walking up to the dog and going over him. He should not react physically to their touch. A dog posing in this stance should show all the beauty and pride of being a sterling example of his breed.

FORMAL SCHOOL TRAINING

We mentioned previously about the various training schools and classes given for dogs. Your local kennel club, newspaper, or the yellow pages of the telephone book will put you in touch with organizations in your area where this service is performed. You and your dog will learn a great deal from these classes. Not only do they offer formal training, but the experience for you and your dog in public, with other dogs of approximately the same age and with the same purpose in mind, is excellent. If you intend to show your dog, this training is valuable ring experience for later on. If you are having difficulty with the training, remember, it is either too soon to start—or YOU are doing something wrong!

indstorm RA's Cordova Thor, owned by Ron and Andi Garback of Imler, Pennsylvania.

Two four-week-old puppies from a litter sired by Ch. Tigara's Karluk *ex* Ch. Inuit's Mehitabel. On the left is future Ch. Inuit's Keemak, owned by Todd Berger, and on the right Inuit's Arctic Thunder, owned by Helen Reid.

ADVANCED TRAINING AND OBEDIENCE TRIALS

The A.K.C. obedience trials are divided into three classes: Novice, Open and Utility.

In the Novice Class, the dog will be judged on the following basis:

TEST	MAXIMUM SCORE
Heel on lead	35
Stand for examination	30
Heel free—on lead	45
Recall (come on command)	30
One-minute sit (handler in ring)	30
Three-minute down (handler in ring)	30
Maximum total score	200

If the dog "qualifies" in three shows by earning at least 50% of the points for each test, with a total of at least 170 for the trial, he has earned the Companion Dog degree and the letters C.D. (Companion Dog) are entered after his name in the A.K.C. records.

After the dog has qualified as a C.D., he is eligible to enter the Open Class competition, where he will be judged on this basis:

TEST	MAXIMUM SCORE
Heel free 40	
Drop on Recall 30	
Retrieve (wooden dumbbell) on flat 25	
Retrieve over obstacle (hurdle) 35	
Broad jump 20	
Three-minute sit (handler out of ring) 25	
Five-minute down (handler out of ring) 25	

maximum total score 200

Again he must qualify in three shows for the C.D.X. (Companion Dog Excellent) title and then is eligible for the Utility Class, where he can earn the Utility Dog (U.D.) degree in these rugged tests:

TEST	MAXIMUM SCORE
Scent discrimination (Article #1) 30	
Scent discrimination (Article #2) 30	
Directed retrieve 30	
Signal exercise (heeling, etc., on hand signal) 35	
Directed jumping (over hurdle and bar jump) 40	
Group examination 35	

Maximum total score 200

For more complete information about these obedience trials, write for the American Kennel Club's *Regulations and Standards for Obedience Trials*. Dogs that are disqualifed from breed shows because of alteration or physical defects are eligible to compete in these trials.

THE COMPANION DOG EXCELLENT DEGREE

There are seven exercises which must be executed to achieve the C.D.X. degree, and the percentages for achieving these are the same as for the U.D. degree. Candidates must qualify in three different obedience trials and under three different judges and must have received scores of more than 50% of the available points in each exercise, with a total of 170 points or more out of the possible 200. At that time they may add the letters C.D.X. after their name.

THE UTILITY DOG DEGREE

The Utility Dog degree is awarded to dogs which have qualified by successfully completing six exercises under three different judges

Ch. Cordova's Tasha pictured being judged by Eva B. Seeley at a recent show. Tasha finished for her championship at the 1973 Eastern Malamute Specialty Show under judge Nelson Groh. She has also won Bests of Breed from the classes over male Specials. Sire was Canadian, American and Bermudian Ch. Inuit's Wooly Bully *ex* Inuit's Kelly of Cordova. Owner Carol Perham of Lakeside, Connecticut.

at three different obedience trials, with a score of more than 50% of available points in each exercise, and with a score of 170 or more out of a possible 200 points.

These six exercises consist of Scent Discrimination, with two different articles for which they receive thirty points each if successfully completed; Direct Retrieving, for 30 points; Signal Exercise for 35 points; Directed Jumping for 40 points and a Group Examination for 35 points.

THE TRACKING DOG DEGREE

The Tracking Dog trials are not held, as the others are, with the dog shows, and need be passed only once.

The dog must work continuously on a strange track at least 440 yards long and with two right angle turns. There is no time limit, and the dog must retrieve an article laid at the other end of the trail. There is no score given; the dog either earns the degree or fails. The dog is worked by his trainer on a long leash, usually in harness.

Ch. Icefloe's Yukon Jake, sled and show dog out of the famous lead dog Ch. Icefloe's North Star. Owner is Jeri Lea Hooks, Icefloe Malamutes, Los Lunas, New Mexico.

Aurora's Tam pictured winning Best of Opposite Sex at a show recently on the way to her championship. Her sire was Arctic Storm of Frostie Trails *ex* Kotzebue's Taku of Seegoo. Owners are Philip and Judith Lake, Aurora Kennels, Holbrook, Massachusetts.

20. SHOWING YOUR ALASKAN MALAMUTE

Let us assume that after a few months of tender loving care, you realize your dog is developing beyond your wildest expectations and that the dog you selected is very definitely a show dog! Of course, every owner is prejudiced. But if you are sincerely interested in going to dog shows with your dog and making a champion of him, now is the time to start casting a critical eye on him from a judge's point of view.

There is no such thing as a perfect dog. Every dog has some faults, perhaps even a few serious ones. The best way to appraise your dog's degree of perfection is to compare him with the Standard for the breed, or before a judge in a show ring.

MATCH SHOWS

For the beginner there are "mock" dog shows, called Match Shows, where you and your dog go through many of the procedures of a regular dog show, but do not gain points toward championship. These shows are usually held by kennel clubs, annually or semiannually, and much ring poise and experience can be gained there. The age limit is reduced to two months at match shows to give puppies four months of training before they compete at the regular shows when they reach six months of age. Classes range from two to four months; four to six months; six to nine months; and nine to twelve months. Puppies compete with others of their own age for comparative purposes. Many breeders evaluate their litters in this manner, choosing which is the most outgoing, which is the most poised, the best showman, etc.

For those seriously interested in showing their dogs to full championship, these match shows provide important experience for both the dog and the owner. Class categories may vary slightly, according to number of entries, but basically include all the classes that are included at a regular point show. There is a nominal entry fee and, of course, ribbons and usually trophies are given for your efforts as well. Unlike the point shows, entries can be made on the day of the show right on the show grounds. They are unbenched and provide an informal, usually congenial atmosphere for the amateur, which helps to make the ordeal of one's first adventures in the show ring a little less nerve-wracking.

THE POINT SHOWS

It is not possible to show a puppy at an American Kennel Club sanctioned point show before the age of six months. When your dog reaches this eligible age, your local kennel club can provide you with the names and addresses of the show-giving superintendents in your area who will be staging the club's dog show for them, and where you must write for an entry form.

Ch. Inuit's Kotzebue Spy pictured winning at the 1972 Wilmington Kennel Club Show under judge Henry Stoecker. Sired by American, Canadian and Bermudian Ch. Inuit's Wooly Bully *ex* Kotzebue of Chinook, a breeding which produced three champions. Spy is owner-handled by Lee Matyola of Somerville, New Jersey.

Ch. Voyageur's Elke, one of a litter of five champions, was Best Opposite Sex at the 1967 National Specialty Show before her first birthday. Bred by Penny Devaney of Albuquerque, New Mexico, the sire was Ch. Tigara's Torch of Arctica ex Ch. Kinao's Silver Trumpet. Owner is Sheila Land.

The Cleveland Amorys and their Alaskan Malamutes, Ivan the Terrible and Peter the Great, pose at the doorway of their New York City apartment. Mrs. Amory takes the dogs to the park every morning to work out. The dogs also have a carriage which they are trained to pull while Cleveland rides his bicycle!

The forms are mailed in a pamphlet called a premium list. This also includes the names of the judges for each breed, a list of the prizes and trophies, the name and address of the show-giving club and where the show will be held, as well as rules and regulations set up by the American Kennel Club which must be abided by if you are to enter.

A booklet containing the complete set of show rules and regulations may be obtained by writing to the American Kennel Club, Inc., 51 Madison Avenue, New York, N.Y., 10010.

When you write to the Dog Show Superintendent, request not only your premium list for this particular show, but ask that your name be added to their mailing list so that you will automatically receive all premium lists in the future. List your breed or breeds and they will see to it that you receive premium lists for Specialty shows as well.

Unlike the match shows where your dog will be judged on ring behavior, at the point shows he will be judged on conformation to the breed Standard. In addition to being at least six months of age (on the

Ch. Chargi's Buckeye finishing his championship with a 4-point major win and Best of Breed over top-winning Specials under judge Peggy Adamson. Buckeye was also a winner at the New England Area Specialty Show under judge Melbourne Downing in the fall of 1973. Owner-handled by Shannon Sollinger of the Kunoe Kennels in Newburgh, New York.

American, Canadian and Bermudian Ch. Inuits Wooly Bully pictured
finishing his Canadian championship from the Bred by Exhibitor Class
in his tenth year! The judge was Lorna Demidoff. Bred and owned by
Sheila Balch. "Floyd" finished this Canadian championship with a
Group First and two Group Thirds.

day of the show) he must be a purebred for a point show. This means both of his parents and he are registered with the American Kennel Club. There must be no alterations or falsifications regarding his appearance. Females cannot have been spayed and males must have both testicles in evidence. No dyes or powders may be used to enhance the appearance, and any lameness or deformity or major deviation from the Standard for the breed constitutes a disqualification.

With all these things in mind, groom your dog to the best of your ability in the specified area for this purpose in the show hall and walk into the show ring with great pride of ownership and ready for an appraisal of your dog by the judge.

The presiding judge on that day will allow each and every dog a certain amount of time and consideration before making his decisions. It is never permissible to consult the judge regarding either

Best of Breed at the 1974 Alaskan Malamute Club of America Specialty Show under judge Roy Kibler was Ch. Inuit's Sweet Lucifer, bred by Sheila Land and owned by Sheila Balch, Inuit Kennels, Valley Cottage, New York. Lucifer was handled by Philip Marsman. Gilbert photo.

your dog or his decision while you are in the ring. An exhibitor never speaks unless spoken to, and then only to answer such questions as the judge may ask—the age of the dog, the dog's bite, or to ask you to move your dog around the ring once again.

However, before you reach the point where you are actually in the ring awaiting the final decisions of the judge, you will have had to decide in which of the five classes in each sex your dog should compete.

Point Show Classes

The regular classes of the AKC are: Puppy, Novice, Bred-by-Exhibitor, American-Bred, Open; if your dog is undefeated in any of the regular classes (divided by sex) in which it is entered, he or she is *required* to enter the Winners Class. If your dog is placed second in the class to the dog which won Winners Dog or Winners Bitch, hold the dog or bitch in readiness as the judge must consider it for Reserve Winners.

PUPPY CLASSES shall be for dogs which are six months of age and over but under twelve months, which were whelped in the U.S.A. or Canada, and which are not champions. Classes are often divided 6 and (under) 9, and 9 and (under) 12 months. The age of a dog shall be calculated up to and inclusive of the first day of a show. For example, a dog whelped on Jan. 1st is eligible to compete in a puppy class on July 1st, and may continue to compete up to and including Dec. 31st of the same year, but is not eligible to compete Jan. 1st of the following year.

THE NOVICE CLASS shall be for dogs six months of age or over, whelped in the U.S.A. or Canada which have not, prior to the closing of entries, won three first prizes in the Novice Class, a first prize in Bred-by-Exhibitor, American-Bred or Open Class, nor one or more points toward a championship title.

THE BRED-BY-EXHIBITOR CLASS shall be for dogs whelped in the U.S.A. which are six months of age and over, which are not champions, and which are owned wholly or in part by the person or by the spouse of the person who was the breeder or one of the breeders of record. Dogs entered in the BBE Class must be handled by an owner or by a member of the immediate family of an owner, i.e., the husband, wife, father, mother, son, daughter, brother or sister.

THE AMERICAN-BRED CLASS is for all dogs (except champions) six months of age or over, whelped in the U.S.A. by reason of a mating that took place in the U.S.A.

THE OPEN CLASS is for any dog six months of age or over, except in a member specialty club show held for only American-Bred dogs, in which case the class is for American-Bred dogs only.

"And don't forget to put in another dime. . ." Ch. Balch's Ingrid of Brenmar and Balch's Pooka photographed downtown in 1965.

WINNERS DOG and WINNERS BITCH: After the above male classes have been judged, the first-place winners are then *required* to compete in the ring. The dog judged "Winners Dog" is awarded the points toward his championship title.

RESERVE WINNERS are selected immediately after the Winners Dog. In case of a disqualification of a win by the AKC, the Reserve Dog moves up to "Winners" and receives the points. After all male classes are judged, the bitch classes are called.

BEST OF BREED OR BEST OF VARIETY COMPETITION is limited to Champions of Record or dogs (with newly acquired points, for a 90-day period prior to AKC confirmation) which have completed championship requirements, and Winners Dog and Winners Bitch (or the dog awarded Winners if only one Winners prize has been awarded), together with any undefeated dogs which have been shown only in non-regular classes; all compete for Best of Breed or Best of Variety (if the breed is divided by size, color, texture or length of coat hair, etc.).

BEST OF WINNERS: If the WD or WB earns BOB or BOV, it automatically becomes BOW; otherwise they will be judged together for BOW (following BOB or BOV judging).

BEST OF OPPOSITE SEX is selected from the remaining dogs of the opposite sex to Best of Breed or Best of Variety.

OTHER CLASSES may be approved by the AKC: STUD DOGS, BROOD BITCHES, BRACE CLASS, TEAM CLASS; classes consist-

Sy Goldberg and a five-month-old Alaskan Malamute puppy. Sy and Ann Goldberg own the Cinnaminson Kennels in Cream Ridge, New Jersey.

American and Canadian Ch. Bernard, pictured winning Best of Breed from the classes over five Specials at the 1974 Eastern Dog Club under judge Arnold Woolf. Owned by Philip and Judith Lake, Aurora Kennels, Holbrook, Massachusetts, Bernard was purchased from a "pet home" at three-and-a-half years of age and finished to his dual championship by the Lakes.

ing of local dogs and bitches may also be included in a show if approved by the AKC (special rules are included in the AKC Rule Book).

The MISCELLANEOUS CLASS shall be for purebred dogs of such breeds as may be designated by the AKC. No dog shall be eligible for entry in this class unless the owner has been granted an Indefinite Listing Privilege (ILP) and unless the ILP number is given on the entry form. Application for an ILP shall be made on a form provided by the AKC and when submitted must be accompanied by a fee set by the Board of Directors.

All Miscellaneous Breeds shall be shown together in a single class except that the class may be divided by sex if so specified in the premium list. There shall be *no* further competition for dogs entered in this class. Ribbons for 1st, 2nd, 3rd and 4th shall be Rose, Brown, Light Green and Gray, respectively. This class is open to the following Miscellaneous dog breeds: Australian Cattle Dogs, Australian Kelpies, Border Collies, Cavalier King Charles Spaniels, Ibizan Hounds, Miniature Bull Terriers, and Spinoni Italiani.

If Your Dog Wins a Class. . .

Study the classes to make certain your dog is entered in a proper class for his or her qualifications. If your dog wins his class, the rule states: *You are required* to enter classes for Winners, Best of Breed and Best of Winners (no additional entry fees). The rule states, "No eligible dog may be withheld from competition." It is not mandatory that you stay for group judging. *If your dog wins a group*, however, *you must stay for Best-in-Show competition.*

THE PRIZE RIBBONS AND WHAT THEY STAND FOR

No matter how many entries there are in each class at a dog show, if you place first through fourth position you will receive a ribbon. These ribbons commemorate your win and can be impressive when collected and displayed to prospective buyers when and if you have puppies for sale, or if you intend to use your dog at public stud.

All ribbons from the American Kennel Club licensed dog shows will bear the American Kennel Club seal, the name of the show, the date and the placement. In the classes the colors are blue for first, red for second, yellow for third, and white for fourth. Winners Dog or Winners Bitch ribbons are purple, while Reserve Dog and Reserve Bitch ribbons are purple and white. Best of Winners ribbons are blue and white; Best of Breed, purple and gold; and Best of Opposite Sex ribbons are red and white.

In the six groups, first prize is a blue rosette or ribbon, second placement is red, third yellow, and fourth white. The Best In Show rosette is either red, white and blue, or incorporates the colors used in the show-giving club's emblem.

QUALIFYING FOR CHAMPIONSHIP

Championship points are given for Winners Dog and Winners Bitch in accordance with a scale of points established by the American Kennel Club based on the popularity of the breed in entries, and the number of dogs competing in the classes. This scale of points varies in different sections of the country, but the scale is published in the front of each dog show catalog. These points may differ between the dogs and the bitches at the same show. You may, however, win additional points by winning Best of Winners, if there are fewer dogs than bitches entered, or vice versa. Points never exceed five at any one show, and a total of fifteen points must be won to constitute a championship. These fifteen points must be won under at least three different judges, and you must acquire at least two major wins. Anything from a three to five point win is a major, while one and two point wins are minor wins. Two major wins must be won under two different judges to meet championship requirements.

OBEDIENCE TRIALS

Some shows also offer Obedience Trials, which are considered as separate events. They give the dogs a chance to compete and score on performing a prescribed set of exercises intended to display their training in doing useful work.

There are three obedience titles for which they may compete. First, the Companion Dog or C.D. title; second, the Companion Dog Excellent or C.D.X.; and third, the Utility Dog or U.D. Detailed information on these degrees is contained in a booklet entitled Official Obedience Regulations and may be obtained by writing to the American Kennel Club.

JUNIOR SHOWMANSHIP COMPETITION

Junior Showmanship Competition is for boys and girls in different age groups handling their own dogs or one owned by their immediate family. There are four divisions: Novice A, for the ten to 12 year olds; Novice B, for those 13 to 16 years of age, with no previous junior showmanship wins; Open C, for ten to 12 year olds; and Open D, for 13 to 16 year olds who have earned one or more JS awards.

As Junior Showmanship at the dog shows increased in popularity, certain changes and improvements had to be made. As of April 1, 1971, the American Kennel Club issued a new booklet containing the Regulations for Junior Showmanship which may be obtained by writing to the A.K.C. at 51 Madison Avenue, New York, N.Y. 10010.

Summer Sunday at a dog show! Sheila Balch's children and Balch's Lil Spook of Roy-El, photographed in 1963.

DOG SHOW PHOTOGRAPHERS

Every show has at least one official photographer who will be more than happy to take a photograph of your dog with the judge, ribbons and trophies, along with your or your handler. These make marvelous remembrances of your top show wins and are frequently framed along with the ribbons for display purposes. Photographers can be paged at the show over the public address system, if you wish to obtain this service. Prices vary, but you will probably find it costs little to capture these happy moments, and the photos can always be used in the various dog magazines to advertise your dog's wins.

TWO TYPES OF DOG SHOWS

There are two types of dog shows licensed by the American Kennel Club. One is the all-breed show which includes classes for all the recognized breeds, and groups of breeds; i.e., all terriers, all toys, etc. Then there are the specialty shows for one particular breed which also offer championship points.

Ch. Inuit's Sweet Lucifer, eleven months old, shown winning his fourth Best of Breed over Specials from the Puppy Class. This win came under judge Earl Adair. Handled by Philip Marsman for owner Sheila Balch, Inuit Kennels, Valley Cottage, New York. Bushman photo.

Ch. Sittiak Kosak Warrior shown winning Best in Match in September, 1971 under judge Sheila Balch. Owner is Gary Galliker.

Ch. Kobuk's Manassass Mischief, owned by Eleanore Du-Buis, Sena-Lak Kennels, Valois, New York.

BENCHED OR UNBENCHED DOG SHOWS

The show-giving clubs determine, usually on the basis of what facilities are offered by their chosen show site, whether their show will be benched or unbenched. A benched show is one where the dog show superintendent supplies benches (cages for toy dogs). Each bench is numbered and its corresponding number appears on your entry identification slip which is sent to you prior to the show date. The number also appears in the show catalog. Upon entering the show you should take your dog to the bench where he should remain until it is time to groom him before entering the ring to be judged. After judging, he must be returned to the bench until the official time of dismissal from the show. At an unbenched show the club makes no provision whatsoever for your dog other than an enormous tent (if an outdoor show) or an area in a show hall where all crates and grooming equipment must be kept.

Benched or unbenched, the moment you enter the show grounds you are expected to look after your dog and have it under complete control at all times. This means short leads in crowded aisles or getting out of cars. In the case of a benched show, a "bench chain" is needed. It should allow the dog to move around, but not get down off the bench. It is also not considered "cute" to have small tots leading enormous dogs around a dog show where the child might be dragged into the middle of a dog fight.

The children of Sheila Balch with Balch's Pooka and a puppy, future Ch. Balch's Ingrid of Brenmar, photographed when she was eight weeks old.

PROFESSIONAL HANDLERS

If you are new in the fancy and do not know how to handle your dog to his best advantage, or if you are too nervous or physically unable to show your dog, you can hire a licensed professional handler who will do it for you for a specified fee. The more successful or well-known handlers charge slightly higher rates, but generally speaking there is a pretty uniform charge for this service. As the dog progresses with his wins in the show ring, the fee increases proportionately. Included in this service is professional advice on when and where to show your dog, grooming, a statement of your wins at each show, and all trophies and ribbons that the dog accumulates. Any cash award is kept by the handler as a sort of "bonus."

When engaging a handler, it is advisable to select one that does not take more dogs to a show than he can properly and comfortably handle. You want your dog to receive his individual attention and not

"Come on in, the water's fine!" Ch. Sena-Lak's Thor II and his pal take to the water at Eleanore DuBuis's Sena-Lak Kennels, Valois, New York.

Ch. Sena-Lak's Copper Knight, C.D., and his dam, Ch. Sena-Lak's Chena of Lakeview, pictured winning at a dog show. Both are owned by Eleanore DuBuis.

Lovely seascape photo of Eileen and Chris Gabriel's Alaskan Malamute Sena-Lak's Sitka of Khazar, photographed near their Golden Bridge, New York home.

be rushed into the ring at the last moment because the handler has been busy with too many other dogs in other rings. Some handlers require that you deliver the dog to their establishment a few days ahead of the show so they have ample time to groom and train him. Others will accept well-behaved and previously trained and groomed dogs at ringside, if they are familiar with the dog and the owner. This should be determined well in advance of the show date. NEVER expect a handler to accept a dog at ringside that is not groomed to perfection!

There are several sources for locating a professional handler. Dog magazines carry their classified advertising; a note or telephone call to the American Kennel Club will put you in touch with several in your area. Usually, you will be billed after the day of the show.

DO YOU REALLY NEED A HANDLER?

The answer to the above question is sometimes yes! However, the answer most exhibitors give is, "But I can't *afford* a professional handler!" or, "I want to show my dog myself. Does that mean my dog will never do any big winning?"

Do you *really* need a handler to win? If you are mishandling a good dog that should be winning and isn't, because it is made to look simply terrible in the ring by its owner, the answer is yes. If you don't know how to handle a dog properly, why make your dog look bad when a handler could show it to its best advantage?

Some owners simply cannot handle a dog well and still wonder why their dogs aren't winning in the ring, no matter how hard they try. Others are nervous and this nervousness travels down the leash to the dog and the dog behaves accordingly. Some people are extroverts by nature, and these are the people who usually make excellent handlers. Of course, the biggest winning dogs at the shows usually have a lot of "show off" in their nature, too, and this helps a great deal.

THE COST OF CAMPAIGNING A DOG WITH A HANDLER

At present many champions are shown an average of 25 times before completing a championship. In entry fees at today's prices, that adds up to about $200. This does not include motel bills, traveling expenses, or food. There have been dog champions finished in fewer shows, say five to ten shows, but this is the exception rather than the rule. When and where to show should be thought out carefully so that you can perhaps save money on entries. Here is one of the services a professional handler provides that can mean a considerable saving. Hiring a handler can save money in the long run if you just wish to make a champion. If your dog has been winning reserves and not taking the points and a handler can finish him in five to ten shows, you would be ahead financially. If your dog is not really top quality, the length of time it takes even a handler to finish it (depending upon competition in the area) could add up to a large amount of money.

Campaigning a show specimen that not only captures the wins in his breed but wins group and Best in Show awards gets up into the big money. To cover the nation's major shows and rack up a record as one of the top dogs in the nation usually costs an owner between ten and fifteen thousand dollars a year. This includes not only the professional handler's fee for taking the dog into the ring, but the cost of conditioning and grooming, board, advertising in the dog magazines, photographs, etc.

There is great satisfaction in winning with your own dog, especially if you have trained and cared for it yourself. With today's enormous entries at the dog shows and so many worthy dogs competing for top wins, many owners who said "I'd rather do it myself!" and meant it became discouraged and eventually hired a handler anyway.

However, if you really are in it just for the sport, you can and should handle your own dog if you want to. You can learn the tricks by attending training classes, and you can learn a lot by carefully observing the more successful professional handlers as they perform in the ring. Model yourself after the ones that command respect as being the leaders in their profession. But, if you find you'd really rather be at ringside looking on, then do get a handler so that your worthy dog gets his deserved recognition in the ring. To own a good dog and win with it is a thrill, so good luck, no matter how you do it.

21. FEEDING AND NUTRITION

FEEDING PUPPIES

There are many diets today for young puppies, including all sorts of products on the market for feeding the newborn, for supplementing the feeding of the young and for adding this or that to diets, depending on what is lacking in the way of a complete diet.

When weaning puppies, it is necessary to put them on four meals a day, even while you are tapering off with the mother's milk. Feeding at six in the morning, noontime, six in the evening and midnight is about the best schedule, since it fits in with most human eating plans. Meals for the puppies can be prepared immediately before or after your own meals, without too much of a change in your own schedule.

6 A.M.

Two meat and two milk meals serve best and should be served alternately, of course. Assuming the 6 A.M. feeding is a milk meal, the contents should be as follows: Goat's milk is the very best milk to feed puppies but is expensive and usually available only a drug stores, unless you live in farm country where it could be readily available fresh and still less expensive. If goat's milk is not available, use evaporated milk (which can be changed to powdered milk later on) diluted two parts evaporated milk and one part water, along with raw egg yoke, honey or Karo syrup, sprinkled with high-protein baby cereal and some wheat germ. As the puppies mature, cottage cheese may be added or, at one of the two milk meals, it can be substituted for the cereal.

NOONTIME

A puppy chow which has been soaked in warm water or beef broth according to the time specified on the wrapper should be mixed with raw or simmered chopped meat in equal proportions with vitamin powder added.

6 P.M.

Repeat the milk meal—perhaps varying the type of cereal from wheat to oats, or corn or rice.

MIDNIGHT

Repeat the meat meal. If raw meat was fed at noon, the evening meal might be simmered.

Please note that specific proportions on this suggested diet are not given. However, it's safe to say that the most important ingredients are the milk and cereal, and the meat and puppy chow which forms the basis of the diet. Your veterinarian can advise on the portion sizes if there is any doubt in your mind as to how much to use.

If you notice that the puppies are cleaning their plates you are perhaps not feeding enough to keep up with their rate of growth. Increase the amount at the next feeding. Observe them closely; puppies should each "have their fill," because growth is very rapid at this age. If they have not satisfied themselves, increase the amount so that they do not have to fight for the last morsel. They will not overeat if they know there is enough food available. Instinct will usually let them eat to suit their normal capacity.

Ch. Kiana of Klondike, owned by Eleanore DuBuis, Sena-Lak Kennels.

Ch. Sena-Lak's Kiana of Klondike, owned by Eleanore DuBuis, Sena-Lak Kennels, Valois, New York.

If there is any doubt in your mind as to any ingredient you are feeding, ask yourself, "Would I give it to my own baby?" If the answer is no, then don't give it to your puppies. At this age, the comparison between puppies and human babies can be a good guide.

If there is any doubt in your mind, I repeat: ask your veterinarian to be sure.

Many puppies will regurgitate their food, perhaps a couple of times, before they manage to retain it. If they do bring up their food, allow them to eat it again, rather than clean it away. Sometimes additional saliva is necessary for them to digest it, and you do not want them to skip a meal just because it is an unpleasant sight for you to observe.

This same regurgitation process holds true sometimes with the bitch, who will bring up her own food for her puppies every now and then. This is a natural instinct on her part which stems from the days when dogs were giving birth in the wilds. The only food the mother could provide at weaning time was too rough and indigestible for her puppies. Therefore, she took it upon herself to pre-digest the food until it could be taken and retained by her young. Bitches today will sometimes resort to this, especially bitches which love having litters and have a strong maternal instinct. Some dams will help you wean their litters and even give up feeding entirely once they see you are taking over.

WEANING THE PUPPIES

When weaning the puppies the mother is kept away from the little ones for longer and longer periods of time. This is done over a period of several days. At first she is separated from the puppies for several hours, then all day, leaving her with them only at night for comfort and warmth. This gradual separation aids in helping the mother's milk to dry up gradually, and she suffers less distress after feeding a litter.

If the mother continues to carry a great deal of milk with no signs of its tapering off, consult your veterinarian before she gets too uncomfortable. She may cut the puppies off from her supply of milk too abruptly if she is uncomfortable, before they should be completely on their own.

There are many opinions on the proper age to start weaning puppies. If you plan to start selling them between six and eight weeks, weaning should begin between two and three weeks of age. Here again, each bitch will pose a different situation. The size and weight of the litter should help determine the time, and your veterinarian will have an opinion, as he determines the burden the bitch is carrying by the size of the litter and her general condition. If she is being pulled down by feeding a large litter, he may suggest that you start at two weeks. If she is glorying in her motherhood without any apparent taxing of her strength, he may suggest three to four weeks. You and he will be the best judges. But remember, there is no substitute that is as perfect as mother's milk—and the longer the puppies benefit from it, the better. Other food yes, but mother's milk first and foremost for the healthiest puppies!

Bertrand Sprague and a four-day-old puppy.

FEEDING THE ADULT DOG

The puppies' schedule of four meals a day should drop to three by six months and then to two by nine months; by the time the dog reaches one year of age, it is eating one meal a day.

The time when you feed the dog each day can be a matter of the dog's preference or your convenience, so long as once in every 24 hours the dog receives a meal that provides him with a complete, balanced diet. In addition, of course, fresh clean water should be available at all times.

There are many brands of dry food, kibbles and biscuits on the market which are all of good quality. There are also many varieties of canned dog food which are of good quality and provide a balanced diet for your dog. But, for those breeders and exhibitors who show their dogs, additional care is given to providing a few "extras" which enhance the good health and good appearance of show dogs.

A good meal or kibble mixed with water or beef broth and raw meat is perhaps the best ration to provide. In cold weather many breeders add suet or corn oil (or even olive or cooking oil) to the mixture and others make use of the bacon fat after breakfast by pouring it over the dog's food.

Salting a dog's food in the summer helps replace the salt he "pants away" in the heat. Many breeders sprinkle the food with garlic powder to sweeten the dog's breath and prevent gas, especially in breeds that gulp or wolf their food and swallow a lot of air. I prefer garlic powder; the salt is too weak and the clove is too strong.

There are those, of course, who cook very elaborately for their dogs, which is not necessary if a good meal and meat mixture is provided. Many prefer to add vegetables, rice, tomatoes, etc., in with everything else they feed. As long as the extras do not throw the nutritional balance off, there is little harm, but no one thing should be fed to excess. Occasionally liver is given as a treat at home. Fish, which

American and Canadian Ch. Tote-Um's Oo-Malik, bred and owned by Dianne Ross, Tote-Um Kennels, Cle Elum, Washington. His sire was American and Canadian Ch. Nikik du Nordkyn *ex* Bearpaw Egavik of Tote-Um. His championship in Canada was earned with three majors and a Group Third win. This handsome team dog was unbeaten in the breed in Canada.

most veterinarians no longer recommend even for cats, is fed to puppies, but should not be given in excess of once a week. Always remember that no one thing should be given as a total diet. Balance is most important; a 100 per cent meat diet can kill a dog.

THE ALL MEAT DIET CONTROVERSY

In March of 1971, the National Research Council investigated a great stir in the dog fancy about the all-meat dog-feeding controversy. It was established that meat and meat by-products constitute a complete balanced diet for dogs only when it is further fortified with vitamins and minerals.

Therefore, a good dog chow or meal mixed with meat provides the perfect combination for a dog's diet. While the dry food is a complete diet in itself, the fresh meat additionally satisfies the dog's anatomically and physiologically meat-oriented appetite. While dogs are actually carnivores, it must be remembered that when they were feeding themselves in the wild they ate almost the entire animal they captured, including its stomach contents. This provided some of the vitamins and minerals we must now add to the diet.

In the United States, the standard for diets which claim to be "complete and balanced" is set by the Subcommittee on Canine Nutrition of the National Research Council (NRC) of the National Academy of Sciences. This is the official agency for establishing the nutritional requirements of dog foods. Most foods sold for dogs and cats meet these requirements, and manufactuers are proud to say so on their labels, so look for this when you buy. Pet food labels must be approved by the Association of American Feed Control Officials, Pet Foods Committee. Both the Food and Drug Administration and the Federal Trade Commission of the AAFCO define the word "balanced" when referring to dog food as:

"Balanced is a term which may be applied to pet food having all known required nutrients in a proper amount and proportion based upon the recommendations of a recognized authority (The National Research Council is one) in the field of animal nutrition, for a given set of physiological animal requirements."

With this much care given to your dog's diet, there can be little reason for not having happy well-fed dogs in proper weight and proportions for the show ring.

OBESITY

As we mentioned before, there are many "perfect" diets for your dogs on the market today. When fed in proper proportions, they should keep your dogs in "full bloom." However, there are those owners who, more often than not, indulge their own appetites and are inclined to overfeed their dogs as well: A study in Great Britain in the early 1970's found that a major percentage of obese people also had obese dogs. The entire family was overfed and all suffered from the same condition.

Obesity in dogs is a direct result of the animal's being fed more food that he can properly "burn up" over a period of time, so it is stored as fat or fatty tissue in the body. Pet dogs are more inclined to become obese than show dogs or working dogs, but obesity also is a factor to be considered with the older dog, since his exercise is curtailed.

A lack of "tuck up" on a dog, or not being able to feel the ribs, or great folds of fat which hang from the underside of the dog can all be considered as obesity. Genetic factors may enter into the picture, but usually the owner is at fault.

The life span of the obese dog is decreased on several counts. Excess weight puts undue stress on the heart as well as the joints. The dog becomes a poor anesthetic risk and has less resistance to viral or bacterial infections. Treatment is seldom easy or completely effective, so emphasis should be placed on not letting your dog get FAT in the first place!

ORPHANED PUPPIES

The ideal solution to feeding orphaned puppies is to be able to put them with another nursing dam who will take them on as her own. If this is not possible within your own kennel, or a kennel that you know of, it is up to you to care for and feed the puppies. Survival is possible but requires a great deal of time and effort on your part.

Your substitute formula must be precisely prepared, always served heated to body temperature and refrigerated when not being fed. Esbilac, a vacuum-packed powder, with complete feeding instructions on the can, is excellent and about as close to mother's milk as you can get. If you can't get Esbilac, or until you do get Esbilac, there are two alternative formulas that you might use.

Mix one part boiled water with five parts of evaporated milk and add one teaspoonful of di-calcium phosphate per quart of formula. Di-calcium phosphate can be secured at any drug store. If they have it in tablet form only, you can powder the tablets with the back part of a tablespoon. The other formula for newborn puppies is a combination of eight ounces of homogenized milk mixed well with two egg yolks.

You will need baby bottles with three-hole nipples. Sometimes doll bottles can be used for the newborn puppies, which should be fed at six-hour intervals. If they are consuming sufficient amounts, their stomachs should look full, or slightly enlarged, though never distended. The amount of formula to be fed is proportionate to the size, age, growth and weight of the puppy, and is indicated on the can of Esbilac or on the advice of your veterinarian. Many breeders like to keep a baby scale nearby to check the weight of the puppies to be sure they are thriving on the formula.

At two to three weeks you can start adding Pablum or some other high protein baby cereal to the formula. Also, baby beef can be licked from your finger at this age, or added to the formula. At four weeks the surviving puppies should be taken off the diet of Esbilac and put on a more substantial diet, such as wet puppy meal or chopped beef. However, Esbilac powder can still be mixed in with the food for additional nutrition. The jarred baby foods of pureed meats make for a smooth changeover also, and can be blended into the diet.

HOW TO FEED THE NEWBORN PUPPIES

When the puppy is a newborn, remember that it is vitally important to keep the feeding procedure as close to the natural mother's routine as possible. The newborn puppy should be held in your lap in

A Siamese cat visits with Sena-Lak's Tijuana Brass and one of her babies at the Sena-Lak Kennels in Valois, New York.

One-week-old puppies from a Christmas litter at the Inuit Kennels in New York.

Inuit's Wild Thing and
two-year-old owner
Dorian Pascoe.

your hand in an almost upright position with the bottle at an angle to allow the entire nipple area to be full of the formula. Do not hold the bottle upright so the puppy's head has to reach straight up toward the ceiling. Do not let the puppy nurse too quickly or take in too much air and possibly get the colic. Once in a while, take the bottle away and let him rest a while and swallow several times. Before feeding, test the nipple to see that the fluid does not come out too quickly, or by the same token, too slowly so that the puppy gets tired of feeding before he has had enough to eat.

When the puppy is a little older, you can place him on his stomach on a towel to eat, and even allow him to hold on to the bottle or to "come and get it" on his own. Most puppies enjoy eating and this will be a good indication of how strong an appetite he has and his ability to consume the contents of the bottle.

It will be necessary to "burp" the puppy. Place a towel on your shoulder and hold the puppy on your shoulder as if it were a human baby, patting and rubbing it gently. This will also encourage the puppy to defecate. At this time, you should observe for diarrhea or other intestinal disorders. The puppy should eliminate after each feeding with occasional eliminations between times as well. If the puppies do not eliminate on their own after each meal, massage their stomachs and under their tails gently until they do.

You must keep the puppies clean. If there is diarrhea or if they bring up a little formula, they should be washed and dried off. Under no circumstances should fecal matter be allowed to collect on their skin or fur.

All this—plus your determination and perseverance—might save an entire litter of puppies that would otherwise have died without their real mother.

GASTRIC TORSION

Gastric torsion, or bloat, sometimes referred to simply as "twisted stomach," has become more and more prevalent. Many dogs that in the past had been thought to die of blockage of the stomach or intestines because they had swallowed toys or other foreign objects are now suspected of having been the victims of gastric torsion and the bloat that followed.

Though life can be saved by immediate surgery to untwist the organ, the rate of fatality is high. Symptoms of gastric torsion are unusual restlessness, excessive salivation, attempts to vomit, rapid respiration, pain and the eventual bloating of the abdominal region.

The cause of gastric torsion can be attributed to overeating, excess gas formation in the stomach, poor function of the stomach or intestine, or general lack of exercise. As the food ferments in the stomach, gases form which may twist the stomach in a clockwise direction so that the gas is unable to escape. Surgery, where the stomach is untwisted counter-clockwise, is the safest and most successful way to correct the situation.

To avoid the threat of gastric torsion, it is wise to keep your dog well exercised to be sure the body is functioning normally. Make sure that food and water are available for the dog at all times, thereby reducing the tendency to overeat. With self-service dry feeding, where the dog is able to eat intermittently during the day, there is not the urge to "stuff" at one time.

If you notice any of the symptoms of gastric torsion, call your veterinarian immediately! Death can result within a matter of hours!

22. GENERAL CARE AND MANAGEMENT

TATTOOING

Ninety per cent success has been reported on the return of stolen or lost dogs that have been tattooed. More and more this simple, painless, inexpensive method of positive identification for dogs is being reported all over the United States. Long popular in Canada, along with nose prints, the idea gained interest in this country when dognapping started to soar as unscrupulous people began stealing dogs for resale to research laboratories. Pet dogs that wander off and lost hunting dogs have always been a problem. The success of tattooing has been significant.

Tattooing can be done by the veterinarian for a minor fee. There are several dog "registries" that will record your dog's number and help you locate it should it be lost or stolen. The number of the dog's American Kennel Club registration is most often used on thoroughbred dogs, or the owner's Social Security number in the case of mixed breeds. The best place for the tattoo is the groin. Some prefer the inside of an ear, and the American Kennel Club has rules that the judges officiating at the AKC dog shows not penalize the dog for the tattoo mark.

The tattoo mark serves not only to identify your dog should it be lost or stolen, but offers positive identification in large kennels where several litters of the same approximate age are on the premises. It is a safety measure against unscrupulous breeders "switching" puppies. Any age is a proper age to tattoo, but for safety's sake, the sooner the better.

The buzz of the needle might cause your dog to be apprehensive, but the pricking of the needle is virtually painless. The risk of infection is negligible when done properly, and the return of your beloved pet may be the reward for taking the time to insure positive identification for your dog. Your local kennel club will know of a dog registry in your area.

Major Dick Sollinger's Christmas picture showing Ch. Chargi's Buckeye in his favorite position. Their Kunoe Kennels are in Newburgh, New York.

OUTDOOR HOUSEBREAKING

If you are particular about your dog's behavior in the house, where you expect him to be clean and respectful of the carpets and furniture, you should also want him to have proper manners outdoors. Just because the property belongs to you doesn't necessarily mean he should be allowed to empty himself any place he chooses. Before long the entire yard will be fouled and odorous and the dog will be completely irresponsible on other people's property as well. Dogs seldom recognize property lines.

If your dog does not have his own yard fenced in, he should be walked on leash before being allowed to run free and before being penned up in his own yard. He will appreciate his own run being kept clean. You will find that if he has learned his manners outside, his manners inside will be better. Good manners in "toilet training" are especially important with big dogs!

OTHER IMPORTANT OUTDOOR MANNERS

Excessive barking is perhaps the most objectionable habit a dog indulges in out of doors. It annoys neighbors and makes for a noisy dog in the house as well. A sharp jerk on the leash will stop a dog from excessive barking while walking; trees and shrubs around a dog run will cut down on barking if a dog is in his own run. However, it is unfair to block off his view entirely. Give him some view—preferably of his own home—to keep his interest. Needless to say, do not leave a dog that barks excessively out all night.

You will want your dog to bark at strangers, so allow him this privilege. Then after a few "alerting" barks tell the dog to be quiet (with the same word command each time). If he doesn't get the idea, put him on leash and let him greet callers·with you at the door until he does get the idea.

Do not let your dog jump on visitors either. Leash training may be necessary to break this habit as well. As the dog jumps in the air, pull back on the lead so that the dog is returned to the floor abruptly. If he attempts to jump up on you , carefully raise your knee and push him away by leaning against his chest.

Inuit's Zanna of Aleut, co-owned by Delores Jeffers and Sheila Balch.

Do not let your dog roam free in the neighborhood no matter how well he knows his way home. Especially do not let your dog roam free to empty himself on the neighbors' property or gardens!

A positive invitation to danger is to allow your dog to chase cars or bicycles. Throwing tin cans or chains out of car windows at them has been suggested as a cure, but can also be dangerous if they hit the dog instead of the street. Streams of water from a garden hose or water pistol are the least dangerous, but leash control is still the most scientific and most effective.

If neighbors report that your dog barks or howls or runs from window to window while you are away, crate training or room training for short periods of time may be indicated. If you expect to be away for longer periods of time, put the dog in the basement or a single room where he can do the least damage. The best solution of all is to buy him another dog or cat for companionship. Let them enjoy each other while you are away and have them both welcome you home!

GERIATRICS

If you originally purchased good healthy stock and cared for your dog throughout his life, there is no reason why you cannot expect your dog to live to a ripe old age. With research and the remarkable foods produced for dogs, especially this past decade or so, his chances of longevity have increased considerably. If you have cared for him well, your dog will be a sheer delight in his old age, just as he was while in his prime.

We can assume you have fed him properly if he is not too fat. Have you ever noticed how fat people usually have fat dogs because

Ch. Wobiska's Pogey, owned by Anita Murphy's Wilinda Kennels in Ontario, Canada. Pogey, finished in 1966, was Anita Murphy's first champion.

they indulge their dogs' appetite as they do their own? If there has been no great illness, then you will find that very little additional care and attention are needed to keep him well. Exercise is still essential, as is proper food, booster shots, and tender loving care.

Even if a heart condition develops, there is still no reason to believe your dog cannot live to an old age. A diet may be necessary, along with medication and limited exercise, to keep the condition under control. In the case of deafness, or partial blindness, additional care must be taken to protect the dog, but neither infirmity will in any way shorten his life. Prolonged exposure to temperature variances, overeating, excessive exercise, lack of sleep, or being housed with younger, more active dogs may take an unnecessary toll on the dog's energies and introduce serious trouble. Good judgment, periodic veterinary checkups and individual attention will keep your dog with you for many added years.

When discussing geriatrics, the question of when a dog becomes old or aged usually is asked. We have all heard the old saying that one year of a dog's life is equal to seven years in a human. This theory is strictly a matter of opinion, and must remain so, since so many outside factors enter into how quickly each individual dog "ages." Recently, a new chart was devised which is more realistically equivalent:

DOG	MAN
6 months	10 years
1 year	15 years
2 years	24 years
3 years	28 years
4 years	32 years
5 years	36 years
6 years	40 years
7 years	44 years
8 years	48 years
9 years	52 years
10 years	56 years
15 years	76 years
21 years	100 years

It must be remembered that such things as serious illnesses, poor food and housing, general neglect and poor beginnings as puppies will take their toll on a dog's general health and age him more quickly than a dog that has led a normal, healthy life. Let your veterinarian help you determine an age bracket for your dog in his later years.

While good care should prolong your dog's life, there are several "old age" disorders to be on the lookout for no matter how well he may be doing. The tendency toward obesity is the most common, but constipation is another. Aging teeth and a slowing down of the digestive processes may hinder digestion and cause constipation, just as any major change in diet can bring on diarrhea. There is also the possibility of loss or impairment of hearing or eyesight which will also tend to make the dog wary and distrustful. Other behavioral changes may result as well, such as crankiness, loss of patience and lack of interest; these are the most obvious changes. Other ailments may manifest themselves in the form of rheumatism, arthritis, tumors and warts, heart disease, kidney infections, male prostatism and female disorders. Of course, all of these require a veterinarian's checking the degree of seriousness and proper treatment.

Take care to avoid infectious diseases. When these hit the older dog, they can debilitate him to an alarming degree, leaving him open to more serious complications and a shorter life.

DOG INSURANCE

Much has been said for and against canine insurance, and much more will be said before this kind of protection for a dog becomes universal and/or practical. There has been talk of establishing a Blue Cross-type plan similar to that now existing for humans. However, the best insurance for your dog is *you*! Nothing compensates for tender, loving care. Like the insurance policies for humans, there will be a lot of fine print in the contracts revealing that the dog is not covered after all. These limited conditions usually make the acquisition of dog insurance expensive and virtually worthless.

Blanket coverage policies for kennels or establishments which board or groom dogs can be an advantage, especially in transporting dogs to and from their premises. For the one-dog owner, however, whose dog is a constant companion, the cost for limited coverage is not necessary.

THE HIGH COST OF BURIAL

Pet cemeteries are mushrooming across the nation. Here, as with humans, the sky can be the limit for those who wish to bury their pets ceremoniously. The costs of satin-lined caskets, grave stones, flowers, etc. run the gamut of prices to match the emotions and means of the owner. This is strictly a matter of what the bereaved owner wishes to do.

IN THE EVENT OF YOUR DEATH. . .

This is a morbid thought perhaps, but ask yourself the question, "If death were to strike at this moment, what would become of my beloved dogs?"

Perhaps you are fortunate enough to have a relative, friend or spouse who could take over immediately, if only on a temporary basis. Perhaps you have already left instructions in your last will and testament for your pet's dispensation, as well as a stipend for their perpetual care.

Provide definite instructions before a disaster occurs and your dogs are carted off to the pound, or stolen by commercially minded neighbors with "resale" in mind. It is a simple thing to instruct your lawyer about your wishes in the event of sickness or death. Leave instructions as to feeding, etc., posted on your kennel room or kitchen bulletin board, or wherever your kennel records are kept. Also, tell several people what you are doing and why. If you prefer to keep such instructions private, merely place them in sealed envelopes in a known place with directions that they are to be opened only in the

Ch. Inuit's Nikolai of Colcord pictured winning at a recent show under judge Eva B. Seeley. Nikolai also was Best of Winners at the 1971 Trenton Kennel Club Show on the way to his championship. 100% Kotzebue breeding, Nikolai is handled by Philip Marsman for co-owners Sheila Balch and Delores Jeffers of Middletown, New York.

event of your demise. Eliminate the danger of your animals suffering in the event of an emergency that prevents your personal care of them.

KEEPING RECORDS

Whether or not you have one dog, or a kennel full of them, it is wise to keep written records. It takes only a few moments to record dates of inoculations, trips to the vet, tests for worms, etc. It can avoid confusion or mistakes, or having your dog not covered with immunization if too much time elapses between shots because you have to guess at the last shot.

Make the effort to keep all dates in writing rather than trying to commit them to memory. A rabies injection date can be a problem if you have to recall that "Fido had the shot the day Aunt Mary got back from her trip abroad, and, let's see, I guess that was around the end of June."

In an emergency, these records may prove their value if your veterinarian cannot be reached and you have to use another, or if you move and have no case history on your dog for the new veterinarian. In emergencies, you do not always think clearly or accurately, and if dates, and types of serums used, etc., are a matter of record, the veterinarian can act more quickly and with more confidence.

23. YOUR DOG, YOUR VETERINARIAN, AND YOU

The purpose of this chapter is to explain why you should never attempt to be your own veterinarian. Quite the contrary, we urge emphatically that you establish good liaison with a reputable veterinarian who will help you maintain happy, healthy dogs. Our purpose is to bring you up to date on the discoveries made in modern canine medicine and to help you work with your veterinarian by applying these new developments to your own animals.

Seacourt Midnight Magic, bred by Mrs. J. Parkyns and owned by Stella Gouding. Elka was sired by Tote-Um's Tamahine of Seacourt *ex* Highnoons Chitimacha.

A white Alaskan Malamute appropriately named Sena-Lak's Abominable Snowman. Owned by Eleanore DuBuis, Sena-Lak Kennels, Valois, New York.

Sitka and her puppy with friend Sarah Lynn Perham, daughter of owner Carol Perham, Cordova Kennels, Lakeside, Connecticut.

We have provided here "thumbnail" histories of many of the most common types of diseases your dog is apt to come in contact with during his lifetime. We feel that if you know a little something about the diseases and how to recognize their symptoms, your chances of catching them in the preliminary stages will help you and your veterinarian effect a cure before a serious condition develops.

Today's dog owner is a realistic, intelligent person who learns more and more about his dog—inside and out—so that he can care for and enjoy the animal to the fullest. He uses technical terms for parts of the anatomy, has a fleeting knowledge of the miracles of surgery and is fully prepared to administer clinical care for his animals at home. This chapter is designed for study and/or reference and we hope you will use it to full advantage.

We repeat, we do *not* advocate your playing "doctor." This includes administering medication without veterinary supervision, or even doing your own inoculations. General knowledge of diseases, their symptoms and side effects will assist you in diagnosing diseases for your veterinarian. He does not expect you to be an expert, but will appreciate your efforts in getting a sick dog to him before it is too late and he cannot save its life.

ASPIRIN: A DANGER

There is a common joke about doctors telling their patients, when they telephone with a complaint, to take an aspirin, go to bed and let him know how things are in the morning! Unfortunately, that is exactly the way it turns out with a lot of dog owners who think aspirins are curealls and give them to their dogs indiscriminately. Then they call the veterinarian when the dog has an unfavorable reaction.

Aspirins are not panaceas for everything—certainly not for every dog. In an experiment, fatalities in cats treated with aspirin in one laboratory alone numbered ten out of 13 within a two-week period. Dogs' tolerance was somewhat better, as far as actual fatalities, but there was considerable evidence of ulceration in varying degrees on the stomach linings when necropsy was performed.

Aspirin has been held in the past to be almost as effective for dogs as for people when given for many of the everyday aches and pains. The fact remains, however, that medication of any kind should be administered only after veterinary consultation and a specific dosage suitable to the condition is recommended.

While aspirin is chiefly effective in reducing fever, relieving minor pains and cutting down on inflammation, the acid has been proven harmful to the stomach when given in strong doses. Only your veterinarian is qualified to determine what the dosage is, or whether it should be administered to your particular dog at all.

WHAT THE THERMOMETER CAN TELL YOU

You will notice in reading this chapter dealing with the diseases of dogs that practically everything a dog might contract in the way of sickness has basically the same set of symptoms. Loss of appetite, diarrhea, dull eyes, dull coat, warm and/or runny nose, and FEVER!

Therefore, it is most advisable to have a thermometer on hand for checking temperature. There are several inexpensive metal rectal-type thermometers that are accurate and safer than the glass variety which can be broken. This may happen either by dropping, or perhaps even breaking off in the dog because of improper insertion or an aggravated condition with the dog that makes him violently resist the injection of the thermometer. Either kind should be lubricated with Vaseline to make the insertion as easy as possible, after it has been sterilized with alcohol.

The normal temperature for a dog is 101.5° Fahrenheit, as compared to the human 98.6°. Excitement as well as illness can cause this to vary a degree or two, but any sudden or extensive rise in body temperature must be considered as cause for alarm. Your first indication will be that your dog feels unduly "warm" and this is the time to take the temperature, not when the dog becomes very ill or manifests additional serious symptoms. With a thermometer on hand, you can check temperatures quickly and perhaps prevent some illness from becoming serious.

COPROPHAGY

Perhaps the most unpleasant of all phases of dog breeding is to come up with a dog that takes to eating stool. This practice, which is referred to politely as coprophagy, is one of the unsolved mysteries in the dog world. There simply is no explanation to why some dogs do it.

However, there are several logical theories, all or any of which may be the cause. Some say nutritional deficiencies; another says that dogs inclined to gulp their food (which passes through them not entirely digested) find it still partially palatable. There is another

Sheila Balch in an informal pose with Floyd when he was five months old.

A litter of puppies bred and owned by Carol Perham, Cordova Kennels, Lakeside, Connecticut.

theory that the preservatives used in some meat are responsible for an appealing odor that remains through the digestive process. Then again poor quality meat can be so tough and unchewable that dogs swallow it whole and it passes through them in large undigested chunks.

There are others who believe the habit is strictly psychological, the result of a nervous condition or insecurity. Others believe the dog cleans up after itself because it is afraid of being punished as it was when it made a mistake on the carpet as a puppy. Others claim boredom is the reason, or even spite. Others will tell you a dog does not want its personal odor on the premises for fear of attracting other hostile animals to itself or its home.

The most logical of all explanations and the one most veterinarians are inclined to accept is that it is a deficiency of dietary enzymes. Too much dry food can be bad and many veterinarians suggest trying meat tenderizers, monosodium glutamate, or garlic powder which gives the stool a bad odor and discourages the dog. Yeast or certain vitamins or a complete change of diet are even more often suggested. By the time you try each of the above you will probably discover that the dog has outgrown the habit anyway. However, the condition cannot be ignored if you are to enjoy your dog to the fullest.

There is no set length of time that the problem persists, and the only real cure is to walk the dog on leash, morning and night and after every meal. In other words, set up a definite eating and exercising schedule before coprophagy is an established pattern.

MASTURBATION

A source of embarrassment to many dog owners, masturbation can be eliminated with a minimum of training

The dog which is constantly breeding anything and everything, including the leg of the piano or perhaps the leg of your favorite guest, can be broken of the habit by stopping its cause.

The over-sexed dog—if truly that is what he is—which will never be used for breeding can be castrated. The kennel stud dog can be broken of the habit by removing any furniture from his quarters or keeping him on leash and on verbal command when he is around people, or in the house where he might be tempted to breed pillows, people, etc.

Hormone imbalance may be another cause and your veterinarian may advise injections. Exercise can be of tremendous help. Keeping the dog's mind occupied by physical play when he is around people will also help relieve the situation.

Females might indulge in sexual abnormalities like masturbation during their heat cycle, or again, because of a hormone imbalance. But if they behave this way because of a more serious problem, a hysterectomy may be indicated.

Ch. Kailas Wicked
Witch of Inuit and
Kaila's the Ironhorse,
owned by Eileen and
Chris Gabriel of
Golden Bridge,
New York.

A sharp "no!" command when you can anticipate the act, or a sharp "no!" when caught in the act will deter most dogs if you are consistent in your correction. Hitting or other physical abuse will only confuse a dog.

RABIES

The greatest fear in the dog fancy today is still the great fear it has always been—rabies!

What has always held true about this dreadful disease still holds true today. The only way rabies can be contracted is through the saliva of a rabid dog entering the bloodstream of another animal or person. There is, of course, the Pasteur treatment for rabies which is very effective. There was of late the incident of a little boy bitten by a rabid bat having survived the disease. However, the Pasteur treatment is administered immediately if there is any question of exposure. Even more than dogs being found to be rabid, we now know that the biggest carriers are bats, skunks, foxes, rabbits and other warm-blooded animals, which pass it from one to another, since they do not have the benefit of inoculation. Dogs that run free should be inoculated for protection against these animals. For city or house dogs that never leave their owner's side, it may not be as necessary.

Best in Show winner at the 1970 Keomah Kennel Club Show was Lois and James Olmen's Ch. Glaciers Burbon King, handled by Denise Kodner. The judge was Maurice Baker, and presenting the trophy was Mrs. Sadie Emiston. Olson photograph.

For many years, Great Britain, because it is an island and because of the country's strictly enforced six-month quarantine, was entirely free of rabies. But in 1969, a British officer brought back his dog from foreign duty and the dog was found to have the disease soon after being released from quarantine. There was a great uproar about it, with Britain killing off wild and domestic animals in a great scare campaign, but the quarantine is once again down to six months and things seem to have returned to a normal, sensible attitude.

Health departments in rural towns usually provide rabies inoculations free of charge. If your dog is outdoors a great deal, or exposed to other animals that are, you might wish to call the town hall and get information on the program in your area. One cannot be too cautious about this dread disease. While the number of cases diminishes each year, there are still thousands being reported and there is still the constant threat of an outbreak where animals roam free. And never forget, there is no cure.

Rabies is caused by a neurotropic virus which can be found in the saliva, brain and sometimes the blood of the warm-blooded animal afflicted. The incubation period is usually two weeks or as long as six months, which means you can be exposed to it without any visible symptoms. As we have said, while there is still no known cure, it can be controlled. It is up to every individual to help effect this control by reporting animal bites, educating the public to the dangers and symptoms and prevention of it, so that we may reduce the fatalities.

There are two kinds of rabies; one form is called "furious," and the other is referred to as "dumb." The mad dog goes through several stages of the disease. His disposition and behavior change radically and suddenly; he becomes irritable and vicious; the eating habits alter, and he rejects food for things like stones and sticks; he be-

Four-week-old Sachem, Tasha and Charade, puppies bred and owned by the Philip Lakes, Aurora Kennels, Holbrook, Massachusetts.

comes exhausted and drools saliva out of his mouth almost constantly. He may hide in corners, look glassy eyed and suspicious, bite at the air as he races around snarling and attacking with his tongue hanging out. At this point paralysis sets in, starting at the throat so that he can no longer drink water though he desires it desperately; hence, the term hydrophobia is given. He begins to stagger and eventually convulse and death is imminent.

In "dumb" rabies paralysis is swift; the dog seeks dark, sheltered places and is abnormally quiet. Paralysis starts with the jaws, spreads down the body and death is quick. Contact by humans or other animals with the drool from either of these types of rabies on open skin can produce the fatal disease, so extreme haste and proper diagnosis is essential. In other words, you do not have to be bitten by a rabid dog to have the virus enter your system. An open wound or cut that comes in touch with the saliva is all that is needed.

The incubation and degree of infection can vary. You usually contract the disease faster if the wound is near the head, since the virus travels to the brain through the spinal cord. The deeper the wound, the more saliva is injected into the body, the more serious the infection. So, if bitten by a dog under any circumstances—or any warm-blooded animal for that matter—immediately wash out the wound with soap and water, bleed it profusely, and see your doctor as soon as possible.

Also, be sure to keep track of the animal that bit, if at all possible. When rabies is suspected the public health officer will need to send the animal's head away to be analyzed. If it is found to be rabies free, you will not need to undergo treatment. Otherwise, your doctor may advise that you have the Pasteur treatment, which is extremely painful. It is rather simple, however, to have the veterinarian examine a dog for rabies without having the dog sent away for positive diagnosis of the disease. A ten-day quarantine is usually all that is necessary for everyone's peace of mind.

Rabies is no respecter of age, sex or geographical location. It is found all over the world from North Pole to South Pole, and has nothing to do with the old wives' tale of dogs going mad in the hot summer months. True, there is an increase in reported cases during summer, but only because that is the time of the year for animals to roam free in good weather and during the mating season when the battle of the sexes is taking place. Inoculation and a keen eye for symptoms and bites on our dogs and other pets will help control the disease until the cure is found.

VACCINATIONS

If you are to raise a puppy, or a litter of puppies, successfully, you must adhere to a realistic and strict schedule of vaccination. Many puppyhood diseases can be fatal—all of them are debilitating.

Tote-Um's Arctic Hawk, imported from the United States in 1966. This multiple Best of Breed winner was also a Best of Rare Breeds and Best Any Other Variety winner at Crufts, England. Co-owners are Mesdames Parkyns and Edmonds. Breeder Dianne Ross of Cle Elum, Washington.

According to the latest statistics, 98 per cent of all puppies are being inoculated after 12 weeks of age against the dread distemper, hepatitis and leptospirosis and manage to escape these horrible infections. Orphaned puppies should be vaccinated every two weeks until the age of 12 weeks. Distemper and hepatitis live-virus vaccine should be used, since they are not protected with the colostrum normally supplied to them through the mother's milk. Puppies weaned at six to seven weeks should also be inoculated repeatedly because they will no longer be receiving mother's milk. While not all will receive protection from the serum at this early age, it should be given and they should be vaccinated once again at both nine and 12 weeks of age.

Leptospirosis vaccination should be given at four months of age with thought given to booster shots if the disease is known in the area, or in the case of show dogs which are exposed on a regular basis to many dogs from far and wide. While annual boosters are in order for distemper and hepatitis, every two or three years is sufficient for leptospirosis, unless there is an outbreak in your immediate area. The one exception should be the pregnant bitch since there is reason to believe that inoculation might cause damage to the fetus.

Strict observance of such a vaccination schedule will not only keep your dog free of these debilitating diseases, but will prevent an epidemic in your kennel, or in your locality, or to the dogs which are competing at the shows.

SNAKEBITE

As field trials and hunts and the like become more and more popular with dog enthusiasts, the incident of snakebite becomes more of a likelihood. Dogs that are kept outdoors in runs or dogs that work the fields and roam on large estates are also likely victims.

Most veterinarians carry snakebite serum, and snakebite kits are sold to dog owners for just such purpose. To catch a snakebite in time might mean the difference between life and death, and whether your area is populated with snakes or not, it behooves you to know what to do in case it happens to you or your dog.

Your primary concern should be to get to a doctor or veterinarian immediately. The victim should be kept as quiet as possible (excitement or activity spreads the venom through the body more quickly) and if possible the wound should be bled enough to clean it out before applying a tourniquet, if the bite is severe.

First of all, it must be determined if the bite is from a poisonous or non-poisonous snake. If the bite carries two horseshoe shaped pinpoints of a double row of teeth, the bite can be assumed to be non-poisonous. If the bite leaves two punctures or holes—the result of the two fangs carrying venom—the bite is very definitely poisonous and time is of the essence.

Recently, physicians have come up with an added help in the case of snakebite. A first aid treatment referred to as hypothermia, which is the application of ice to the wound to lower body temperature to a point where the venom spreads less quickly, minimizes swelling, helps prevent infection and has some influence on numbing the pain. If ice is not readily available, the bite may be soaked in ice-cold water. But even more urgent is the need to get the victim to a hospital or a veterinarian for additional treatment.

EMERGENCIES

No matter how well you run your kennel or keep an eye on an individual dog, there will almost invariably be some emergency at some time that will require quick treatment until you get the animal to the veterinarian. The first and most important thing to remember is to keep calm! You will think more clearly and your animal will need to know he can depend on you to take care of him. However, he will be frightened and you must beware of fear biting. Therefore, do not shower him with kisses and endearments at this time, no matter how

Six-month-old Inuit's Chickasaw with his owner, Enid Ross of New York.

sympathetic you feel. Comfort him reassuringly, but keep your wits about you. Before getting him to the veterinarian try to alleviate the pain and shock.

If you can take even a minor step in this direction it will be a help toward the final cure. Listed here are a few of the emergencies which might occur and what you can do AFTER you have called the vet and told him your are coming.

BURNS

If you have been so foolish as not to turn your pot handles toward the back of the stove—for your children's sake as well as your dog's— and the dog is burned, apply ice or ice cold water and treat for shock. Electrical or chemical burns are treated the same; but with an acid or alkali burn, use, respectively, a bicarbonate of soda or vinegar solution. Check the advisability of covering the burn when you call the veterinarian.

DROWNING

Most animals love the water, but sometimes get in "over their heads." Should your dog take in too much water, hold him upside down and open his mouth so that water can empty from the lungs, then apply artificial respiration, or mouth-to-mouth resuscitation. Then treat for shock by covering him with a blanket, administering a stimulant such as coffee with sugar, and soothing him with voice and hand.

FITS AND CONVULSIONS

Prevent the dog from thrashing about and injuring himself, cover with a blanket and hold down until you can get him to the veterinarian.

FROSTBITE

There is no excuse for an animal getting frostbite if you are on your toes and care for the animal. However, should frostbite set in, thaw out the affected area slowly with a circulatory motion and stimulation. Use vaseline to help keep the skin from peeling off and/or drying out.

HEART ATTACK

Be sure the animal keeps breathing by applying artificial respiration. A mild stimulant may be used and give him plenty of air. Treat for shock as well, and get to the veterinarian quickly.

Aurora's Marko at eleven months of age with owner John Breda. Marko was sired by American and Canadian Ch. Bernard *ex* Aurora's Kantishna Meadow Winter Wind. Breeder, Judith Lake. Marko is pictured winning Reserve Winners Dog at the 1975 Providence Kennel Club Show.

SUFFOCATION

Artificial respiration and treat for shock with plenty of air.

SUN STROKE

Cooling the dog off immediately is essential. Ice packs, submersion in ice water, and plenty of cool air are needed.

WOUNDS

Open wounds or cuts which produce bleeding must be treated with hydrogen peroxide and tourniquets should be used if bleeding is excessive. Also, shock treatment must be given, and the animal must be kept warm.

THE FIRST AID KIT

It would be sheer folly to try to operate a kennel or to keep a dog without providing for certain emergencies that are bound to crop up when there are active dogs around. Just as you would provide a first aid kit for people you should also provide a first aid kit for the animals on the premises.

The first aid kit should contains the following items:

BFI or other medicated powder
jar of Vaseline
Q-tips
bandage—1 inch gauze
adhesive tape
Band-Aids
cotton
boric acid powder

Fourteen-month-old Aleut's Kanuck of Inuit, photographed in Anchorage, Alaska, with owner Barbara Litwin and a friend.

A trip to your veterinarian is always safest, but there are certain preliminaries for cuts and bruises of a minor nature that you can care for yourself.

Cuts, for instance, should be washed out and medicated powder or Vaseline applied with a bandage. The lighter the bandage the better so that the most air possible can reach the wound. Q-tips can be used for removing debris from the eyes after which a mild solution of boric acid wash can be applied. As for sores, use dry powder on wet sores, and Vaseline on dry sores. Use cotton for washing out wounds and drying them.

A particular caution must be given here on bandaging. Make sure that the bandage is not too tight to hamper the dog's circulation. Also, make sure the bandage is made correctly so that the dog does not bite at it trying to get it off. A great deal of damage can be done to a wound by a dog tearing at a bandage to get it off. If you notice the dog is starting to bite at it, do it over or put something on the bandage that smells and tastes bad to him. Make sure, however, that the solution does not soak through the bandage and enter the wound. Sometimes, if it is a leg wound, a sock or stocking slipped on the dog's leg will cover the bandage edges and will also keep it clean.

HOW NOT TO POISON YOUR DOG

Ever since the appearance of Rachel Carson's book *Silent Spring,* people have been asking, "Just how dangerous are chemicals?" In the animal world where disinfectants, room deodorants, parasitic sprays, solutions and aerosols are so widely used, the question has taken on even more meaning. Veterinarians are beginning to ask, "What kind of disinfectant do you use?" or "Have you any fruit trees that have been sprayed recently?" When animals are brought in to their offices in a toxic condition, or for unexplained death, or when entire litters of puppies die mysteriously, there is good reason to ask such questions.

The popular practice of protecting animals against parasites has given way to their being exposed to an alarming number of commercial products, some of which are dangerous to their very lives. Even flea collars can be dangerous, especially if they get wet or somehow touch the genital regions or eyes. While some products are a great deal more poisonous than others, great care must be taken that they be applied in proportion to the size of the dog and the area to be covered. Many a dog has been taken to the vet with an unusual skin problem that was a direct result of having been bathed with a detergent rather than a proper shampoo. Certain products that are safe for dogs can be fatal for cats. Extreme care must be taken to read all ingredients and instructions carefully before use on any animal.

The same caution must be given to outdoor chemicals. Dog owners must question the use of fertilizers on their lawns. Lime, for in-

Eileen Gabriel and four-month-old Kaila's The Wicked Witch of Inuit.

stance, can be harmful to a dog's feet. The unleashed dog that covers the neighborhood on his daily rounds is open to all sorts of tree and lawn sprays and insecticides that may prove harmful to him, if not as a poison, as a producer of an allergy. Many puppy fatalities are reported when they consume mothballs.

There are various products found around the house which can be lethal, such as rat poison, boric acid, hand soap, detergents, and insecticides. The garage too may provide dangers: antifreeze for the car, lawn, garden and tree sprays, paints, etc., are all available for tipping over and consuming. All poisons should be placed on high shelves for the sake of your children as well as your animals.

Perhaps the most readily available of all household poisons are plants. Household plants are almost all poisonous, even if taken in small quantities. Some of the most dangerous are the elephant ear, the narcissus bulb, any kind of ivy leaves, burning bush leaves, the jimson weed, the dumb cane weed, mock orange fruit, castor beans, Scotch broom seeds, the root or seed of the plant called four o'clock, cyclamen, pimpernel, lily of the valley, the stem of the sweet pea, rhododendrons of any kind, spider lily bulbs, bayonet root, foxglove leaves, tulip bulbs, monkshood roots, azalea, wisteria, poinsettia leaves, mistletoe, hemlock, locoweed and arrowglove. In all, there are over 500 poisonous plants in the United States. Peach, elderberry and cherry trees can cause cyanide poisoning if the bark is consumed. Rhubarb leaves either raw or cooked can cause death or violent convulsions. Check out your closets, fields and grounds around your home to see what might be of danger to your pets.

Backpacking in Geneva, Switzerland. . . the children of Roman Beier with Inuit's Honkita of Sillanouk and a Husky bitch photographed in September, 1974.

SYMPTOMS OF POISONING

Be on the lookout for vomiting, hard or labored breathing, whimpering, stomach cramps, and trembling as a prelude to the convulsions. Any delay in a visit to your veterinarian can mean death. Take along the bottle or package or a sample of the plant you suspect to be the cause to help the veterinarian determine the correct antidote.

The most common type of poisoning, which accounts for nearly one-fourth of all animal victims, is staphylococcic-infected food. Salmonella ranks third. These can be avoided by serving fresh food and not letting it lie around in hot weather.

There are also many insect poisonings caused by animals eating cockroaches, spiders, flies, butterflies, etc. Toads and some frogs give off a fluid which can make a dog foam at the mouth—and even kill him—if he bites just a little too hard!

Some misguided dog owners think it is "cute" to let their dogs enjoy a cocktail with them before dinner. There can be serious effects resulting from encouraging a dog to drink—sneezing fits, injuries as a result of intoxication, and heart stoppage are just a few. Whiskey for medicinal purposes, or beer for brood bitches should be administered only on the advice of your veterinarian.

There have been cases of severe damage and death when dogs emptied ash trays and consumed cigarettes, resulting in nicotine poisoning. Leaving a dog alone all day in a house where there are cigarettes available on a coffee table is asking for trouble. Needless to say, the same applies to marijuana. The narcotic addict who takes his dog along with him on "a trip" does not deserve to have a dog. All the ghastly side effects are as possible for the dog as for the addict, and for a person to submit an animal to this indignity is indeed despicable. Don't think it doesn't happen. Ask the veterinarians that practice near some of your major hippie havens! Unfortunately, in all our major cities the practice is becoming more and more a problem for the veterinarian.

Be on the alert and remember that in the case of any type of poisoning, the best treatment is prevention.

Alaskan Malamute Club of America members Sheila Land and Warren Rice's children pictured in Utah with their Alaskan Malamute puppies.

Darling little male puppy Alamal's Pax Alaska, bred and owned by Nick and Dianne Koch. Sire was American, Canadian and Bermudian Ch. Inuit's Wooly Bully ex Sena-Lak Eldor Northwind.

THE CURSE OF ALLERGY

The heartbreak of a child being forced to give up a beloved pet because he is suddenly found to be allergic to it is a sad but true story. Many families claim to be unable to have dogs at all; others seem to be able only to enjoy them on a restricted basis. Many children know animals only through occasional visits to a friend's house or the zoo.

While modern veterinary science has produced some brilliant allergists, such as Dr. Edward Baker of New Jersey, the field is still working on a solution for those who suffer from exposure to their pets. There is no permanent cure as yet.

Over the last quarter of a century there have been many attempts at a permanent cure, but none has proven successful, because the treatment was needed too frequently, or was too expensive to maintain over extended periods of time.

Ten-week-old Lucifer winning Best of Breed over 32 other Malamute puppies at a Naugatuk, Connecticut match show under judge Bob Tongren. Owner-handler-breeder: Sheila Balch.

However, we find that most people who are allergic to their animals are also allergic to a variety of other things as well. By eliminating the other irritants, and by taking medication given for the control of allergies in general, many are able to keep pets on a restricted basis. This may necessitate the dog's living outside the house, being groomed at a professional grooming parlor instead of by the owner, or merely being kept out of the bedroom at night. A discussion of this "balance" factor with your medical and veterinary doctors may give new hope to those willing to try.

A paper presented by Mathilde M. Gould, M.D., a New York allergist, before the American Academy of Allergists in the 1960's, and reported in the September-October 1964 issue of the *National Humane Review* magazine, offered new hope to those who are allergic by a method referred to as hyposensitization. You may wish to write to the magazine and request the article for discussion with your medical and veterinary doctors on your individual problem.

Ch. Cordova's Tasha shown winning Best of Breed from the classes over Specials under Mrs. Milton Seeley at the 1973 Northshore Kennel Club Show. Owner-handled by Carol Perham, Cordova Kennels, Lakeside, Connecticut.

DO ALL DOGS CHEW?

All young dogs chew! Chewing is the best possible method of cutting teeth and exercising gums. Every puppy goes through this teething process. True, it can be destructive if not watched carefully, and it is really the responsibility of every owner to prevent the damage before it occurs.

When you see a puppy pick up an object to chew, immediately remove it from his mouth with a sharp "No!" and replace the object with a Nylon or rawhide bone which should be provided for him to do his serious chewing. Puppies take anything and everything into their mouths so they should be provided with proper toys which they cannot chew up and swallow.

BONES

There are many opinions on the kind of bones a dog should have. Anyone who has lost a puppy or dog because of a bone chip puncturing the stomach or intestinal wall will say "no bones" except for the

Nylon or rawhide kind you buy in pet shops. There are those who say shank or knuckle bones are permissible. Use your own judgment, but when there are adequate processed bones which you know to be safe, why risk a valuable animal? Cooked bones, soft enough to be pulverized and put in the food can be fed if they are reduced almost to a powder. If you have the patience for this sort of thing, okay. Otherwise, stick to the commercial products.

As for dogs and puppies chewing furniture, shoes, etc., replace the object with something allowable and safe and put yourself on record as remembering to close closet doors. Keep the puppy in the same room with you so you can stand guard over the furniture.

Electrical cords and sockets, or wires of any kind, present a dangerous threat to chewers. Glass dishes which can be broken are hazardous if not picked up right after feeding.

Chewing can also be a form of frustration or nervousness. Dogs sometimes chew for spite, if owners leave them alone too long or too often. Bitches will sometimes chew if their puppies are taken away from them too soon; insecure puppies often chew thinking they're nursing. Puppies which chew wool or blankets or carpet corners or certain types of materials may have a nutritional deficiency or something lacking in their diet, such as craving the starch that might be left in material after washing. Perhaps the articles have been near something that tastes good and they retain the odor.

The act of chewing has no connection with particular breeds or ages, any more than there is a logical reason for dogs to dig holes outdoors or dig on wooden floors indoors.

So we repeat, it is up to you to be on guard at all times until the need—or habit—passes.

HIP DYSPLASIA

Hip dysplasia, or HD, is one of the most widely discussed of all animal afflictions, since it has appeared in varying degrees in just about every breed of dog. True, the larger breeds seem most susceptible, but it has hit the small breeds and is beginning to be recognized in cats as well.

While HD in man has been recorded as far back as 370 B.C., HD in dogs was more than likely referred to as rheumatism until veterinary research came into the picture. In 1935, Dr. Otto Schales, at Angell Memorial Hospital in Boston, wrote a paper on hip dysplasia and classified the four degrees of dysplasia of the hip joint as follows:

Grade 1—slight (poor fit between ball and socket)

Grade 2—moderate (moderate but obvious shallowness of the socket)

Grade 3—severe (socket quite flat)

Grade 4—very severe (complete displacement of head of femur at early age)

HD is an incurable, hereditary, though not congenital disease of the hip sockets. It is transmitted as a dominant trait with irregular manifestations. Puppies appear normal at birth but the constant wearing away of the socket means the animal moves more and more on muscle, thereby presenting a lameness, a difficulty in getting up and severe pain in advanced cases.

The degree of severity can be determined around six months of age, but its presence can be noticed from two months of age. The problem is determined by X-ray, and if pain is present it can be relieved temporarily by medication. Exercise should be avoided since motion encourages the wearing away of the bone surfaces.

Dogs with HD should not be shown or bred, if quality in the breed is to be maintained. It is essential to check a pedigree for dogs known to be dysplastic before breeding, since this disease can be dormant for many generations.

ELBOW DYSPLASIA

The same condition can also affect the elbow joints and is known as elbow dysplasia. This also causes lameness, and dogs so affected should not be used for breeding.

PATELLAR DYSPLASIA

Some of the smaller breeds of dogs also suffer from patella dysplasia, or dislocation of the knee. This can be treated surgically, but the surgery by no means abolishes the hereditary factor. Therefore, these dogs should not be used for breeding.

All dogs—in any breed—should be X-rayed before being used for breeding. The X-ray should be read by a competent veterinarian, and the dog declared free and clear.

HD PROGRAM IN GREAT BRITAIN

The British Veterinary Association (BVA) has made an attempt to control the spread of HD by appointing a panel of members of their profession who have made a special study of the disease to read X-rays. Dogs over one year of age may be X-rayed and certified as free. Forms are completed in triplicate to verify the tests. One copy remains with the panel, one copy is for the owner's veterinarian, and one for the owner. A record is also sent to the British Kennel Club for those wishing to check on a particular dog for breeding purposes.

THE UNITED STATES REGISTRY

In the United States we have a central Hip Dysplasia Foundation, known as the OFA (Orthopedic Foundation for Animals). This HD control registry was formed in 1966. X-rays are sent for expert evaluation by qualified radiologists.

All you need do for complete information on getting an X-ray for your dog is to write to the Orthopedic Foundation for Animals at 817 Virginia Ave., Columbia, Mo., 65201, and request their dysplasia packet. There is no charge for this kit. It contains an envelope large enough to hold your X-ray film (which you will have taken by your own veterinarian), and a drawing showing how to position the dog properly for X-ray. There is also an application card for proper identification of the dog. Then, hopefully, your dog will be certified "normal." You will be given a registry number which you can put on his pedigree, use in your advertising, and rest assured your breeding program is in good order.

All X-rays should be sent to the address above. Any other information you might wish to have may be requested from Mrs. Robert Bower, OFA, Route 1, Constantine, Mo., 49042.

We cannot urge strongly enough the importance of doing this. While it involves time and effort, the reward in the long run will more than pay for your trouble. To see the heartbreak of parents and children when their beloved dog has to be put to sleep because of severe hip dysplasia as the result of bad breeding is a sad experience. Don't let this happen to your or to those who will purchase your puppies!

Additionally, we should mention that there is a method of palpation to determine the extent of affliction. This can be painful if the animal is not properly prepared for the examination. There have also been attempts to replace the animal's femur and socket. This is not only expensive, but the percentage of success is small.

For those who refuse to put their dog down, there is a new surgical technique which can relieve pain, but in no way constitutes a cure. This technique involves the severing of the pectinius muscle which for some unknown reason brings relief from pain over a period of many months—even up to two years. Two veterinary colleges in the United States are performing this operation at the present time. However, the owner must also give permission to "de-sex" the dogs at the time of the muscle severance. This is a safety measure to help stamp out hip dysplasia, since obviously the condition itself remains and can be passed on.

24. THE BLIGHT OF PARASITES

Anyone who has ever spent countless hours peering down intently at his dog's warm, pink stomach waiting for a flea to appear will readily understand why we call this chapter the "blight of parasites." For it is that dreaded onslaught of the pesky flea that heralds the subsequent arrival of worms.

If you have seen even one flea scoot across that vulnerable expanse of skin you can be sure there are more fleas lurking on other favorite areas of your dog. They seldom travel alone. So it is now an established fact that *la puce*, as the French would say when referring to the flea, has set up housekeeping on your dog and it is going to demand a great deal of your time before you manage to evict them completely, and probably just temporarily, no matter which species your dog is harboring.

Fleas are not always choosy about their host, but chances are your dog has what is commonly known as *Ctenocephalides canis*, the dog flea. If you are a lover of cats also, your dog might even be playing host to a few *Ctenocephalides felis*, the cat flea, or vice versa! The only thing you can be really sure of is that your dog is supporting an entire community of them, all hungry and all sexually oriented, and you are going to have to be persistent in your campaign to get rid of them.

One of the chief reasons they are so difficult to catch is that what they lack in beauty and eyesight (they are blind at birth, throughout infancy and see very poorly or are blind during adulthood,) they make up for in their fantastic ability to jump and scurry about.

While this remarkable ability to jump—some say 150 times the length of their bodies—stands them in good stead with circus entrepeneurs and has given them claim to fame as chariot pullers and acrobats in side show attractions, the dog owner can be reduced to tears at the very thought of the onset of fleas.

Modern research has provided a remedy in the form of flea sprays, dips, collars and tags which can be successful in varying degrees. But there are those who swear by the good old-fashioned methods of removing them by hand, which can be a challenge to your sanity as well as your dexterity.

Since the fleas' conformation (they are built like envelopes, long and flat) with their spiny skeletal system on the outside of their bodies is specifically provided for slithering through hair forests, they are given a distinct advantage to start with. Two antennae on the head select the best spot for digging and then two mandibles penetrate the skin and hit a blood vessel. It is also at this moment that the flea brings into play his spiny contours to prop himself against a few surrounding hairs which prevent him from being scratched off as he puts the bite on your dog. A small tubular tongue is then lowered into the hole to draw out blood and another tube is injected into the hole to pump the saliva of the flea into the wound which prevents the blood from clotting. This allows the flea to drink freely. Simultaneously your dog jumps into the air and gets one of those back legs into action scratching endlessly and in vain.

Now while you may catch an itinerant flea as he mistakenly shortcuts across your dog's stomach, the best hunting grounds are usually in the deep fur down along the dog's back from neck to the base of the tail. However, the flea like every other creature on earth must have water, so several times during its residency it will make its way to the moister areas of your dog, such as the corners of the mouth, the eyes or the genital areas. This is when the flea collars and tags are useful. The fumes from them prevent the fleas from passing the neck to get to the head of your dog.

Your dog can usually support several generations of fleas if he doesn't scratch himself to death or go out of his mind with the itching in the interim. The population of the flea is insured by the strong mating instinct and the wise personal decision of the female flea as to the best time to deposit her eggs. She has the useful capacity to store semen until the time is right to lay the eggs after some previous brief encounter with a passing member of the opposite sex.

When that time comes for her to lay the eggs, she does so without so much as a backward glance and moves on. The dog, during a normal day's wandering, shakes the eggs off along his way, and there the eggs remain until hatched and the baby fleas are ready to jump back on a dog. If any of the eggs remain on the dog, chances are your dog will help them emerge from their shells with his scratching when some adult flea passes in the vicinity.

Larval fleas look like very small and slender maggots; they begin their lives feasting off their own egg shells until your dog comes along and offers the return to the world of adult fleas, whose excrement provides the predigested blood pellets they must have to thrive. They cannot survive on fresh blood, nor are they capable at this tender age of digging for it themselves. We are certain that the expression "two can eat as cheaply as one" originated after some curious scientist made a detailed study of the life cycle of the flea.

After a couple of weeks of this free loading, the baby flea makes his own cocoon and becomes a pupa. This stage lasts long enough for the larval flea to grow legs, mandibles, and sharp spines and to flatten out and in general get to be identifiable as the commonly known and obnoxious *Ctenocephalides canis*. The process can take several weeks or several months, depending on weather conditions, heat, moisture, etc., but generally three weeks is all that is required to enable it to start chomping on your dog in its own right.

And so the life of the flea is renewed and begun again, and if you don't have plans to stem the tide, you will certainly see a population explosion that will make the human one resemble an endangered species. Getting rid of fleas can be accomplished by the aforementioned spraying of the dog, or the flea collars and tags, but air, sunshine and a good shaking out of beds, bedding, carpets, cushions, etc., certainly must be undertaken to get rid of the eggs or larvae lying around the premises.

However, if you love the thrill of the chase, and have the stomach for it, you can still try to catch them on safari across your dog's stomach. Your dog will love the attention, that is, if you don't keep pinching a bit of skin instead of that little blackish critter. Chances are

Aurora's Suque, bred and owned by Judith A. Lake, Aurora Kennels, Holbrook, Massachusetts. This darling puppy is pictured here at ten weeks of age.

Ch. Spawn's T'Domar's Panda, Best of Breed at one of the National Specialties. This lovely bitch is owned by Robert Spawn.

great you will come up with skin rather than the flea and your dog will lose interest and patience.

Should you be lucky enough to get hold of one, you must either squeeze it to death (which isn't likely) or break it in two with a sharp, strong fingernail (which also isn't likely) or you must release it *underwater* in the toilet bowl and flush immediately. This prospect is only slightly more likely. We strongly suggest that you shape up, clean up, shake out and spray—on a regular basis.

There are those people, however, who are much more philosophical about the flea, since, like the cockroach, it has been around since the beginning of the world. For instance, that old-time philosopher, David Harum, who has been much quoted with his remark, "A reasonable amount of fleas is good for a dog. They keep him from broodin' on bein' a dog." We would rather agree with John Donne who in his *Devotions* reveals that, "The flea, though he kill none, he does all the harm he can." This is especially true if your dog is a show dog! If the scratching doesn't ruin the coat, the inevitable infestations of the parasites the fleas will leave with your dog will!

So we readily see that dogs can be afflicted by both internal and external parasites. The external parasites are known as the aforementioned fleas, plus ticks and lice; while all of these are bothersome, they can be treated. However, the internal parasites, or worms of various kinds, are usually well-infested before discovery and require more substantial means of ridding the dog of them completely.

341

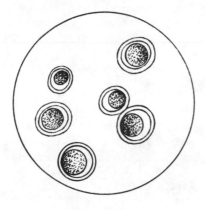

**Round Worm
(Ascarid)**

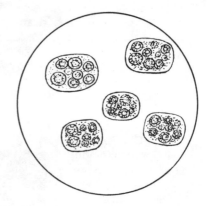

Tapeworm

Hookworm

Whipworm

Eggs of certain parasites commonly seen in dogs.

INTERNAL PARASITES

The most common worms are the round worms. These, like many other worms, are carried and spread by the flea and go through a cycle within the dog host. They are excreted in egg or larval form and passed on to other dogs in this manner.

Worm medicine should be prescribed by a veterinarian, and dogs should be checked for worms at least twice a year, or every three months if there is a known epidemic in your area, and during the summer months when fleas are plentiful.

Major types of worms are hookworms, whipworms, tapeworms (the only non-round worm in this list), ascarids (the "typical" round worms), heartworms, kidney and lung worms. Each can be peculiar to a part of the country or may be carried by a dog from one area to another. Kidney and lung worms are quite rare, fortunately. The others are not. Symptoms for worms might be vomiting intermittently, eating grass, lack of pep, bloated stomach, rubbing their tail along the ground, loss of weight, dull coat, anemia and pale gums, eye discharge, or unexplained nervousness and irritability. A dog with worms will usually eat twice as much as he normally would also.

Never worm a sick dog, or a pregnant bitch after the first two weeks she has been bred, and never worm a constipated dog. . . it will retain the strong medicine within the body for too long a time. The best, safest way to determine the presence of worms is to test for them before they do excessive damage.

HOW TO TEST FOR WORMS

Worms can kill your dog if the infestation is severe enough. Even light infestations of worms can debilitate a dog to the point where he is more susceptible to other serious diseases that can kill, if the worms do not.

Today's medication for worming is relatively safe and mild, and worming is no longer the traumatic experience for either dog or owner that it used to be. Great care must be given, however, to the proper administration of the drugs. Correct dosage is a "must" and clean quarters are essential to rid your kennel of these parasites. It is almost impossible to find an animal that is completely free of parasites, so we must consider worming as a necessary evil.

However mild today's medicines may be, it is inadvisable to worm a dog unnecessarily. There are simple tests to determine the presence of worms and this chapter is designed to help you learn how to make these tests yourself. Veterinarians charge a nominal fee for this service, if it is not part of their regular office visit examination. It is a simple matter to prepare fecal slides that you can read yourself on a periodic basis. Over the years it will save you much time and money, especially if you have more than one dog or a large kennel.

All that is needed by way of equipment is a microscope with 100x power. These can be purchased in the toy department in a department or regular toy store for a few dollars, depending on what else you want to get with it, but the basic, least expensive sets come with the necessary glass slides and attachments.

After the dog has defecated, take an applicator stick, or a toothpick with a flat end, or even an old-fashioned wooden matchstick, and gouge off a piece of the stool about the size of a small pea. Have one of the glass slides ready with a large drop of water on it. Mix the two together until you have a cloudy film over a large area of the slide. This smear should be covered with another slide, or a cover slip—though it is possible to obtain readings with just the one open slide. Place your slide under the microscope and prepare to focus in on it. To read the slide you will find that your eye should follow a certain pattern. Start at the top and read from left to right, then right back to the left side and then left over to the right side once again until you have looked at every portion of the slide from the top left to the bottom right side, as illustrated here:

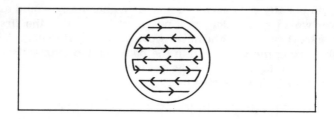

Make sure that your smear is not too thick or watery or the reading will be too dark and confused to make proper identification. Included in this chapter are drawings which will show you what to look for when reading the slides to identify the four most common varieties of worms. If you decide you would rather not make your own fecal examinations, but would prefer to have the veterinarian do it, the proper way to present a segment of the stool for him to examine is as follows:

After the dog has defecated, a portion of the stool, say a square inch from different sections of it, should be placed in a glass jar or plastic container, and labeled with the dog's name and address of the owner. If the sample cannot be examined within three to four hours after passage, it should be refrigerated. Your opinion as to what variety of worms you suspect is sometimes helpful to the veterinarian and may be noted on the label of the jar you submit to him for the examination.

Checking for worms on a regular basis is advisable not only for the welfare of the dog but for the protection of your family, since most worms are transmissible, under certain circumstances, to humans.

25. DICTIONARY OF DOG DISEASES

AN AID TO DIAGNOSIS

—A—

ABORTION—The premature expulsion of embryos from the uterus. If part of a fetus is left in the uterus, serious infection may occur. The first indication of this will be high fever, dry nose and lethargy. The immediate services of a veterinarian are necessary.

ABSCESS—A skin eruption characterized by a localized collection of pus formed as a result of disintegrating tissues of the body. Abscesses may be acute or chronic. An acute abscess forms rapidly and will more than likely burst within a week. It is accompanied by pain, redness, heat and swelling, and may cause a rise in temperature. An abscess is usually the result of infection of a bacterial nature. Treatment consists of medication in the form of antibiotics and salves, ointments, powders or a poultice designed to bring it to a head. A chronic abscess is a slow-developing headless lump surrounded by gathering tissue. This infection is usually of internal origin, and painless unless found in a sensitive area of the body. The same antibiotics and medications are used. Because abscesses of this nature are slow in developing, they are generally slow in dissolving.

ACARUS—One of the parasitic mites which cause mange.

ACHONDROPLASIA—A disease which results in the stunting of growth, or dwarfing of the limbs before birth.

ADENOMA—A non-inflammatory growth or benign tumor found in a prominent gland; most commonly found in the mammary gland of the bitch.

AGALACTIA—A contagious, viral disease resulting in lowered or no production of milk by a nursing bitch. It usually appears in warm weather, and is accompanied by fever and loss of appetite. Abscesses may also form. In chronic cases the mammary gland itself may atrophy.

ALARIASIS—An infection caused by flukes (*Alaria arisaemoides*), which are ingested by the dog. They pass on to the bronchial tract and into the small intestine where they grow to maturity and feed on intestinal contents.

Ch. Tote-Um's Arctic Panther finished his championship in five consecutive shows with four majors. A team dog, he was bred and owned by Dianne Ross, Tote-Um Kennels, Cle Elum, Washington. Panther's sire was Ch. Voyageur's Cougar *ex* Tote-Um's Tigar Woman.

ALLERGY—Dogs can be allergic as well as people to outdoor or indoor surroundings, such as carpet fuzz, pillow stuffings, food, pollen, etc. Recent experiments in hyposensitization have proved effective in many cases when injections are given with follow-up "boosters." Sneezing, coughing, nasal discharges, runny, watery eyes, etc., are all symptomatic.

ALOPECIA—A bare spot, or lack of full growth of hair on a portion of the body; another name for baldness and can be the end result of a skin condition.

AMAUROSIS—Sometimes called "glass eye." A condition that may occur during a case of distemper if the nervous system has been affected, or head injuries sustained. It is characterized by the animal bumping into things or by a lack of coordination. The condition is incurable and sooner or later the optic nerve becomes completely paralyzed.

ANALGESIA—Loss of ability to feel pain with the loss of consciousness or the power to move a part of the body. The condition may be induced by drugs which act on the brain or central nervous system.

ANAL SAC OBSTRUCTION—The sacs on either side of the rectum, just inside the anus, at times may become clogged. If the condition persists, it is necessary for the animal to be assisted in their opening, so that they do not become infected and/or abscess. Pressure is applied by the veterinarian and the glands release a thick, horrible-smelling excretion. Antibiotics or a "flushing" of the glands if infected is the usual treatment, but at the first sign of discomfort in the dog's eliminating, or a "sliding along" the floor, it is wise to check for clogged anal glands.

ANASARCA—Dropsy of the connective tissues of the skin. It is occasionally encountered in fetuses and makes whelping difficult.

ANEMIA—A decrease of red blood cells which are the cells that carry oxygen to the body tissues. Causes are usually severe infestation of parasites, bad diet, or blood disease. Transfusions and medications can be given to replace red blood cells, but the disease is sometimes fatal.

ANEURYSM—A rupture or dilation of a major blood vessel, causing a bulge or swelling of the affected part. Blood gathers in the tissues forming a swelling. It may be caused by strain, injury, or when arteries are weakened by debilitating disease or old age. Surgery is needed to remove the clot.

ANESTROUS—When a female does not come into heat.

ANTIPERISTALSIS—A term given to the reverse action of the normal procedures of the stomach or intestine, which brings their contents closer to the mouth.

ANTIPYRETICS—Drugs or methods used to reduce temperature during fevers. These may take the form of cold baths, purgatives, etc.

ANTISPASMODICS—Medications which reduce spasms of the muscular tissues and soothe the nerves and muscles involved.

ANTISIALICS—Term applied to substances used to reduce excessive salivation.

ARSENIC POISONING—Dogs are particularly susceptible to this type of poisoning. There is nausea, vomiting, stomach pains and convulsions, even death in severe cases. An emetic may save the animal in some cases. Salt or dry mustard (1 tablespoon mixed with 1 teaspoonful of water) can be effective in causing vomiting until the veterinarian is reached.

347

Inuit's Wild Thing and Inuit's Our Man Flint pictured at 10 weeks of age in this charming photograph by Alton Anderson. These two puppies are brother and sister to the famous Wooly Bully, sired by Ch. Spawn's Hot-Shot of Roy-El *ex* Ch. Balch's Ingrid of Brenmar.

Puppy love. . . eight-week-old Inuit's Stormy with owner Jon Arlow.

ARTHRITIS—A painful condition of the joints which results in irritation and inflammation. A disease that pretty much confines itself to older dogs, especially in the larger breeds. Limping, irritability and pain are symptomatic. Anti-inflammatory drugs are effective after X-ray determines the severity. Heat and rest are helpful.

ASCITES—A collection of serous fluid in the abdominal cavity, causing swelling. It may be a result of heavy parasitic infestation or a symptom of liver, kidney, tuberculosis or heart diseases.

ASPERGILLOSIS—A disease contracted from poultry and often mistaken for tuberculosis since symptoms are quite similar. It attacks the nervous system and sometimes has disastrous effects on the respiratory system. This fungus growth in the body tissue spreads quickly and is accompanied by convulsions. The dog rubs his nose and there is a bloody discharge.

ASTHMA—Acute distress in breathing. Attacks may occur suddenly at irregular intervals and last as long as half an hour. The condition may be hereditary or due to allergy or heart condition. Antihistamines are effective in minor attacks.

ATAXIA—Muscular incoordination or lack of movement causing an inhibited gait, although the necessary organs and muscle power are coherent. The dog may have a tendency to stagger.

ATOPY—Manifestations of atopy in the dog are a persistent scratching of the eyes and nose. Onsets are usually seasonal—the dog allergic to, say, ragweed will develop the condition when ragweed is in season, or say, house dust all year round. Most dogs afflicted with atopy are multi-sensitive and are affected by something several months out of the year. Treatment is by antihistamines or systemic corticosteroids, or both.

Ch. Eldor's Botek, owned and handled by Louis Grubisic, winning under judge C. Ross Hamilton, Jr.

—B—

BABESIA GIBSONI (or Babesiosis)—A parasitic disease of the tropics, reasonably rare in the U.S.A. to date. Blood tests can reveal its presence and like other parasitic infections the symptoms are loss of appetite, no pep, anemia and elevations in temperature as the disease advances, and enlarged spleen and liver are sometimes evident.

BALANITIS—The medical term for a constant discharge of pus from the penis which causes spotting of clothing or quarters or causes the dog to clean himself constantly. When bacteria gather at the end of the sheath, it causes irritations in the tissue and pus. If the condition becomes serious, the dog may be cauterized or ointment applied.

BLASTOMYCOSIS—A rare infectious disease involving the kidneys and liver. The animal loses its appetite and vomits. Laboratory examination is necessary to determine presence.

BRADYCARDIA—Abnormal slowness of the heartbeat and pulse.

BRONCHITIS—Inflammation of the mucus lining in the respiratory tract, the windpipe or trachea, and lungs. Dampness and cold are usually responsible and the symptoms usually follow a chill, or may be present with cases of pneumonia or distemper. Symptoms are a nagging dry cough, fever, quickened pulse rate, runny nose, perhaps vomiting, and congested nasal passages which must be kept open. Old dogs are particularly affected. It is a highly transmissible disease and isolation from other animals is important. Antibiotics are given.

BRUCELLA CANIS—An infectious disease associated with abortion in bitches in the last quarter of gestation, sterility or stillbirths. A comparable is testicle trouble in male dogs. It is highly contagious and can be diagnosed through blood tests and animals having the infection should be isolated.

—C—

CANCER (tumors, neoplasia, etc.)—A growth of cells which serve no purpose is referred to as a cancer. The growth may be malignant or benign. Malignancy is the spreading type growth and may invade the entire body. Treatment, if the condition is diagnosed and caught in time, may be successful by surgical methods, drugs, or radioactive therapy. Haste in consulting your veterinarian cannot be urged too strongly.

CANKER (Otitis)—A bacterial infection of the ear where the ear may drain, have a dreadful odor, and ooze a dark brown substance all the way out to the ear flap. Cause of canker can be from mites, dirt, excessive hair growth in the ear canal, wax, etc. A daily cleaning and administering of antifungal ointment or powder are in order until the condition is cured. Symptoms are the dog shaking his head, scratching his ear and holding the head to the side.

CARIES—A pathologic change causing destruction of the enamel on teeth and subsequent invasion of the dentine; in other words, a cavity in a tooth. This may result in bad breath, toothache, digestive disorders, etc., depending upon the severity. Cavities in dogs are rare, though we hear more and more of false teeth being made for dogs and occasionally even root canal work for show dogs.

CASTRATION—Surgical removal of the male gonads or sex organs. An anesthesia is necessary and the animal must be watched for at least a week to see that hemorrhage does not occur. It is best performed at an early age—anywhere from three to nine months. Older dogs suffering from a hormonal imbalance or cancer of the gonads are castrated.

CATARACT—An opaque growth covering the lens of the eye. Surgical removal is the only treatment. Cataract may be a result of an injury to the eye or in some cases may be an inherited trait.

CELLULITIS—Inflammation of the loose subcutaneous tissue of the body. A condition which can be symptomatic of several other diseases.

CHEILITIS—Inflammation of the lips.

CHOLECYSTITIS—A condition affecting the gall bladder. The onset is usually during the time an animal is suffering from infectious canine hepatitis. Removal of the gall bladder, which thickens and becomes highly vascular, can effect a complete cure.

CHOREA—Brain damage as a result of distemper which has been severe is characterized by convulsive movements of the legs. It is progressive and if it affects the facial muscles, salivating or difficulty in eating or moving the jaws may be evident. Sedatives may bring relief, but the disease is incurable.

CHOROIDITIS—Inflammation of the choroid coat of the eye which is to be regarded as serious. Immediate veterinary inspection is required.

COCCIDIOSIS—An intestinal disease of parasitic nature and origin. Microscopic organisms reproduce on the walls of the intestinal tract and destroy tissue. Bloody diarrhea, loss of weight and appetite and general lethargy result. Presence of parasites is determined by fecal examination. Sulfur drugs are administered and a complete clean up of the premises is in order since the parasite is passed from one to to another through floor surfaces or eating utensils.

COLOSTRUM—A secretion of the mammary glands for the first day or so after the bitch gives birth. It acts as a purgative for the young, and contains antibodies against distemper, hepatitis and other bacteria.

CONJUNCTIVITIS—Inflammation of the conjunctiva of the eye.

CONVULSIONS—A fit, or violent involuntary contractions of groups of muscles, accompanied by unconsciousness. They are in themselves a symptom of another disease, especially traceable to one affecting the brain; i.e., rabies, or an attack of encephalitis or distemper. It may also be the result of a heavy infestation of parasites or toxic poisonings. Care must be taken that the animal does not injure itself and a veterinarian must be consulted to determine and eliminate the cause.

Tote-Um's Tamahine of Seacourt, bred by Dianne Ross of Cle Elum, Washington. Imported to England by owner J.S. Parkyns.

CRYPTORCHID—A male animal in which neither testicle is present or descended. This condition automatically bars a dog from the show ring.

CYANOSIS—A definite blueness seen in and around the mucous membranes of the face; i.e. tongue, lips and eyes. It is usually synonymous with a circulatory obstruction or heart condition.

CYSTITIS—A disease of the urinary tract which is characterized by inflammation and/or infection in the bladder. Symptoms are straining, frequent urination with little results or with traces of blood, and perhaps a fever. Antibiotics, usually in the sulfur category, as well as antiseptics are administered. This is a condition which is of great discomfort to the animal and is of lengthy duration. Relief must be given by a veterinarian, who will empty bladder by means of catheter or medication to relax the bladder so that the urine may be passed.

—D—

DEMODECTIC MANGE—A skin condition caused by a parasitic mite, *Demodex*, living in hair follicles. This is a difficult condition to get rid of and is treated internally as well as externally. It requires diligent care to free the animal of it entirely.

DERMATITIS—There are many forms of skin irritations and eruptions but perhaps the most common is "contact dermatitis." Redness and itching are present. The irritation is due to something the animal has been exposed to and to which it is allergic. The irritant must be identified and removed. Antihistamines and anti-inflammatory drugs are administered, and in severe cases sedatives or tranquilizers are prescribed to lessen the dog's scratching.

DIABETES (Insipidus)—A deficiency of antidiuretic hormone produced by the posterior pituitary gland. It occurs in older animals and is characterized by the animal's drinking excessive amounts of water and voiding frequently. Treatment is by periodic injection of an antidiuretic drug for the rest of the animal's life.

DIABETES (Mellitus)—Sometimes referred to as sugar diabetes, this is a disorder of the metabolism of carbohydrates caused by lack of insulin production by the cells of the pancreas. Symptoms are the same as in the insipidus type, and in severe cases loss of weight, vomiting or coma may occur. Blood and urine analysis confirm its presence. It is treated by low carbohydrate diet, oral medication and/or insulin injections.

Nine-week-old future Champion Inuit's Nikolai of Colcord, co-owned by Delores Jeffers and Sheila Balch.

DIGITOXIN—A medication given to a dog with congestive heart failure. Dosage is, of course, adjusted to severeness of condition and size of the individual animal.

DISC ABNORMALITIES (Intervertebral)—Between each bone in the spine is a connecting structure called an intervertebral disc. When the disc between two vertebrae becomes irritated and protrudes into the spinal canal it forms lesions and is painful. (This is a disease which particularly affects the Dachshund because of its long back in comparison to length of legs.) Paralysis of the legs, reluctance to move, and loss of control of body functions may be symptoms. X-ray and physical examination will determine extent of the condition. Massage helps circulation and pain relievers may be prescribed. Surgery is sometimes successful and portable two-wheel carts which support the hindquarters help.

DISTEMPER—Highly transmissible disease of viral origin which spreads through secretions of nose, eyes or direct oral contact. May be fatal in puppies under 12 weeks. Symptoms of this disease are alternately high and low fevers, runny eyes and nose, loss of appetite and general lassitude, diarrhea and loss of weight. This disease sometimes goes into pneumonia or convulsions if the virus reaches the brain. Chorea may remain if infection has been severe or neglected. Antibiotics are administered and fluids and sedation may be advised by your veterinarian. If the dog has been inoculated, the disease may remain a light case, BUT it is not to be treated lightly. Warmth and rest are also indicated.

DROPSY—Abnormal accumulation of fluid in the tissues or body cavities. Also referred to as edema when accumulations manifest themselves below the skin. In the stomach region it is called ascites. Lack of exercise or poor circulation, particularly in older dogs, may be the cause. While the swellings are painless, excess accumulations in the stomach can cause digestive distress or heart disturbances, and may be associated with diabetes. Occasional diarrhea, lack of appetite, loss of weight, exhaustion, emaciation and death may occur if the condition is not treated.

DYSGERMINOMA—A malignant ovarian tumor. Symptoms are fever, vaginal discharge, vomiting and diarrhea. Tumors vary in size, though more commonly are of the large size and from reports to date, the right ovary is more commonly affected. Radiotherapy may be successful; if not, surgery is required.

—E—

EAR MANGE—Otodectic mange, or parasitic otitis externa. Ear mites suck lymph fluids through the walls of the ear canal. Infections are high when mites are present and a brownish, horrible smelling ooze is present deep down in the canal all the way out to the flap where the secretion has a granular texture. The dog shakes his head, rubs and scrapes. In extreme cases convulsions

A seven-week-old Alaskan Malamute puppy playing footsie. . . Owned by Sheila Balch.

or brain damage may result. The ear must be cleaned daily and drugs of an antibiotic and anti-inflammatory nature must be given.

ECLAMPSIA—A toxemia of pregnancy. Shortly before the time a bitch whelps her puppies, her milk may go bad. She will pant as a result of high fever, and go into convulsions. The puppies must be taken away from the mother immediately. This is usually the result of an extreme lack of calcium during pregnancy. Also known as milk fever.

ECTROPION—All breeders of dogs with drooping eyelids or exaggerated haws will be familiar with this condition, where the lower eyelid turns out. It can be a result of an injury, as well as hereditary in some breeds, but can be corrected surgically.

ECZEMA—Eczema is another form of skin irritation which may confine itself to redness and itching, or go all the way to a scaly skin surface or open wet sores. This is sometimes referred to as "hot spots." A hormone imbalance or actual diet deficiency may prevail. Find the cause and remove it. Medicinal baths and ointments usually provide a cure, but cure is a lengthy process and the condition frequently recurs.

EDEMA—Abnormal collections of fluids in the tissues of the body.

ELBOW DYSPLASIA—Term applies to a developmental abnormality of the elbow joints. It is hereditary.

EMPHYSEMA—Labored breathing caused by distended or ruptured lungs. May be acute or chronic and is not uncommon.

EMPYEMA—Accumulation of pus or purulent fluid, in a body cavity resembling an abscess. Another term for pleurisy.

ENCEPHALITIS—Brain fever associated with meningitis. An inflammation of the brain caused by a virus, rabies or perhaps tuberculosis. It may also be caused by poisonous plants, bad food or lead poisoning. Dogs go "wild," running in circles, falling over, etc. Paralysis and death frequently result. Cure depends on extent of infection and speed with which it is diagnosed and treated.

ENDOCARDITIS—Inflammation and bacterial infection of the smooth membrane that lines the inside of the heart.

ENTERITIS—Intestinal inflammation of serious import. It can be massive or confine itself to one spot. Symptoms are diarrhea, bloody at times, vomiting, and general discomfort. Antibiotics are prescribed and fluids, if the diarrhea and vomiting have been excessive. Causes are varied; may follow distemper or other infections or bacterial infection through intestinal worms.

Feeding time at Inuit Kennels for a litter of five-week-old puppies!

ENTROPION—A turning in of the margin of the eyelids. As a result, the eyelashes rub on the eyeball and cause irritation resulting in a discharge from the eye. Here again it is a condition peculiar to certain breeds—particularly Chow Chows—or may be the result of an injury which failed to heal properly. Infection may result as the dog will rub his eyes and cause a swelling. It is painful, but can be cured surgically.

ENTEROTOXEMIA—A result of toxins and gases in the intestine. As bacteria increase in the intestine, intermittent diarrhea and/or constipation results from maldigestion. If the infection reaches the kidney through the circulatory system, nephritis results. The digestive system must be cleaned out by use of castor oil or colonic irrigation, and outwardly by antibiotics.

Inuit's Nunny Brown at three months of age with Cockatiel friend Admiral Byrd. Owned by Sheila Balch, Valley Cottage, New York.

Little Eric Balch and Balch's Pooka.

Jamie, one of Joan Kolman's lovely Malamutes.

EOSINOPHILIC MYOSITIS—Inflammation of the muscles dogs use for chewing. Persistent attacks usually lasting one or more weeks. They come and go over long periods of time, coming closer and closer together. Difficulty in swallowing, swelling of the face, or even the dog holding his mouth open will indicate the onset of an attack. Anti-inflammatory drugs are the only known treatment. Cause unknown, outlook grave.

EPILEPSY—The brain is the area affected and fits and/or convulsions may occur early or late in life. It cannot be cured; however, it can be controlled with medication. Said to be hereditary. Convulsions may be of short duration or the dog may just appear to be dazed. It is rarely fatal. Care must be taken to see that the dog does not injure itself during an attack.

EPIPHORA—A constant tearing which stains the face and fur of dogs. It is a bothersome condition which is not easily remedied either with outside medication or by surgical tear duct removal. There has been some success in certain cases reported from a liquid medication given with the food and prescribed by veterinarians. This condition may be caused by any one or more of a number of corneal irritations, such as nasal malfunction or the presence of foreign matter in the superficial gland of the third eyelid. After complete examination as to the specific cause, a veterinarian can decide whether surgery is indicated.

ESOPHAGEAL DIVERTICULUM—Inflammation or sac-like protrusions on the walls of the esophagus resembling small hernias. It is uncommon in dogs, but operable, and characterized by gagging, listlessness, temperature and vomiting in some cases.

—F—

FALSE PREGNANCY (or pseudopregnancy)—All the signs of the real thing are present in this heart-breaking and frustrating condition. The bitch may even go into false labor near the end of the 63-day cycle and build a nest for her hoped-for puppies. It may be confirmed by X-ray or a gentle feeling for them through the stomach area. Hormones can be injected to relieve the symptoms.

FROSTBITE—Dead tissue as a result of extreme cold. The tissues become red, swollen and painful, and may peel away later, causing open lesions. Ointments and protective coverings should be administered until irritation is alleviated.

FUSOSPIROCHETAL DISEASE—Bad breath is the first and most formidable symptom of this disease of the mouth affecting the gums. Bloody saliva and gingivitis or ulcers in the mouth may also be present, and the dog may be listless due to lack of desire to eat. Cleaning the teeth and gums daily with hydrogen peroxide in prescribed dosage by the veterinarian is required. Further diagnosis of the disease can be confirmed by microscopic examination of smears, though these fusiform bacteria might be present in the mouth of a dog which never becomes infected. Attempts to culture these anaerobes have been unsuccessful.

—G—

GASTRIC DILATION—This is an abnormal swelling of the abdomen due to gas or overeating. Consumption of large amounts of food especially if dry foods are eaten, and then large quantities of water make the dog "swell." The stomach twists so that both ends are locked off. Vomiting is impossible, breathing is hampered and the dog suffers pain until the food is expelled. Dogs that gulp their food and swallow air with it are most susceptible. Immediate surgery may be required to prevent the stomach from bursting. Commonly known as bloat.

GASTRITIS—Inflammation of the stomach caused by many things—spoiled food which tends to turn to gas, overeating, eating foreign bodies, chemicals or even worms. Vomiting is usually the first symptom though the animal will usually drink great quantities of water which more often than not it throws back up. A 24-hour fast which eliminates the cause is the first step toward cure. If vomiting persists chunks of ice cubes put down the throat may help. Hopefully the dog will lick them himself. Keep the dog on a liquid diet for another 24 hours before resuming his regular meals.

GASTRO-ENTERITIS—Inflammation of the stomach and intestines. There is bleeding and ulceration in the stomach and this serious condition calls for immediate veterinary help.

GASTRODUODENITIS—Inflammation of the stomach and duodenum.

GINGIVITIS or gum infection—Badly tartared teeth are usually the cause of this gum infection characterized by swelling, redness at the gum line, bleeding and bloody saliva. Bad breath also. Improper diet may be a cause of it. Feeding of only soft foods as a steady diet allows the tartar to form and to irritate the gums. To effect a cure, clean the teeth and perhaps the veterinarian will also recommend antibiotics.

Six-week-old Brandy, bred and owned by Hope Leanza.

GLAUCOMA—Pressure inside the eyeball builds up, the eyeball becomes hard and bulgy and a cloudiness of the entire corneal area occurs. The pupil is dilated and the eye is extremely sensitive. Blindness is inevitable unless treatment is prompt at the onset of the disease. Cold applications as well as medical prescriptions are required with also the possibility of surgery, though with no guarantee of success.

GLOSSITIS—Inflammation of the tongue.

GOITER—Enlargement of the thyroid gland, sometimes requiring surgery. In minor cases, medication—usually containing iodine—is administered.

HARELIP—A malformation of the upper lip characterized by a cleft palate. Difficulty in nursing in exaggerated cases can result in starvation or puny development. Operations can be performed late in life.

HEART DISEASE—Heart failure is rare in young dogs, but older dogs which show an unusual heavy breathing after exercise or are easily tired may be victims of heart trouble, and an examination is in order. As it grows worse, wheezing, coughing or gasping may be noticed. Other symptoms indicating faulty circulation may manifest themselves as the animal retains more body fluids as the circulation slows down. Rest, less exercise, and non-fattening diets are advised and medication to remove excess fluids from the body are prescribed. In many cases, doses of digitalis may be recommended.

HEARTWORM (*Dirofilaria immitis*)—This condition does not necessarily debilitate a working dog or a dog that is extremely active. It is diagnosed by a blood test and a microscopic examination to determine the extent of the microfilariae. If positive, further differentials are made for comparison with other microfilariae. Treatment consists of considerable attention to the state of nutrition, and liver and kidney functions are watched closely in older dogs. Medication is usually treatment other than surgery and consists of dithiazine iodine therapy over a period of two weeks. Anorexia and/or fever·may occur and supplemental vitamins and minerals may be indicated. Dogs with heavy infestations are observed for possible foreign protein reaction from dying and decomposing worms, and are watched for at least three months.

HEATSTROKE—Rapid breathing, dazed condition, vomiting, temperature, and collapse in hot weather indicate heatstroke. It seems to strike older dogs especially if they are overweight or have indulged in excessive activity. Reduce body temperature immediately by submerging dog in cold water, apply ice packs, cold enemas, etc. Keep dog cool and quiet for at least 24 hours.

HEMATOMA—A pocket of blood that may collect in the ear as a result of an injury or the dog's scratching. Surgery is required to remove the fluid and return skin to cartilage by stitching.

HEMOPHILIA—Excessive bleeding on the slightest provocation. Only male subjects are susceptible and it is a hereditary disease passed on by females. Blood coagulants are now successfully used in certain cases.

HEPATITIS, Infectious canine—This disease of viral nature enters the body through the mouth and attacks primarily the liver. Puppies are the most susceptible to this disease and run a fever and drink excessive amounts of water. Runny eyes, nose, vomiting, and general discomfort are symptoms. In some cases blood builders or even blood transfusions are administered since the virus has a tendency to thin the blood. This depletion of the blood often leaves the dog open to other types of infection and complete recovery is a lengthy process. Antibiotics are usually given and supplemental diet and blood builders are a help. Vaccination for young puppies is essential.

HERNIA (diaphragmatic)—An injury is usually responsible for this separation or break in the wall of the diaphragm. Symptoms depend on severity; breathing may become difficult, there is some general discomfort or vomiting. X-rays can determine the extent of damage and the only cure is surgery.

HERNIA (umbilical)—Caused by a portion of the abdominal viscera protruding through a weak spot near the navel. Tendency toward hernia is said to be largely hereditary.

Indian Warpaint of Seacourt pictured showing in the Working Breeds championship class at a 1973 show in England. Possum was bred and owned by Mrs. J.S. Parkyns of Oxford. Sire was Tote-Um's Arctic Hawk *ex* Highnoons Bella Koda.

HIP DYSPLASIA—or HD is a wearing away of the ball and socket of the hip joint. It is a hereditary disease. The symptoms of this bone abnormality are a limp and an awkwardness in raising or lowering the body. X-ray will establish severity and it is wise in buying or selling a dog of any breed to insist on a radiograph to prove the animal is HD clear. The condition can be detected as early as three months and if proven the dog should have as little exercise as possible. There is no cure for this condition. Only pain relievers can be given for the more severe cases. No animal with HD should be used for breeding.

HOOKWORM—Hookworms lodge in the small intestines and suck blood from the intestinal wall. Anemia results from loss of blood. Loss of weight, pale gums, and general weakness are symptoms. Microscopic examination of the feces will determine presence.

Emphasis on diet improvement and supplements to build up the blood is necessary and, of course, medication for the eradication of the hookworms. This can be either oral or by veterinary injection.

HYDROCEPHALUS—A condition also known as "water head" since a large amount of fluid collects in the brain cavity, usually before birth. This may result in a difficult birth and the young are usually born dead or die shortly thereafter. Euthanasia is recommended on those that do survive since intelligence is absent and violence to themselves or to others is liable to occur.

HYDRONEPHROSIS—Due to a cystic obstruction the kidney collects urine which cannot be passed through the ureter into the bladder, causing the kidney to swell (sometimes to five times its normal size) and giving pain in the lumbar region. The kidney may atrophy, if the condition goes untreated.

—I—

ICHTHYOSIS—A skin condition over elbows and hocks. Scaliness and cracked skin cover the area particularly that which comes in contact with hard surfaces. Lubricating oils well rubbed into the skin and keeping the animal on soft surfaces are solutions.

IMPETIGO—Skin disease seen in puppies infested by worms, distemper, or teething problems. Little soft pimples cover the surface of the skin. Sulfur ointments and ridding the puppy of the worms are usually sufficient cure as well.

INTERDIGITAL CYSTS—Growths usually found in the legs. They are painful and cause the dog to favor the paw or not walk on it at all. Surgery is the only cure and antibiotic ointments to keep dirt and infection out are necessary.

INTESTINAL OBSTRUCTIONS—When a foreign object becomes lodged in the intestines and prevents passage of stool constipation results from the blockage. Hernia is another cause of obstruction or stoppage. Pain, vomiting, loss of appetite are symptoms. Fluids, laxatives or enemas should be given to remove blockage. Surgery may be necessary after X-ray determines cause. Action must be taken since death may result from long delay or stoppage.

IRITIS—Inflammation of the iris or colored part of the eye. May be caused by the invasion of foreign bodies or other irritants.

—J—

JAUNDICE—A yellow discoloration of the skin. Liver malfunction causes damage by bile seeping into the circulatory system and being dispensed into the body tissue, causing discoloration of the skin. It may be caused by round worms, liver flukes or gall stones. It may be either acute or chronic and the animal loses ambition, convulses or vomits, sometimes to excess. It may be cured once the cause has been eliminated. Neglect can lead to death.

Anernek, owned by Betsey Correy Ketclaar-Triller of Holland, enjoys a romp with a German Shepherd and another friend.

—K—

KERATITIS—Infection of the cornea of the eye. Distemper or hepatitis may be a cause. Sensitivity to light, watery discharge and pain are symptomatic. Treatment depends on whether the lesion is surface irritation or a puncture of the cornea. Warm compresses may help until the veterinarian prescribes the final treatment. Sedatives or tranquilizers may be prescribed to aid in preventing the dog from rubbing the eye.

KIDNEY WORM—The giant worm that attacks the kidney and kidney tissue. It can reach a yard in length. The eggs of this rare species of worm are passed in the dog's urine rather than the feces. These worms are found in raw fish. It is almost impossible to detect them until at least one of the kidneys is completely destroyed or an autopsy reveals its presence. There is no known cure at this point and, therefore, the only alternative is not to feed raw fish.

—L—

LEAD POISONING—Ingestion of lead-based paints or products such as linoleum containing lead is serious. Symptoms are vomiting, behavior changes and/or hysteria or even convulsions in severe cases. It can be cured by medication if caught early enough. Serious damage can be done to the central nervous system. Blood samples are usually taken to determine amount in the blood. Emetics may be required if heavy intake is determined.

LEPTOSPIROSIS—This viral infection is dangerous and bothersome because it affects many organs of the body before lodging itself in the kidneys. Incubation is about two weeks after exposure to the urine of another affected dog. Temperature, or subtemperature, pain and stiffness in the hindquarters are not uncommon, nor is vomiting. Booster shots after proper vaccination at a young age are usually preventative, but once afflicted, antibiotics are essential to cure.

LOCKJAW (tetanus)—Death rate is very high in this bacterial disease. Puncture wounds may frequently develop into lockjaw. Symptoms are severe. As the disease progresses high fever and stiffness in the limbs becomes serious though the dog does not lose consciousness. Sedatives must be given to help relax the muscles and dispel the spasms. When the stiffness affects the muscles of the face, intravenous feeding must be provided. If a cure is effected, it is a long drawn out affair. Lockjaw bacteria are found in soil and in the feces of animals and humans.

LYMPHOMA (Hodgkins disease)—Malignant lymphoma most frequently is found in dogs under four years of age, affects the lymph glands, liver and spleen. Anorexia and noticeable loss of weight are apparent as well as diarrhea. Depending on area and organ, discharge may be present. The actual neoplasm or tumorous growth may be surrounded by nodules or neoplastic tissue which should be surgically removed under anesthesia.

—M—

MAMMARY NEOPLASMS—25 per cent of all canine tumors are of mammary origin. About half of all reported cases are benign. They are highly recurrent and, when cancerous, fatalities are high. Age or number of litters has nothing to do with the condition itself or the seriousness.

MANGE—The loss of a patch of hair usually signals the onset of mange, which is caused by any number of types of microscopic mites. The veterinarian will usually take scrapings to determine which of the types it is. Medicated baths and dips plus internal and external medication is essential as it spreads rapidly and with care can be confined to one part of the body. Antibiotics are prescribed.

MASTITIS (mammary gland infection)—After the birth of her young, a bitch may be beset by an infection causing inflammation of the mammary glands which produce milk for the puppies. Soreness and swelling make it painful for her when the puppies nurse. Abscess may form and she will usually run a fever. Hot compresses and antibiotics are necessary and in some instances hormone therapy.

MENINGITIS—Inflammation affecting the membranes covering the brain and/or spinal cord. It is a serious complication which may result from a serious case of distemper, tuberculosis, hardpad, head injury, etc. Symptoms are delirium, restlessness, high temperature, and dilated pupils in the eyes. Paralysis and death are almost certain.

METRITIS—This infection, or inflammation of the uterus, causes the dog to exude a bloody discharge. Vomiting and a general lassitude are symptoms. Metritis can occur during the time the bitch is in season or right after giving birth. Antibiotics are used, or in severe cases hysterectomy.

MONORCHIDISM—Having only one testicle.

MOTION SICKNESS—On land, on sea, or in the air, your dog may be susceptible to motion sickness. Yawning, or excessive salivation, may signal the onset, and there is eventual vomiting. One or all of the symptoms may be present and recovery is miraculously fast once the motion ceases. Antinauseant drugs are available for animals which do not outgrow this condition.

MYELOMA—Tumor of the bone marrow. Lameness and evidence of pain are symptoms as well as weight loss, depression and palpable tumor masses. Anemia or unnatural tendency to bleed in severe cases may be observed. The tumors may be detected radiographically, but no treatment has yet been reported for the condition.

—N—

NEONATAL K-9 HERPESVIRUS INFECTION—Though K-9 herpesvirus infection, or CHV, has been thought to be a disease of the respiratory system in adult dogs, the acute necrotizing and hemorrhagic disease occurs only in infant puppies. The virus multiplies in the respiratory system and female genital tracts of older dogs. Puppies may be affected in the vaginal canal. Unfortunately the symptoms resemble other neonatal infections, even hepatitis, and only after autopsy can it be detected.

NEPHROTIC SYNDROME—Symptoms may be moist or suppurative dermatitis, edema or hypercholesteremia. It is a disease of the liver and may be the result of another disease. Laboratory data and biopsies may be necessary to determine the actual cause if it is other than renal disease. This is a relatively uncommon thing in dogs, and liver and urinal function tests are made to determine its presence.

Aninvak of Kananak, multiple Best of Breed winner in England, owned by Mrs. J. Parkyns. Sire was Pawnee Flash of North Wind ex Ambara's Nuviya.

Canadian Ch. Oak's Kanuyak Kakka of Wilinda, photographed in 1971 at one-and-a-half years of age with his owner, Mrs. Linda Smith. This dog was one of the first red Alaskan Malamutes to finish in Canada.

NEURITIS—Painful inflammation of a nerve.

NOSEBLEED (epistaxis)—A blow or other injury which causes injury to the nasal tissues is usually the cause. Tumors, parasites, foreign bodies, such as thorns or burs or quills, may also be responsible. Ice packs will help stem the tide of blood, though coagulants may also be necessary. Transfusions in severe cases may be indicated.

—O—

ORCHITIS—Inflammation of the testes.

OSTEOGENESIS IMPERFECTA—Or "brittle bones" is a condition that can be said to be both hereditary and dietary. It may be due to lack of calcium or phosphorus or both. Radiographs show "thin" bones with deformities throughout the skeleton. Treatment depends on cause.

OSTEOMYELITIS (enostosis)—Bone infection may develop after a bacterial contamination of the bone, such as from a compound fracture. Pain and swelling denote the infection and wet sores may accompany it. Lack of appetite, fever and general inactivity can be expected. Antibiotics are advised after X-ray determines severity. Surgery eliminates dead tissue or bone splinters to hasten healing.

OTITIS—Inflammation of the ear.

—P—

PANCREATITIS—It is difficult to palpate for the pancreas unless it is enlarged, which it usually is if this disease is present. Symptoms to note are as in other gastronomic complaints such as vomiting, loss of appetite, anorexia, stomach pains and general listlessness. This is a disease of older dogs though it has been diagnosed in young dogs as well. Blood, urine and stool examination and observation of the endocrine functions of the dog are in order. Clinical diseases that may result from a serious case of pancreatitis are acute pancreatitis which involves a complete degeneration of the pancreas, atrophy, fibrous and/or neoplasia, cholecystitis. Diabetes mellitus is also a possibility.

PATELLAR LUXATION—"Trick knees" are frequent in breeds that have been "bred down" from Standard to Toy size, and is a condition where the knee bone slips out of position. It is an off again, on again condition that can happen as a result of a jump or excessive exercise. It if is persistent, anti-inflammatory drugs may be given or in some cases surgery can correct it.

PERITONITIS—Severe pain accompanies this infection or inflammation of the lining of the abdominal cavity. Extreme sensitivity to touch, loss of appetite and vomiting occur. Dehydration and weight loss is rapid and anemia is a possibility. Antibiotics should

Pooh Bear, a darling Malamute puppy owned by Herbert R. Nichols of Tunkhannock, Pennsylvania, photographed in June, 1972.

Ch. Icefloe's North Star, dam of six champions during 1972, making her the top-producing bitch for the breed that year. Star is owned by Jeri Lea Hooks, Icefoe Kennels, Los Lunas, New Mexico.

kill the infection and a liquid diet for several days is advised. Pain-killers may be necessary or drainage tubes in severe cases.

PHLEBITIS—Inflammation of a vein.

PLACENTA—The afterbirth which accompanies and has been used to nourish the fetus. It is composed of three parts; the chorion, amnion, and allantois.

POLYCYTHEMIA VERA—A disease of the blood causing an elevation of hemoglobin concentration. Blood-letting has been effective. The convulsions that typify the presence can be likened to epileptic fits and last for several minutes. The limbs are stiff and the body feels hot. Mucous membranes are congested, the dog may shiver, and the skin has a ruddy discoloration. Blood samples must be taken and analyzed periodically. If medication to reduce the production of red blood cells is given, it usually means the dog will survive.

PROCTITIS—Inflammation of the rectum.

PROSTATITIS—Inflammation of the prostate gland.

PSITTACOSIS—This disease which affects birds and people has been diagnosed in rare instances in dogs. A soft, persistent cough indicates the dog has been exposed, and a radiograph will show a cloudy portion on the affected areas of the lung. Antibiotics such as aureomycin have been successful in the known cases and cure has been effected in two to three weeks' time. This is a highly contagious disease, to the point where it can be contracted during a post mortem.

PYOMETRA—This uterine infection presents a discharge of pus from the uterus. High fever may turn to below normal as the infection persists. Lack of appetite with a desire for fluids and frequent urination are evidenced. Antibiotics and hormones are known cures. In severe cases, hysterectomy is performed.

—R—

RABIES (hydrophobia)—The most deadly of all dog diseases. The Pasteur treatment is the only known cure for humans. One of the viral diseases that affects the nervous system and damages the brain. It is contracted by the intake, through a bite or cut, of saliva from an infected animal. It takes days or even months for the symptoms to appear, so it is sometimes difficult to locate, or isolate, the source. There are two reactions in a dog to this disease. In the paralytic type of rabies the dog can't swallow and salivates from a drooping jaw, and progressive paralysis eventually overcomes the entire body. The animal goes into coma and eventually dies. In the furious type of rabies the dog turns vicious, eats strange objects, in spite of a difficulty in swallowing, foams at the mouth, and searches out animals or people to attack—hence the expression "mad dog." Vaccination is available for dogs that run loose.

Examination of the brain is necessary to determine actual diagnosis.

RECTAL PROLAPSE—Diarrhea, straining from constipation or heavy infestations of parasites are the most common cause of prolapse which is the expulsion of a part of the rectum through the anal opening. It is cylindrical in shape, and must be replaced within the body as soon as possible to prevent damage. Change in diet, medication to eliminate the cause, etc. will effect a cure.

RETINAL ATROPHY—A disease of the eye that is highly hereditary and may be revealed under ophthalmoscopic examination. Eventual blindness inevitably results. Dogs with retinal atrophy should not be used for breeding. Particularly prominent in certain breeds where current breeding trends have tended to change the shape of the head.

RHINITIS—Acute or chronic inflammation of the mucous membranes of the nasal passages. It is quite common in both dogs and cats. It is seldom fatal, but requires endless "nursing" on the part of the owner for survival, since the nose passages must be kept open so the animal will eat. Dry leather on the nose though there is excessive discharge, high fever, sneezing, etc., are symptoms. Nose discharge may be bloody and the animal will refuse to eat, making it listless. The attacks may be recurrent and medication must be administered.

RICKETS—The technical name for rickets is osteomalacia and is due to not enough calcium in the body. The bones soften and the legs become bowed or deformed. Rickets can be cured if caught in early stages by improvement in diet.

RINGWORM—The dread of the dog and cat world! This is a fungus disease where the hair falls out in circular patches. It spreads rapidly and is most difficult to get rid of entirely. Drugs must be administered "inside and out!" The cure takes many weeks and much patience. Ultraviolet lights will show hairs green in color so it is wise to have your animal, or new puppy, checked out by the veterinarian for this disease before introducing him to the household. It is contracted by humans.

ROOT CANAL THERAPY—Injury to a tooth may be treated by prompt dental root canal therapy which involves removal of damaged or necrotic pulp and placing of opaque filling material in the root canal and pulp chamber.

—S—

SALIVARY CYST—Surgery is necessary when the salivary gland becomes clogged or non-functional, causing constant salivation. A swelling becomes evident under the ear or tongue. Surgery will release the accumulation of saliva in the duct of the salivary gland, though it is at times necessary to remove the salivary gland in its

Sena-Lak's Houdini with a young friend. Owned
by Eleanore DuBuis, Valois, New York.

entirety. Zygomatic salivary cysts are usually a result of obstructions in the four main pairs of salivary glands in the mouth. Infection is more prevalent in the parotid of the zygomatic glands located at the rear of the mouth, lateral to the last upper molars. Visual symptoms may be protruding eyeballs, pain when moving the jaw, or a swelling in the roof of the mouth. If surgery is necessary, it is done under general anesthesia and the obstruction removed by dissection. Occasionally, the zygomatic salivary gland is removed as well. Stitches or drainage tubes may be necessary or dilation of the affected salivary gland. Oral or internal antibiotics may be administered.

SCABIES—Infection from a skin disease caused by a sarcoptic mange mite.

SCURF (dandruff)—A scaly condition of the body in areas covered with hair. Dead cells combined with dried sweat and sebaceous oil gland materials.

SEBORRHEA—A skin condition also referred to as "stud tail," though studding has nothing to do with the condition. The sebaceous or oil-forming glands are responsible. Accumulation of dry skin, or scurf, is formed by excessive oily deposits while the hair becomes dry or falls out altogether.

SEPTICEMIA—When septic organisms invade the bloodstream, it is called septicemia. Severe cases are fatal as the organisms in the blood infiltrate the tissues of the body and all the body organs are affected. Septicemia is the result of serious wounds, especially joints and bones. Abscess may form. High temperature and/or shivering may herald the onset, and death occurs shortly thereafter since the organisms reproduce and spread rapidly. Close watch on all wounds, antibiotics and sulfur drugs are usually prescribed.

SHOCK (circulatory collapse)—The symptoms and severity of shock vary with the cause and nervous system of the individual dog. Severe accident, loss of blood, and heart failure are the most common cause. Keep the dog warm, quiet and get him to a veterinarian right away. Symptoms are vomiting, rapid pulse, thirst, diarrhea, "cold, clammy feeling" and then eventually physical collapse. The veterinarian might prescribe plasma transfusion, fluids, perhaps oxygen, if pulse continues to be too rapid. Tranquilizers and sedatives are sometimes used as well as antibiotics and steroids. Relapse is not uncommon, so the animal must be observed carefully for several days after initial shock.

SINUSITIS—Inflammation of a sinus gland that inhibits breathing.

SNAKEBITE—The fact must be established as to whether the bite was poisonous or non-poisonous. A horse-shoe shaped double row of toothmarks is a non-poisonous bite. A double, or two-hole puncture, is a poisonous snake bite. Many veterinarians now carry anti-venom serum and this must be injected intramuscularly almost immediately. The veterinarian will probably inject a tranquilizer and other antibiotics as well. It is usually a four-day wait before the dog is normal once again, and the swelling completely gone. During this time the dog should be kept on medication.

SPIROCHETOSIS—Diarrhea which cannot be checked through normal anti-diarrhea medication within a few days may indicate spirochetosis; while spirochetes are believed by some authorities to be present and normal to gastrointestinal tracts, unexplainable diarrhea may indicate its presence in great numbers. Large quantities could precipitate diarrhea by upsetting the normal balance of the organ, though it is possible for some dogs which are infected to have no diarrhea at all.

SPONDYLITIS—Inflammation and loosening of the vertebrae.

STOMATITIS—Mouth infection. Bleeding or swollen gums or excessive salivation may indicate this infection. Dirty teeth are usually the cause. Antibiotics and vitamin therapy are indicated; and, of course, scraping the teeth to eliminate the original cause. See also GINGIVITIS.

STRONGYLIDOSIS—Disease caused by strongyle worms that enter the body through the skin and lodge in the wall of the small intestine. Bloody diarrhea, stunted growth, and thinness are general symptoms, as well as shallow breathing. Heavy infestation or neglect leads to death. Isolation of an affected animal and medication will help eliminate the problem, but the premises must also be cleaned thoroughly since the eggs are passed through the feces.

SUPPOSITORY—A capsule comprised of fat or glycerine introduced into the rectum to encourage defecation. A paper match with the ignitible sulfur end torn off may also be used. Medicated suppositories are also used to treat inflammation of the intestine.

—T—

TACHYCARDIA—An abnormal acceleration of the heartbeat. A rapid pulse signaling a disruption in the heart action. Contact a veterinarian at once.

TAPEWORM—There are many types of tapeworms, the most common being the variety passed along by the flea. It is a white, segmented worm which lives off the wall of the dog's intestine and keeps growing by segments. Some of these are passed and can be

Cleveland Amory, famed television critic and president of Funds for Animals, and his wife play chess while their Alaskan Malamutes, Ivan and Peter, provide back-to-back support.

seen in the stool or adhering to the hairs on the rear areas of the dog or even in his bedding. It is a difficult worm to get rid of since, even if medication eliminates segments, the head may remain in the intestinal wall to grow again. Symptoms are virtually the same as for other worms: debilitation, loss of weight, occasional diarrhea, and general listlessness. Medication and treatment should be under the supervision of a veterinarian.

TETANUS (lockjaw)—A telarius bacillus enters the body through an open wound and spreads where the air does not touch the wound. A toxin is produced and affects the nervous system, particularly the brain or spine. The animal exhibits a stiffness, slows down considerably and the legs may be extended out beyond the body even when the animal is in a standing position. The lips have a twisted appearance. Recovery is rare. Tetanus is not common in dogs, but it can result from a bad job of tail docking or ear cropping, as well as from wounds received by stepping on rusty nails.

THALLOTOXICOSIS or thallium poisoning—Thallium sulfate is a cellular-toxic metal used as a pesticide or rodenticide and a ready cause of poisoning in dogs. Thallium can be detected in the urine by a thallium spot test or by spectrographic analysis by the veterinarian. Gastrointestinal disturbances signal the onset with vomiting, diarrhea, anorexia and stomach cramps. Sometimes a cough or difficulty in breathing occurs. Other intestinal disorders may also manifest themselves as well as convulsions. In mild cases the disease may be simply a skin eruption, depending upon the damage to the kidneys. Enlarged spleens, edema or nephrosis can develop. Antibiotics and a medication called dimercaprol are helpful, but the mortality rate is over 50 per cent.

THROMBUS—A clot in the blood vessel or the heart.

TICK PARALYSIS— Seasonal tick attacks or heavy infestations of ticks can result in a dangerous paralysis. Death is a distinct reality at this point and immediate steps must be taken to prevent total paralysis. The onset is observed usually in the hindquarters. Lack of coordination, a reluctance to walk, and difficulty in getting up can be observed. Complete paralysis kills when infection reaches the respiratory system. The paralysis is the result of the saliva of the tick excreted as it feeds.

TOAD POISONING—Some species of toads secrete a potent toxin. If while chasing a toad your dog takes it in his mouth, more than likely the toad will release the toxin from its parotid glands which will coat the mucous membranes of the dog's throat. The dog will salivate excessively, suffer prostration, cardiac arrhythmia. Some tropical and highly toxic species cause convulsions that result in death. Caught in time, there are certain drugs that can be used to counteract the dire effects. Try washing the dog's mouth with large amounts of water and get him to a veterinarian quickly.

TONSILLECTOMY—Removal of the tonsils. A solution called epine-phrine, injected at the time of surgery, makes excessive bleeding almost a thing of the past in this otherwise routine operation.

TOXEMIA—The presence of toxins in the bloodstream, which nor-mally should be eliminated by the excretory organs.

TRICHIASIS—A disease condition of the eyelids, the result of neglect of earlier infection or inflammation.

—U—

UREMIA—When poisonous materials remain in the body, because they are not eliminated through the kidneys, and are recirculated in the bloodstream. A nearly always fatal disease—sometimes within hours—preceded by convulsions and unconsciousness. Vet-erinary care and treatment are urgent and imperative.

URINARY BLADDER RUPTURE—Injury or pelvic fractures are the most common causes of a rupture in this area. Anuria usually occurs in a few days when urine backs up into the stomach area. Stomach pains are characteristic and a radiograph will determine the seriousness. Bladder is flushed with saline solution and sur-gery is usually required. Quiet and little exercise is recommended during recovery.

—V—

VENTRICULOCORDECTOMY—Devocalization of dogs, also known as aphonia. In diseases of the larynx this operation may be used. Portions of the vocal cords are removed by manual means or by electrocautery. Food is withheld for a day prior to surgery and premedication is administered. Food is again provided 24 hours after the operation. At the end of three or four months, scar tissue develops and the dog is able to bark in a subdued manner. Compli-cations from surgery are few, but the psychological effects on the animal are to be reckoned with. Suppression of the barking varies from complete to merely muted, depending on the veterinarian's ability and each individual dog's anatomy.

—W—

WHIPWORMS—Parasites that inhabit the large intestine and the ce-cum. Two to three inches in length, they appear "whip-like" and symptoms are diarrhea, loss of weight, anemia, restlessness or even pain, if the infestation is heavy enough. Medication is best prescribed by a veterinarian. Cleaning of the kennel is essential, since infestation takes place through the mouth. Whipworms reach maturity within thirty days after intake.

26. PURSUING A CAREER IN DOGS

One of the biggest joys for those of us who love dogs is to see someone we know or someone in our family grow up in the fancy and go on to enjoy the sport of dogs in later life. Many dog lovers, in addition to leaving codicils in their wills, are providing in other ways for veterinary scholarships for deserving youngsters who wish to make their association with dogs their profession.

Unfortunately, many children who have this earnest desire are not always able to afford the expense of an education that will take them through veterinary school, and they are not eligible for scholarships. In recent years, however, we have had a great innovation in this field—a college course for those interested in earning an Animal Science degree, which costs less than half of what it costs to complete veterinary courses. These students have been a boon to the veterinarians, and a number of colleges are now offering the program.

With each passing year, the waiting rooms of veterinarians have become more crowded, and the demands on the doctors' time for research, consultation, surgery and treatment have consumed more and more of the working hours over and above his regular office hours. The tremendous increase in the number of dogs and cats and other domestic animals, both in cities and in the suburbs, has resulted in an almost overwhelming consumption of veterinarians' time.

Until recently most veterinary help consisted of kennel men or women who were restricted to services more properly classified as office maintenance rather than actual veterinary assistance. Needless to say, their part in the operation of a veterinary office is both essential and appreciated, as are the endless details and volumes of paperwork capably handled by office secretaries and receptionists. However, still more of a veterinarian's duties could be handled by properly trained semiprofessionals.

With exactly this additional service in mind, many colleges are now conducting two-year courses in animal science for the training of such semiprofessionals, thereby opening a new field for animal technologists. The time saved by the assistance of these trained semiprofessionals will relieve veterinarians of the more mechanical chores and will allow them more time for diagnosing and general servicing of their clients.

"Delhi Tech," the State University Agricultural and Technical College at Delhi, New York, has recently graduated several classes of these technologists, and many other institutions of learning are offering comparable two-year courses at the college level. Entry requirements are usually that each applicant must be a graduate of an approved high school or have taken the State University admissions examination. In addition, each applicant for the Animal Science Technology program must have some previous credits in mathematics and science, with chemistry an important part of the science background.

The program at Delhi was a new educational venture dedicated to the training of competent technicians for employment in the biochemical field and has been generously supported by a five-year grant, designated as a "Pilot Development Program in Animal Science." This grant provided both personal and scientific equipment with such obvious good results when it was done originally pursuant to a contract with the United States Department of Health, Education, and Welfare. Delhi is a unit of the State University of New York and is accredited by the Middle States Association of Colleges and Secondary Schools. The campus provides offices, laboratories and animal quarters and is equipped with modern instruments to train technicians in laboratory animal care, physiology, pathology, microbiology, anesthesia, X-ray and germ-free techniques. Sizable animal colonies are maintained in air-conditioned quarters: animals housed include mice, rats, hamsters, guinea-pigs, gerbils and rabbits, as well as dogs and cats.

First-year students are given such courses as livestock production, dairy food science, general, organic and biological chemistry, mammalian anatomy, histology and physiology, pathogenic microbiology and quantitative and instrumental analysis, to name a few. Second year students matriculate in general pathology, animal parasitology, animal care and anesthesia, introductory psychology, animal breeding, animal nutrition, hematology and urinalysis, radiology, genetics, food sanitation and meat inspection, histological techniques, animal laboratory practices and axenic techniques. These, of course, may be supplemented by electives that prepare the student for contact with the public in the administration of these duties. Such recommended electives include public speaking, botany, animal reproduction and other related subjects.

In addition to Delhi and the colleges which got in early on the presentation of these courses, more and more universities are offering training for animal technologists. Students at the State University of Maine, for instance, receive part of their practical training at the Animal Medical Center in New York City, and after this actual experience can perform professionally immediately upon entering a veterinarian's employ.

Typical Malamute puppies bred at Mrs. Anita Murphy's Ontario, Canada, Wilinda Kennels. These two cuties were born December 2, 1968. They are four weeks of age in this photo and were sired by Ch. Tarbo's Bobcat *ex* Ch. Wobiska's Pogey.

Under direct veterinary supervision they are able to perform all of the following procedures as a semi-professional:

*Recording of vital information relative to a case. This would include such information as the client's name, address, telephone number and other facts pertinent to the visit. The case history would include the breed, age of the animal, its sex, temperature, etc.

*Preparation of the animal for surgery

*Preparation of equipment and medicaments to be used in surgery.

*Preparation of medicaments for dispensing to clients on prescription of the attending veterinarian.

*Administration and application of certain medicines.

*Administration of colonic irrigations.

*Application or changing of wound dressings.

*Cleaning of kennels, exercise runs and kitchen utensils.

*Preparation of food and the feeding of patients.

*Explanation to clients on the handling and restraint of their pets, including needs for exercise, house training and elementary obedience training.

*First-aid treatment for hemorrhage, including the proper use of tourniquets.

*Preservation of blood, urine and pathologic material for the purpose of laboratory examination.

*General care and supervision of the hospital or clinic patients to insure their comfort.

*Nail trimming and grooming of patients.

High school graduates with a sincere affection and regard for animals and a desire to work with veterinarians and perform such clinical duties as mentioned above will find they fit in especially well. Women particularly will be useful since, over and beyond the strong maternal instinct that goes so far in the care and the recovery phase when dealing with animals, women will find the majority of the positions will be in the small animal field, their dexterity will also fit in well. Students having financial restrictions that preclude their education and licensing as full-fledged veterinarians can in this way pursue careers in an area close to their actual desire. Their assistance in the pharmaceutical field, where drug concerns deal with laboratory animals, covers another wide area for trained assistance. The career opportunities are varied and reach into job opportunities in medical centers, research institutions and government health agencies; at present, the demand for graduates far exceeds the current supply of trained personnel.

As far as the financial remunerations, yearly salaries are estimated at an average of $5,000.00 for a starting point. As for the estimate of basic college education expenses, they range from $1800.00 to $2200.00 per year for out-of-state residents, and include tuition, room and board, college fees, essential textbooks and limited personal expenses. These personal expenses, of course, will vary with individual students, as well as the other expenses, but we present an average. It is obvious that the costs are about half of the costs involved in becoming a full-fledged veterinarian, however.

Tote-Um's Arctic Hawk, an American import bred by Dianne Ross, photographed in the show ring at the 1970 Nordic Show. Co-owned by Mesdames Parkyns and Edmonds of England.

Ch. Sena'Lak's Laskana pictured winning at a dog show several years ago. Owned by Eleanore DuBuis, Valois, New York.

Ch. Kiana of Klondike poses with one of her trophies at the Sena-Lak Kennels in Valois, New York. Owner is Eleanore DuBuis.

PART TIME KENNEL WORK

Youngsters who do not wish to go on to become veterinarians or animal technicians can get valuable experience and extra money by working part-time after school and weekends, or full-time during summer vacations, in a veterinarian's office. The exposure to animals and office procedure will be time well spent.

Another great help to veterinarians has been the housewife who loves animals and wishes to put in some time at a job away from the house, especially if her children are grown or away at college. If she can clean up in her own kennel she can certainly clean up in a veterinarian's office, and she will learn much about handling and caring for her own animals while she is making money.

Kennel help is also an area that is wide open for retired men. They are able to help out in many areas where they can learn and stay active, and most of the work allows them to set their own pace.

The gentility that age and experience brings is also beneficial to the animals they will deal with; for their part, the men find great reward in their contribution to animals and will be keeping their hand in the business world as well.

PROFESSIONAL HANDLERS

For those who wish to participate in the sport of dogs and whose interests or abilities do not center around the clinical aspects of the fancy, there is yet another avenue of involvement.

For those who excel in the show ring, who enjoy being in the limelight and putting their dogs through their paces, a career in professional handling may be the answer. Handling may include a weekend of showing a few dogs for special clients, or it may be a full-time career which can also include boarding, training, conditioning, breeding and showing of dogs for several clients.

Depending on how deeply your interest runs, the issue can be solved by a lot of preliminary consideration before it becomes necessary to make a decision. The first move would to to have a long, serious talk with a successful professional handler to learn the pros and cons of such a profession. Watching handlers in action from ringside as they perform their duties can be revealing. A visit to their kennels for

Sheila Balch and a typical litter of four-week-old Inuit Alaskan Malamute puppies. These puppies were sired by Tigara's Bandit of Brenmar *ex* Ch. Balch's Ingrid of Brenmar.

Eleanore DuBuis with her Ch. Sena-Lak's Thor II, pictured at her Sena-Lak Kennels in Valois, New York.

Inuit's In the Nick of Time, shown as a puppy. Bred by Hope Leanza and owned by Sheila Balch. Sire was Ch. Inuit's Sweet Lucifer *ex* Inuit's Can-De Aleut.

Six-month-old Floyd wins Best Puppy in Match at the 1966 Wallkill Kennel Club Match Show under judge Bernard Berman. Owner Sheila Balch, Valley Cottage, New York.

an on-the-spot revelation of the behind-the-scenes responsibilities is essential! And working for them full or part time would be the best way of all to resolve any doubt you might have!

Professional handling is not all glamour in the show ring. There is plenty of "dirty work" behind the scenes 24 hours of every day. You must have the necessary ability and patience for this work, as well as the ability and patience to deal with CLIENTS—the dog owners who value their animals above almost anything else and would expect a great deal from you in the way of care and handling. The big question you must ask yourself first of all is: do you *really* love dogs enough to handle it. . .

DOG TRAINING

Like the professional handler, the professional dog trainer has a most responsible job! You not only need to be thoroughly familiar with the correct and successful methods of training a dog but also

Ch. Husky-Pak Marclar's Sioux, bred by C.W. and Mary Cramer. This beautiful Malamute was sired by Ch. Apache Chief of Husky-Pak *ex* Ch. Cheyenne of Husky-Pak. Owned by the Robert Zollers of Blue Ridge Summit, Pennsylvania, Sioux is pictured here being handled by Mrs. Zoller.

Ch. Roy-El's Fantom Hawk, handled by owner Kim Johnson. Bred by Elsie Truchon, the sire was Erik of Roy-El *ex* Marclar's Una. Photo by Evelyn Shafer.

must have the ability to communicate with dogs. True, it is very rewarding work, but training for the show ring, obedience, or guard dog work must be done exactly right for successful results to maintain a business reputation.

Training schools are quite the vogue nowadays, with all of them claiming success. But careful investigation should be made before enrolling a dog. . . and even more careful investigation should be made of their methods and of their actual successes before becoming associated with them.

GROOMING PARLORS

If you do not wish the 24-hour a day job which is required by a professional handler or professional trainer, but still love working with and caring for dogs, there is always the very profitable grooming business. Poodles started the ball rolling for the swanky, plush grooming establishments which sprang up like mushrooms all over the major cities, many of which seem to be doing very well. Here again, handling dogs and the public is necessary for a successful operation, as well as skill in the actual grooming of the dogs, and of all breeds.

While shops flourish in the cities, some of the suburban areas are now featuring mobile units which by appointment will visit your home with a completely equipped shop on wheels and will groom your dog right in your own driveway!

THE PET SHOP

Part-time or full-time work in a pet shop can help you make up your mind rather quickly as to whether or not you would like to have a shop of your own. For those who love animals and are concerned with their care and feeding, the pet shop can be a profitable and satisfying association. Supplies which are available for sale in these shops are almost limitless, and a nice living can be garnered from pet supplies if the location and population of the city you choose warrant it.

DOG JUDGING

There are also those whose professions or age or health prevent them from owning or breeding or showing dogs, and who turn to judging at dog shows after their active years in the show ring are no longer possible. Breeder-judges make a valuable contribution to the fancy by judging in accordance with their years of experience in the fancy, and the assignments are enjoyable. Judging requires experience, a good eye for dogs and an appreciation of a good animal.

MISCELLANEOUS

If you find all of the aforementioned too demanding or not within your abilities, there are still other aspects of the sport for you to enjoy and participate in at will. Writing for the various dog magazines, books or club newsletters, dog photography, portrait painting, club activities, making dog coats, or needlework featuring dogs, typing pedigrees or perhaps dog walking. All, in their own way, contribute to the sport of dogs and give great satisfaction. Perhaps, where Samoyeds are concerned, you may wish to learn to train for racing, or sled hauling, or you might even wish to learn the making of the sleds!

27. GLOSSARY OF DOG TERMS

ACHILLES HEEL—The major tendon attaching the muscle of the calf from the thigh to the hock

AKC—The American Kennel Club. Address: 51 Madison Avenue, N.Y., N.Y. 10010

ALBINO—Pigment deficiency, usually a congenital fault, which renders skin, hair and eyes pink

AMERICAN KENNEL CLUB—Registering body for canine world in the United States. Headquarters for the stud book, dog registrations, and federation of kennel clubs. They also create and enforce the rules and regulations governing dog shows in the U.S.A.

ALMOND EYE—The shape of the eye opening, rather than the eye itself, which slants upwards at the outer edge, hence giving it an almond shape

ANUS—Anterior opening found under the tail for purposes of alimentary canal elimination

ANGULATION—The angles formed by the meeting of the bones

APPLE-HEAD—An irregular roundedness of topskull. A domed skull

APRON—On long-coated dogs, the longer hair that frills outward from the neck and chest

BABBLER—Hunting dog that barks or howls while out on scent

BALANCED—A symmetrical, correctly proportioned animal; one with correct balance with one part in regard to another

BARREL—Rounded rib section; thorax; chest

BAT EAR—An erect ear, broad at base, rounded or semicircular at top, with opening directly in front

BAY—The howl or bark of the hunting dog

BEARD—Profuse whisker growth

BEAUTY SPOT—Usually roundish colored hair on a blaze of another color. Found mostly between the ears

BEEFY—Overdevelopment or overweight in a dog, particularly hindquarters

BELTON—A color designation particularly familiar to Setters. An intermingling of colored and white hairs

BITCH—The female dog

Eldon's Little Bo in a lovely outdoor setting. Owned by D.E. and Ella Mae Tarr of Lynchburg, Virginia.

Opposite:
Owner Nancy C. Russell and her famous Ch. Glaciers Storm Kloud C.D., one of the most renowned Alaskan Malamutes that ever lived.

BLAZE—A type of marking. White strip running up the center of the face between the eyes

BLOCKY—Square head

BLOOM—Dogs in top condition are said to be "in full bloom"

BLUE MERLE—A color designation. Blue and gray mixed with black. Marbled-like appearance

BOSSY—Overdevelopment of the shoulder muscles

BRACE—Two dogs which move as a pair in unison

BREECHING—Tan-colored hair on inside of the thighs

Nine-week-old Kotzebue Chandlar of Chinook with Philip Lake, Jr. Sired by Ch. Kotzebue Bering of Chinook ex Kotzebue Muffin Chinook, Kusko was bred by Eva B. Seeley and is owned by Philip and Judith Lake, Aurora Kennels, Holbrook, Massachusetts.

BRINDLE—Even mixture of black hairs with brown, tan or gray

BRISKET—The forepart of the body below the chest

BROKEN COLOR—A color broken by white or another color

BROKEN-HAIRED—A wiry coat

BROKEN-UP FACE—Receding nose together with deep stop, wrinkle, and undershot jaw

BROOD BITCH—A female used for breeding

BRUSH—A bushy tail

BURR—Inside part of the ear which is visible to the eye

BUTTERFLY NOSE—Parti-colored nose or entirely flesh color

BUTTON EAR—The edge of the ear which folds to cover the opening of the ear

CANINE—Animals of the family Canidae which includes not only dogs but foxes, wolves, and jackals

CANINES—The four large teeth in the front of the mouth often referred to as fangs

CASTRATE—The surgical removal of the testicles on the male dog

CAT-FOOT—Round, tight, high-arched feet said to resemble those of a cat

CHARACTER—The general appearance or expression said to be typical of the breed

CHEEKY—Fat cheeks or protruding cheeks

CHEST—Forepart of the body between the shoulder blades and above the brisket

CHINA EYE—A clear blue wall eye

CHISELED—A clean cut head, especially when chiseled out below the eye

CHOPS—Jowls or pendulous lips

CLIP—Method of trimming coats according to individual breed standards

CLODDY—Thick set or plodding dog

CLOSE-COUPLED—A dog short in loins; comparatively short from withers to hipbones

COBBY—Short-bodied; compact

COLLAR—Usually a white marking, resembling a collar, around the neck

CONDITION—General appearance of a dog showing good health, grooming and care

CONFORMATION—The form and structure of the bone or framework of the dog in comparison with requirements of the Standard for the breed

CORKY—Active and alert dog

COUPLE—Two dogs

COUPLING—Leash or collar-ring for a brace of dogs

COUPLINGS—Body between withers and the hipbones indicating either short or long coupling

COW HOCKED—when the hocks turn toward each other and sometimes touch

CRANK TAIL—Tail carried down

CREST—Arched portion of the back of the neck

CROPPING—Cutting or trimming of the ear leather to get ears to stand erect

CROSSBRED—A dog whose sire and dam are of two different breeds

CROUP—The back part of the back above the hind legs. Area from hips to tail

CROWN—The highest part of the head; the topskull

CRYPTORCHID—Male dog with neither testicle visible

CULOTTE—The long hair on the back of the thighs

CUSHION—Fullness of upper lips

DAPPLED—Mottled marking of different colors with none predominating

DEADGRASS—Dull tan color

DENTITION—Arrangement of the teeth

DEWCLAWS—Extra claws, or functionless digits on the inside of the four legs; usually removed at about three days of age

DEWLAP—Loose, pendulous skin under the throat

DISH-FACED—When nasal bone is so formed that nose is higher at the end than in the middle or at the stop

DISQUALIFICATION—A dog which has a fault making it ineligible to compete in dog show competition

DISTEMPER TEETH—Discolored or pitted teeth as a result of having had distemper

DOCK—To shorten the tail by cutting

DOG—A male dog, though used freely to indicate either sex

Best of Breed and Best Opposite Sex winners under judge Arnold Wolff at the 1973 Ladies Kennel Association of America dog show were a son and daughter of American, Canadian and Bermudian Ch. Inuit's Wooly Bully. At left is the son, Ch. Inuits Sweet Lucifer, and on the right is Ch. Cordova's Tasha. Shafer photograph.

DOMED—Evenly rounded in topskull; not flat but curved upward

DOWN-FACED—When nasal bone inclines toward the tip of the nose

DOWN IN PASTERN—Weak or faulty pastern joints; a let-down foot

DROP EAR—The leather pendant which is longer than the leather of the button ear

DRY NECK—Taut skin

DUDLEY NOSE—Flesh-colored or light brown pigmentation in the nose

ELBOW—The joint between the upper arm and the forearm

ELBOWS OUT—Turning out or off the body and not held close to the sides

EWE NECK—Curvature of the top of neck

EXPRESSION—Color, size and placement of the eyes which give the dog the typical expression associated with his breed

FAKING—Changing the appearance of a dog by artificial means to make it more closely resemble the Standard. White chalk to whiten fur, etc.

FALL—Hair which hangs over the face

FEATHERING—Long hair fringe on ears, legs, tail, or body

FEET EAST AND WEST—Toes turned out

FEMUR—The large heavy bone of the thigh

FIDDLE FRONT—Forelegs out at elbows, pasterns close, and feet turned out

FLAG—A long-haired tail

FLANK—The side of the body between the last rib and the hip

FLARE—A blaze that widens as it approaches the topskull

FLAT BONE—When girth of the leg bones is correctly elliptical rather than round

FLAT-SIDED—Ribs insufficiently rounded as they meet the breastbone

FLEWS—Upper lips, particularly at inner corners

FOREARM—Bone of the foreleg between the elbow and the pastern

FOREFACE—Front part of the head, before the eyes; muzzle

FROGFACE—Usually overshot jaw where nose is extended by the receding jaw

FRINGES—Same as feathering

FRONT—Forepart of the body as viewed head-on

FURROW—Slight indentation or median line down center of the skull to the top

GAY TAIL—Tail carried above the top line

GESTATION—The period during which the bitch carries her young; 63 days in the dog

GOOSE RUMP—Too steep or sloping a croup

GRIZZLE—Bluish-gray color

GUN-SHY—When a dog fears gun shots

GUARD HAIRS—The longer stiffer hairs which protrude through the undercoat

HARD-MOUTHED—The dog that bites or leaves tooth marks on the game he retrieves

HARE-FOOT—A narrow foot

HARLEQUIN—A color pattern, patched or pied coloration, predominantly black and white

HAW—A third eyelid or membrane at the inside corner of the eye

HEEL—The same as the hock

HEIGHT—Vertical measurement from the withers to the ground, or shoulder to the ground

HOCK—The tarsus bones of the hind leg which form the joint between the second thigh and the metatarsals.

HOCKS WELL LET DOWN—When distance from hock to the ground is close to the ground

HOUND—Dog commonly used for hunting by scent

HOUND-MARKED—Three-color dogs; white, tan and black, predominating color mentioned first

HUCKLEBONES—The top of the hipbones

HUMERUS—The bone of the upper arm

Eleanore DuBuis's Ch. Sena-Lak's Thor II pictured winning under prominent judge Albert Van Court. Brown photograph.

INBREEDING—The mating of closely related dogs of the same standard, usually brother to sister

INCISORS—The cutting teeth found between the fangs in the front of the mouth

ISABELLA—Fawn or light bay color

KINK TAIL—A tail which is abruptly bent, appearing to be broken

KNUCKLING-OVER—An insecurely knit pastern joint often causes irregular motion while dog is standing still

LAYBACK—Well placed shoulders

LAYBACK—Receding nose accompanied by an undershot jaw

LEATHER—The flap of the ear

LEVEL BITE—The front or incisor teeth of the upper and lower jaws meet exactly

Inuit's Trouble and Strife "on point" in the fields at Martha's Vineyard, where she lived with her owner, Roy Hayes.

LINE BREEDING—The mating of related dogs of the same breed to a common ancestor. Controlled inbreeding. Usually grandmother to grandson, or grandfather to granddaughter.

LIPPY—Lips that do not meet perfectly

LOADED SHOULDERS—When shoulder blades are out of alignment due to overweight or overdevelopment on this particular part of the body

LOIN—The region of the body on either side of the vertebral column between the last ribs and the hindquarters

LOWER THIGH—Same as second thigh

LUMBER—Excess fat on a dog

LUMBERING—Awkward gait on a dog

MANE—Profuse hair on the upper portion of neck

MANTLE—Dark-shaded portion of the coat or shoulders, back and sides

MASK—Shading on the foreface

MEDIAN LINE—Same as furrow

MOLARS—Rear teeth used for actual chewing

MOLERA—Abnormal ossification of the skull

MONGREL—Puppy or dog whose parents are of two different breeds

MONORCHID—A male dog with only one testicle apparent

MUZZLE—The head in front of the eyes—this includes nose, nostrils and jaws as well as the foreface

Ch. Tigara's Togiak Chieftan pictured taking an important win under judge Beatrice Godsol. Owned by Kathy Frick of La Crescenta, California. Photo by Joan Ludwig.

American and Canadian Ch. Bernard, owned by Philip D. and Judith Lake of Holbrook, Massachusetts. This win, under judge Robert Wills, was for Best of Breed at the Providence County Kennel Club Show in February, 1975. Handler, Phillip Marsman. Breeders, Joseph and Irene Delamater.

MUZZLE-BAND—White markings on the muzzle

NICTITATING EYELID—The thin membrane at the inside corner of the eye which is drawn across the eyeball. Sometimes referred to as the third eyelid

NOSE—Scenting ability

OCCIPUT—The upper crest or point at the top of the skull

OCCIPITAL PROTUBERANCE—The raised occiput itself

OCCLUSION—The meeting or bringing together of the upper and lower teeth.

OLFACTORY—Pertaining to the sense of smell

OTTER TAIL—A tail that is thick at the base, with hair parted on under side

OUT AT SHOULDER—The shoulder blades are set in such a manner that the joints are too wide, hence jut out from the body

OUTCROSSING—The mating of unrelated individuals of the same breed

OVERHANG—A very pronounced eyebrow

OVERSHOT—The front incisor teeth on top overlap the front teeth of the lower jaw. Also called pig jaw.

PACK—Several hounds kept together in one kennel

PADDLING—Moving with the forefeet wide, to encourage a body roll motion

PADS—The underside, or soles, of the feet

Six-week-old Stacy and her owner, Donald Thayer of Maine.

Looch-A-Pooch and his friend Chris Gabriel.

PARTI-COLORED—Variegated in patches of two or more colors
PASTERN—The collection of bones forming the joint between the radius and ulna and the metacarpals
PEAK—Same as occiput
PENCILING—Black lines dividing the tan colored hair on the toes
PIED—Comparatively large patches of two or more colors. Also called parti-colored or piebald
PIGEON-BREAST—A protruding breastbone
PIG·JAW—Jaw with overshot bite
PILE—The soft hair in the undercoat
PINCER BITE—A bite where the incisor teeth meet exactly
PLUME—A feathered tail which is carried over the back
POINTS—Color on face, ears, legs and tail in contrast to the rest of the body color
POMPON—Rounded tuft of hair left on the end of the tail after clipping
PRICK EAR—Carried erect and pointed at tip

Alaskaland's Wolfgang Inuit, shown with owner David Lynch in Geneva, Switzerland in July, 1974. The sire was Inuit's Wooly Bully *ex* Ch. Voyageurs Elke.

PUPPY—Dog under one year of age

QUALITY—Refinement, fineness

QUARTERS—Hind legs as a pair

RACY—Tall, of comparatively slight build

RAT TAIL—The root thick and covered with soft curls—tip devoid of hair or having the appearance of having been clipped

RINGER—A substitute for close resemblance

RING TAIL—Carried up and around and almost in a circle

ROACH BACK—Convex curvature of back

ROAN—A mixture of colored hairs with white hairs. Blue roan, orange roan, etc.

ROMAN NOSE—A nose whose bridge has a convex line from forehead to nose tip. Ram's nose

ROSE EAR—Drop ear which folds over and back revealing the burr

ROUNDING—Cutting or trimming the ends of the ear leather

RUFF—The longer hair growth around the neck

SABLE—A lacing of black hair in or over a lighter ground color

SADDLE—A marking over the back, like a saddle

SCAPULA—The shoulder blade

SCREW TAIL—Naturally short tail twisted in spiral formation

SCISSORS BITE—A bite in which the upper teeth just barely overlap the lower teeth

SELF COLOR—One color with lighter shadings

SEMIPRICK EARS—Carried erect with just the tips folding forward

SEPTUM—The line extending vertically between the nostrils

SHELLY—A narrow body which lacks the necessary size required by the Breed Standard

SICKLE TAIL—Carried out and up in a semicircle

SLAB SIDES—Insufficient spring of ribs

SLOPING SHOULDER—The shoulder blade which is set obliquely or "laid back"

SNIPEY—A pointed nose

SNOWSHOE FOOT—Slightly webbed between the toes

SOUNDNESS—The general good health and appearance of a dog in its entirety

SPAYED—A female whose ovaries have been removed surgically

SPECIALTY CLUB—An organization to sponsor and promote an individual breed

SPECIALTY SHOW—A dog show devoted to the promotion of a single breed

Kotzebue Chandlar of Chinook with eight-year-old Philip Lake, Jr. Philip's parents own the Aurora Kennels in Holbrook, Massachusetts. These two are a great combination at the races.

SPECTACLES—Shading or dark markings around the eyes or from eyes to ears

SPLASHED—Irregularly patched color on white or vice versa

SPLAY FOOT—A flat or open-toed foot

SPREAD—The width between the front legs

SPRING OF RIBS—The degree of rib roundness

SQUIRREL TAIL—Carried up and curving slightly forward

STANCE—Manner of standing

STARING COAT—Dry harsh hair, sometimes curling at the tips

STATION—Comparative height of a dog from the ground—either high or low

STERN—Tail of a sporting dog or hound

STERNUM—Breastbone

STIFLE—Joint of hind leg between thigh and second thigh. Sometimes called the ham

STILTED—Choppy, up-and-down gait of straight-hocked dog

STOP—The step-up from nose to skull between the eyes

STRAIGHT-HOCKED—Without angulation; straight behind

SUBSTANCE—Good bone. Or in good weight, or well muscled dog

SUPERCILIARY ARCHES—The prominence of the frontal bone of the skull over the eye

Alaskaland's Wolfgang Inuit photographed in West Germany in 1973 where he lives with owners David and Leslie Lynch. The sire was American, Canadian and Bermudian Ch. Inuit's Wooly Bully ex Voyageur's Elke.

Tigara's War Drum of Apple Hill with owner Mary Ellen Narkis, photographed when Drum was sixteen months of age. Sire was Ch. Dangerous Dan McGrew *ex* SnoBears Amber of Arctica.

SWAYBACK—Concave curvature of the back between the withers and the hipbones

TEAM—Four dogs usually working in unison

THIGH—The hindquarter from hip joint to stifle

THROATINESS—Excessive loose skin under the throat

THUMB-MARKS—Black spots in the tan markings on the pasterns

TICKED—Small isolated areas of black or colored hairs on a white background

TIMBER—Bone, especially of the legs

TOPKNOT—Tuft of hair on the top of head

TRIANGULAR EYE—The eye set in surrounding tissue of triangular shape. A three-cornered eye

TRI-COLOR—Three colors on a dog, white, black and tan

TRUMPET—Depression or hollow on either side of the skull just behind the eye socket; comparable to the temple area in man

TUCK-UP—Body depth at the loin

TULIP EAR—Ear carried erect with slight forward curvature along the sides

TURN-UP—Uptilted jaw

TYPE—The distinguishing characteristics of a dog to measure its worth against the Standard for the breed

UNDERSHOT—The front teeth of the lower jaw overlapping or projecting beyond the front teeth of the upper jaw

UPPER-ARM—The humerus bone of the foreleg between the shoulder blade and forearm

VENT—Tan-colored hair under the tail

WALLEYE—A blue eye also referred to as a fish or pearl eye

WEAVING—When the dog is in motion, the forefeet or hind feet cross

WEEDY—A dog too light of bone

WHEATEN—Pale yellow or fawn color

WHEEL-BACK—Back line arched over the loin; roach back

WHELPS—Unweaned puppies

WHIP TAIL—Carried out stiffly straight and pointed

WIRE-HAIRED—A hard wiry coat

WITHERS—The peak of the first dorsal vertebra; highest part of the body just behind the neck

WRINKLE—Loose, folding skin on forehead and/or foreface

INDEX